More praise for

D0752679

Many of today's CEOs purport to serve the public good. They are wealth takers re-branded as wealth creators. This book illuminates the dangers of CEO worship in an age of entrenched austerity.'

Linsey McGoey, author of *The Unknowers: How Strategic Ignorance Rules the World*

'In spite of the thorough and still growing critique of the leadership cult, CEOs proliferate in both private and public sectors. Let us hope that Bloom and Rhodes' book will serve as an antidote.'

Barbara Czarniawska, author of *Cyberfactories: How News Agencies Produce News*

'Why do we pray at the altar of the celebrity CEOs? What are consequences of such disturbing worship? Bloom and Rhodes answer these questions, showing us the ugly side of our contemporary obsession and the price we collectively pay in the CEO society.'

Alessia Contu, University of Massachusetts

'This unique book sheds light on one of the most tragic paradoxes of contemporary life: Why do we celebrate neoliberalism, through today's "cult of the CEO"? Bloom and Rhodes explain our deep-seated attachments to ideologies that are not only flawed but also dangerous.'

Kate Kenny, Queens University Belfast

'Essential reading for anyone wanting to understand the contemporary fetishisation of corporate leadership. Rhodes and Bloom trace the rise of the cult of the CEO, mounting a strong defence of democracy in the face of this celebratory authoritarianism.'

Chris Land, Anglia Ruskin University

About the authors

Peter Bloom heads the People and Organisations Department at the Open University, UK. His research critically examines the everyday practices of capitalism and democracy and their implications for work and life. Peter's recent books are *Authoritarian Capitalism in the Age of Globalization* (2016) and *The Ethics of Neoliberalism: The Business of Making Capitalism Moral (2017)*. Peter's writing has also featured in *The Washington Post, The Guardian, The Independent, The New Statesmen, The Week, The Conversation* and *Open Democracy* among others.

Carl Rhodes is Professor of Organisation Studies at UTS Business School in Sydney, Australia. He has written widely on issues concerning the ethical and political dimensions of business and working life, including the recent *Companion to Ethics, Politics and Organizations* (2015, with Alison Pullen). Carl is a frequent commentator on business and politics on Australian and international television and radio. He regularly writes for the mainstream and independent press, where his articles can be found in *The Guardian, New Matilda, The Conversation, Independent Australia* and *Open Democracy.*

658.42
B

CEO Society

The Corporate Takeover of Everyday Life

Peter Bloom
and Carl Rhodes

ZED

CEO Society: The Corporate Takeover of Everyday Life
was first published in 2018 by Zed Books Ltd,
The Foundry, 17 Oval Way, London SE11 5RR, UK.

www.zedbooks.net

Copyright © Peter Bloom and Carl Rhodes 2018.

The right of Peter Bloom and Carl Rhodes to be identified as the
authors of this work have been asserted by them in accordance
with the Copyright, Designs and Patents Act, 1988.

Typeset in Haarlemmer by seagulls.net
Index by Bronwyn Edds
Cover design by Emma J. Hardy
Printed and bound by CPI Group (UK) Ltd, Croydon, CR0 4YY

All rights reserved. No part of this publication may be
reproduced, stored in a retrieval system or transmitted in any
form or by any means, electronic, mechanical, photocopying or
otherwise, without the prior permission of Zed Books Ltd.

A catalogue record for this book is available from the British Library

ISBN 978-1-78699-073-0 hb
ISBN 978-1-78699-072-3 pb
ISBN 978-1-78699-074-7 pdf
ISBN 978-1-78699-075-4 epub
ISBN 978-1-78699-076-1 mobi

3 1327 00669 4061

Contents

Introduction: the threat and promise of CEO salvation   1

1. Welcome to the CEO society   17
2. The idolisation of the CEO   47
3. Competing in the executive economy   79
4. The CEO politician   115
5. The CEO as a model for living   141
6. The generous CEO?   177
7. The bad faith of CEO salvation   213

Afterword: the high cost of the CEO society   239

Notes   242
Index   273

Introduction

The threat and promise of CEO salvation

On 9 November 2016, the world awoke to a new political reality. Donald Trump defied all expectations and was elected president of the United States of America, his victory reverberating the world over. For some it was cheered as a blow to a corrupt economic and political establishment, while for others it was feared as a dangerous embrace of racism, sexism, xenophobia and authoritarianism. What almost all agreed was that the future of liberal democracy and capitalism – which only a decade before appeared unassailable – was suddenly uncertain. It was not just Trump who had been questioning the status quo on the campaign trail. Although ultimately unsuccessful, the very existence of the explicitly democratic socialist campaign of Bernie Sanders in the earlier part of the US presidential race was for many a welcome injection of a progressive anti-establishment grassroots energy into an entrenched oligarchic and elitist American political system.

These events did not happen in a social vacuum. They were the capstone to a mounting populist attack on neoliberalism and its free market orthodoxy in both Europe and the United States. In the mid-2010s, Europe, once a bedrock of the international order, was rocked by massive political earthquakes. From the reinvigorated left arose Syriza in Greece, Podemos in Spain and Momentum in the United Kingdom, all of which directly challenged the dominant politics of austerity and financial rule. On the right, the British people's 2016 vote to exit the European Union revealed the rise of a nationalist conservative revival that was anti-immigrant and protectionist. These politics, despite their fundamental ideological differences, started from a shared critique of the tyranny of corporate globalisation.

Perhaps the most obvious insight to be gained from these developments is that economic anxiety and inequality breed extreme reactions for both good and ill. Politicians, decision makers and the broader public, whether their politics lean left or right, seemed to have woken up to the dangers of a runaway neoliberalism. That the popularity of Trump arose as a response to this is especially astounding. The curious case with Trump is that while free market globalisation has been challenged from all sides, millions of Americans en masse voted to elect an ostentatiously super-rich CEO as their president. More generally, even as capitalism appears to be historically endangered, it remains the case that business executives (even the many times bankrupted ones) have a strong hold on the popular imagination as the people who can 'get things done'. The irony is that the very personification of the establishment – the ultimate insiders most responsible for our economic crises, political corruption and environmental destruction – can be idolised and rendered powerful on the promise that they will fight an oppressive status quo. One may well ask why the heroic ideal of the CEO is continuing to thrive when by all moral and ethical rights its incumbents should have been fired once and for all.

Beyond the good and evil CEO

The CEO stands as one of contemporary society's most compelling and conflicted figures, as well as amongst its most famous. Present-day CEOs like Facebook's Mark Zuckerberg and Tesla's Elon Musk, have joined business leaders of the recent past such as Apple's Steve Jobs and The Body Shop's Anita Roddick in becoming figures of envy and adulation. Nevertheless, depending on one's point of view, political persuasion and the vicissitudes of the news cycle, any particular CEO can be either lionised or loathed. They can be characterised at one and the same time as visionaries and realists; ethical innovators and moral hazards; generous benefactors and selfish hoarders; the very key to progress and the very obstacle to its achievement. They are, accordingly, both looked up to with admiration and despised with vehemence. CEOs appear as both a threat and a salvation for the woes of the modern world.

How can we make sense of such a contradictory modern subject, and the persistent resurgence of belief in its virtues? One way is to simply describe the function that these senior business executives fulfil, responsible as they are for leading the corporations that drive the global market economy. Yet this straightforward approach fails to capture the widespread appeal and power of the CEO in the present era, and how this appeal is able to fend off charges that CEOs represent an elite and wealthy class of people who have achieved that privilege at the expense of others. How exactly, and why, has the CEO become one of the 21st century's most pre-eminent idols, in many cases a household name? These are the CEOs who, for many, stand as our greatest prophets and our most productive action heroes. They do not just run companies and make profits, but are also positioned as the primary producers of global prosperity.

Is there anything surprising about this veneration of the executive class? In an age of growing inequality and exploding salaries for senior management, it might seem natural to look up aspiringly to these obvious social 'winners'. To do so reaffirms the corporate funded and friendly media coverage often reserved for CEOs, coverage that preaches their values in the name of the sacred gospel of the competitive free market. The business executive appears deserving of all of their economic rewards and social accolades, as if each one pulled themselves to success by their own bootstraps. Surely, winners deserve their prizes. Such a narrative suggests that CEOs have risen to the top like the cream of society through some individualised business version of Darwinian natural selection. So valorised, the CEO is presented as a supreme capitalist being who ascended to the apex of the pecking order to take their rightful place amongst the rulers of the world.

This characterisation of the CEO has undoubtedly infiltrated and infected the general imaginary, most especially in those countries where neoliberalism has married liberal democracy and global capitalism to produce the world order that governs us today. There is also a different and richer story that must be told. Especially in light of the blame that has been laid on individual business leaders for the 2008 financial crisis, as well as for recent corporate scandals ranging from the BP oil spill in the Gulf of Mexico in 2010, to the Volkswagen emissions scandal of 2015, to the Exxon Mobil climate controversy of 2016. These stories offer a counter-narrative, proposing that those positioned as our greatest heroes should have fallen from grace, relegated to being our most feared villains. While CEOs can be portrayed as value-creating innovators, they can also be characterised as psychopaths and evil parasites. In that latter sense, the question is no longer how CEOs will save the economy but rather how the economy and society can be saved from their greedy clutches.

Despite ample criticisms, setbacks and failings, the CEO continues to be reinvented as more than just a materialistic purveyor of the virtues of capitalism. Even given the disasters so many CEOs are held responsible for, they are still commonly presented as absolutely necessary for realising social and economic progress. There is a dominant logic which holds that the world will be rescued and sustainably developed by their forward thinking and a singular ability for action and achievement. The promise is that CEOs will not just protect corporations but will safeguard the population with prosperity, leading the way to a brighter and more ethical capitalist future. They come bearing the gifts of jobs and innovation, contributions that extend far beyond the stuffy confines of the boardroom and the soft comfort of the executive bathroom. In this rosy view, it is CEOs who can find smarter ways to fight climate change, cut through frustrating public red tape as well as balance desires for fiscal and social responsibility. If the CEOs of old were meant only to be the saviours of their companies, the executives of today are tasked with no less than saving humanity and the world. Have they become the last and greatest hope for the supposed salvation of us all? The election of Trump, and his popularity in various corners of the world, indicates that for some the answer is a resounding 'yes'.

The CEO to the rescue

The business executive is, for many, a compelling hero of the contemporary era, with CEOs having been immortalised in a manner once reserved for royalty. If you go to the Henry Ford Museum of American Innovation in Detroit, for example, you are greeted by imposing statue of the man standing tall in a statesmanlike pose. In 1994 the Australian government put 19th century businesswoman Mary Reibey on the country's $20 note. Meanwhile, in the UK business luminaries readily accept formal honours from the Queen, all the way up to knighthood. Idolised by many for their genius and productivity, CEOs symbolise the perfect mix of drive, intelligence and commitment. More than just corporate functionaries, they are role models held up to be envied by people everywhere.

CEOs are not just to be admired; they are also to be emulated. This reflects the social sedimentation of market rationality, where all our ingenuity and passion must be directed to winning in a social, political and economic life that is presented as a game. Present is a pervading logic of competition with which people are reduced to rivals fighting in an existential and financial contest. The good life, it would seem, belongs to the rich and famous and being an executive is positioned as being able to give you the money and power to make all your dreams come true. All that is required is that you ruthlessly play the game to win; only then will victory and happiness be yours to enjoy.

The 'I came, I saw, I profited' mentality is only part of the CEO appeal; it is also broader in its attraction, revolving around not just the aspiration to be an actual CEO, but also the inculcation of a desire for people to acquire the executive skills and mindset in order to succeed in all walks of life. With such a pursuit, people can hope to boost their productivity and find better methods for achieving their hopes and dreams. CEOs are imagined as the purveyors of the secret wisdom of not only how to survive, but to thrive in an exceedingly complex modern world. Not everyone, of course, can reach the vaunted heights of being an actual CEO, but everyone can strive to be the successful and effective 'CEO' of their own life.

The rise of the CEO society is the topic of this book. The CEO society is a product of decades of neoliberal political and economic reform. It goes beyond managerialism and the export of corporate management practices to non-corporate organisations. It takes the values that have become culturally and affirmatively associated with CEOs and applies them to all dimensions of human endeavour. Fiercely individualistic and anti-democratic, the CEO society prizes instrumentality, decisiveness, rivalry, profitability, efficiency and effectiveness. The adoption of this executive wisdom is touted as being fundamental to leading a successful existence, regardless of prior desires or values. Even more troubling, it is posited as the necessary antidote to addressing the deep structural problems of the global free market; an antidote that involves people accepting that they owe it both to themselves and to society to be like a CEO. This is an unequal society where not only are people judged as winners and losers, but that judgement is deemed morally righteous.

In the CEO society, the role of the CEO is presented not just as an elite job but as a lifestyle, a way of seeing and being in the world that can be taken up and embraced across cultures, class and personal circumstances. It is the simple answer to all of life's problems. If you want a promotion, sage CEO wisdom can tell you how to get ahead in business. Just ask Alex Malley, former CEO of CPA Australia, whose bestselling 2015 book *The Naked CEO* promises to give you "the truth you need to build a big life".[1] Never mind that in 2017 he was fired as CEO while facing allegations ranging from bullying to financial mismanagement.[2] If you want a better community, follow the CEO way to create a marketable and profitable brand of social justice. Indeed, the last ten years has even seen changes in the way corporations deal with charity, with the advent of a new approach where giving money to good causes is expected to yield a financial return to the giver.[3]

If you are seeking a more rewarding love life, then turn to CEO methods for finding how to win the person of your wildest dreams. All a lonely guy has to do is to follow Nina Atwood's advice and 'Date Like a CEO'.[4] If that's not enough you can plumb the depths of romance novels featuring CEO protagonists, with tasty titles such as Miranda Charles' *The Unmasked CEO* (Captured by Love Book 7),[5] or Anna DePalo's *Second Chance with the CEO*.[6] A common aphorism among certain Christians is to approach life's problems by imagining 'what would Jesus do?' Today people might well ask: 'what would a CEO do?' The answer, it is assumed, could lead you to a life that would be otherwise unattainable.

An obsession with being like a CEO has profound and dangerous social implications. The CEO society is one that promotes values of competition, instrumentality and exploitation at the exclusion of all other ideals. It trumps principles of tolerance, justice, cooperation, deliberation, equality and collective transformation. It reduces human existence to a mere set of market calculations fuelled by a desire to triumph individually regardless of the costs. It also offers a romantic vision of the singularly powerful executive; a mirage that only deepens feelings of our powerlessness and puts us in thrall to the very people and values most responsible for our disempowerment. The failure to criticise, question and overturn this will guarantee our social and moral bankruptcy.

It may appear we are arguing that the CEO society has completed its dominance, and that there is no resistance to this 'executisation' of our world and our lives. This is not so, and such a totalistic interpretation is far from our intention.

For example, the financial crisis of the late 2000s in particular profoundly challenged contemporary executive power and influence. In the United States, the modern citadel of the free market revolution, the insurgent presidential candidacy of Bernie Sanders in 2016 also revealed a threat to once sacred corporate leadership. Beneath Sanders' rather moderate social democratic policies was a profoundly revolutionary energy for change that directly took on the privileged and economic values of top executives. This is symptomatic of a broader and potentially fundamental shift in values across the world. Yet if this transformation is to continue to be realised, it requires a deeper critical understanding of the continuing appeal of CEOs in the face of overwhelming evidence of their economic and political destructiveness.

About the rest of the book

With this book we will critically chart the development of the CEO society as it has come to be a dominant feature of more and more dimensions of contemporary life. This begins in chapter 1 with an introduction to the phenomenon of the CEO society as it has arisen through the expansion of the neoliberal political and economic doctrine since at least the 1980s. We consider the CEO not just as a position occupied by a business executive, but as a social ideal, and a dangerous one at that. What we see is how corporate leaders are positioned as embodying generally applicable approaches to life concerning the free pursuit of self-interest, drive and determination to achieve personal goals, moral righteousness, independence, toughness, charisma and, more generally, just being the boss. It is through their association with such ideals that CEOs have come to be amongst the heroes of our time, embodying the power and authority that others strive for both at work and elsewhere in their lives.

In chapter 2 we delve deeper into the rise of the CEO as a character that has been both valorised and vilified. The chapter presents a historical overview of the CEO as a public figure. The 19th century business titans, exemplified in figures such as Andrew Carnegie and John D. Rockefeller, evolved into the executive technocrats of the post-war era. The conservative revolution of the 1980s glamorised the image of successful businesspeople and sexy capitalists, while they were simultaneously blamed for corporate scandals and disasters. As the 20th century turned into the new millennium this fetishising of the CEO spread into a broader promotion of CEO values, and an ongoing project of protecting them against being seen as exploitative creators of inequality. They were not just cherished and admired (largely) male celebrities, as, for example, Richard Branson or Warren Buffett had long been. They were now role models, whose lessons, if heeded, could be applied to all areas of one's existence. Thus we witnessed the birth of the CEO society, populated by individuals seeking to deploy the values and principles of the business executive anytime and anywhere.

Chapter 3 examines the influence of the CEO society specifically in the economic sphere. We discuss how work has become characterised by an attempted inculcation of executive moralities that emphasise competition, winning and self-sufficient individualism. Within all types of organisations, be they business, community organisations, schools, universities or the public services, employees at all levels are cajoled into becoming mini-executives, seeking out and spotting fresh profitable opportunities while maximising the return of their efforts. This mindset extends to workers' relationships with each other, as the modern ethos is to do whatever it takes to out-compete one's colleagues. Beyond this, everyone must be the CEO of their careers, using initiative and experience to increase their employability and their profitability as a worker. This fantasy of all-encompassing market rationality creates renewed anxieties among the present workforce. It also helps mask deeper structural problems of precarious labour, the erosion of workers' rights, and for many a more pressurised workplace and job market. With everyone being heralded as some form of CEO, responsibility for personal success is heaped on the individual, despite few having the actual privilege of being high-level business executives.

Chapter 4 investigates the effect of the CEO society on modern politics. While the expansion of corporate political lobbying since the 1970s has seen CEOs dramatically shape political decision making, today the relationship between business and politics has become more complicated. Business leaders are more and more directly entering into politics as candidates for office. The media promotes their business skills as politically desirable, if not necessary. An MBA and experience in a corporate boardroom is thought to prepare an individual to lead countries in a competitive global marketplace. These are the credentials that have given CEO-politicians, past and present, such as the United States' Donald Trump, Australia's Malcolm Turnbull and Italy's Silvio Berlusconi, an at least temporary aura of decisiveness and a presumed ability to make the tough choices required for fostering a 'productive' and 'efficient' fiscally responsible nation. What is emerging is the rise of corporate politics where commercial values risk eclipsing democratic ones.

Turning attention away from the mainstays of economic and political activity, chapter 5 extends the investigation into the ideals that shape what it means to be a good person in today's world, especially in the wake of the 2008 global financial crisis. Traditionally, the professional and personal spheres were considered separate. One could be a cutthroat CEO at the office and an adoring parent at home, a competitive employee at work and a fun-loving person at the weekend. Of course, this separation was never as distinct as it was portrayed. Work stress bled into home life and domestic concerns impacted on professional success, or lack thereof. Nevertheless, the values of these areas were commonly viewed as being quite different, if not incompatible. In the new millennium, the goal extended to us is to be the 'CEO of your life'. The implications of this are significant both inside and outside of work as our very humanity is recast in the image of competitive individualism, while at the same time actual CEO 'winners' are shielded from responsibility when their schemes harm others, often on a massive scale.

Philanthropy is another area that has been affected by the spread of the CEO society and this is the subject of chapter 6. This chapter highlights the extension of the CEO society into the provision of public goods in the name of corporate social responsibility generally, and philanthropy more specifically. The chapter focuses especially on the recent trend towards what has been called 'philanthrocapitalism', with the super-rich, headed by celebrity CEOs, pledging to give away their fortunes to good causes, for example through Bill Gates' and Warren Buffett's The Giving Pledge. As often is the case with CEO-styled activity, there is more to this apparently selfless generosity than meets the eye, with a simple devotion to giving being a naïve and unsatisfactory explanation. The chapter shows how large-scale philanthropic and socially responsible programmes reinforce a CEO society where control, wealth and power lie in the hands of the minority. Moreover, this is a society where even generosity and charity are ideas that can be manipulated into a CEO mould, a mould that ultimately privileges self-interest over generosity.

Chapter 7 considers the worrying costs and effects of this CEO society by exploring how it stands as a threat to collectively beneficial economic values, political ideals and personal relationships. The chapter also considers the danger this creates for the possibility of imagining of a better world. This is a danger where competition, interpersonal exploitation and a market-driven paradigm for social progress and cultural engagement can take over not just as dominant practices, but also as putative moral virtues. They can usurp cherished values of economic fairness, democracy, social justice, compassion and sustainable development. This evolution comes with a high and dangerous individual and collective cost. Notably, this 'bad faith' in CEO values works to rob us of our imagination to individually and collectively transform our lives and society.

The book concludes by considering the high cost of the CEO society. This raises the question of what is at stake in putting too much faith in the idea that CEOs and their ways of doing things provide the sure-fire route to social, political and economic wellbeing for all. The answer we propose is that the future of a fair, equal and democratic society cannot be delivered by the likes of Mark Zuckerberg, Bill Gates or Donald Trump. Although these people, together with others like them, may have helped transform the world we live in, to make it more cutthroat in its competitiveness and more unequal in its distribution of wealth, that doesn't mean things cannot change again. The book ends with a final warning against the dangers of worshipping at the altar of the CEO; a warning we hope will lead us all to seek better alternatives to the CEO society.

1

Welcome to the CEO society

One of the best known scenes from Oliver Stone's 1987 blockbuster movie *Wall Street* occurs when Gordon Gecko addresses the Teldar Paper shareholders meeting. With slicked back hair, a steely gaze and a half-cocked frown Gecko delivers a portentous sermon on how business should work. "I am not a destroyer of companies", he states, "I am a liberator of them."[1] For Gecko it is ruthless competition that is the font of both wealth and freedom. Gecko then delivers the film's most famous line: "the point is, ladies and gentleman, that greed – for lack of a better word – is good". The belief, and indeed the value that he propounds is that human flourishing, in all of its possible domains, results from the avaricious endeavours of self-seeking individualists. To put it more simply, the only sure path to progress is to allow the winners to take all and for everyone else to aspire to be like them.

Looking back some thirty years later, it feels as though this film was chronicling a still adolescent neoliberalism, while presaging the ruthlessness of the adult to come. If we believe the credo that life imitates art, then we are living through a particularly pernicious imitation right now. This was a film that foreshadowed a world where everything was permissible as long as it was profitable. It was difficult then to even imagine how nefarious this grown-up would turn out to be, maturing into a global society marked by widening inequality, lack of sustainable development and the threat of an environmental apocalypse. That difficulty no longer exists. In our current age, the corporate ethos that Gecko epitomised has spread to almost all areas of human existence. As contemporary political scientist Wendy Brown describes it, even dimensions of life that are not wealth generating, for example learning, dating or exercise, are now construed in market terms, controlled through market metrics, and administered through market methods.[2] Brown contends that

> Today, market actors – from individuals to firms, universities to states, restaurants to magazines – are more often concerned with their speculatively determined value, their ratings and rankings that shape future value, than with immediate profit. All are tasked with enhancing present and future value through self-investments that in turn attract investors. Financialised market conduct entails increasing or maintaining one's ratings, whether through blog hits, retweets, Yelp stars, college rankings, or Moody's bond ratings.

Even after a catastrophic financial crisis and mountains of evidence that business executives and Wall Street operators do more social harm than economic good, their mantra of competition, efficiency and profiteering continue to hold sway. With this, the CEO has emerged as the quintessential hero of our times.

It is what Gecko says immediately after the renowned 'greed is good' line that holds a special prescience for the themes explored in this book. It is at this point that he broadens the ambit of what he sees as greed's moral value. His conviction is that the "upward surge of mankind" that greed has made happen is not limited to business. The monologue ends: "greed – you mark my words – will not only save Teldar Paper, but that other malfunctioning corporation called the USA". The crowd applauds. What Oliver Stone both pointed to, and to a large extent foretold, through Gecko's hardnosed and moralistic competitiveness is how, in the context of neoliberalism, the corporation has become the ideal model for aspects of human enterprise all the way up to and including democratic government. Fast-forwarding to the late 2010s Stone's dystopian image of corporate greed as an idealised future seems to have come to fruition, with corporations having not just massively expanded in terms of their size and global reach, but also having become the model form of organising beyond compare.

It is the case today that, as a consequence of neoliberalism, corporate managerialism is a socially dominant value. In this sense, we can understand neoliberalism as the extension of market-based values to all dimensions of human endeavour. With neoliberalism comes managerialism, such that the management of market-based organisations is established as the preferred way to manage all other types of organisation as well. In this society all forms of human activity can be seen as analogous to corporate activity, with the players involved equivalent to businesses and their 'stakeholders'. In ancient spheres of life once thought of as being antithetical to business, corporate cultures, language and practices have taken hold. In universities, for example, students are now thought of as customers, courses are products, and the whole success of the institution has become newly reliant on corporate strategy, market rivalry, competitive positioning and branding. While this has become a well-supported means for universities to fill their coffers at the expense of student debt, not all agree. Indeed, in 2014 the International Student Movement (ISM) held a global week of action under the slogan 'we are students, not customers'. The point was to protest at the commercialisation of universities and promote the value of free education.

The management of public services from post offices, to local government, to libraries (that is, the ones that have not yet been privatised) have also suffered. Corporate management techniques have been brought in on the back of a narrative of progress that deems this approach to have the twin qualities of superiority and inevitability. The same goes for non-profit organisations, non-governmental organisations, charities, churches and community organisations. This all amounts to a managerialist domination whereby the means through which both the economy and society are run should "mirror the way that corporations are managed".[3]

There seems no limit to this fantastic enthusiasm for CEOs and their ways of getting things done. Self-styled American executive coach Larry Julian has even gone so far as to claim 'God is my CEO'.[4] In his book of that title, Julian brings his Christian deity into the boardroom, showing that following his principles of faith and becoming a "godly leader" can yield "tangible outcomes" such as "financial success, increased sales, reduced costs, productivity improvements, etc."[5] Julian's Christian God is not the one who banished the merchants and money dealers from the temple, but a modernised version who preaches business from the pulpit as some kind of holy CEO, newly installed at the apex of the trinity. This is a worldwide phenomenon. In Guangzhou, China, children as young as three are being sent to schools so that they can take CEO classes. Emblazoned on a poster outside one such school was the slogan 'Hand us a kid, we give you back a future leader';[6] an apparent modern-day corporate reformulation of the Jesuit slogan 'give me the boy, and I'll show you the man'

These tendencies also strike at the heart of contemporary work practice by impacting on newly emerging modes of employment, albeit in different ways. In the so-called 'gig economy' the risks once borne by wealthy corporations can be seamlessly transferred to the worker-cum-corporation. Can't get a job? Then start a company with you as the only employee. As employment contracts are torn up, and commercial ones are signed, the one-person micro-corporation is founded. No longer a precarious jobber, the worker is now the CEO of their very own business. If you are impoverished and living on the street, that's your fault: you should be a self-employed entrepreneur selling the *Big Issue* for pity and change. Self-employed personal trainer? Uber-driving moonlighter? Domestic cleaner? All can be reconceived as profit-maximising mini-CEOs. As innovation and entrepreneurship are touted as the route to prosperity, even individuals are fashioned to be corporations, and humanity reconceived in an image located in the nexus of business acumen and blinkered self-interest.

The turn to the corporation as a model for human endeavour echoes two major tenets of neoliberalism: market efficiency and individualism. As sociologist Michael Peters has explained, the ethos of neoliberalism values freedom over equality, and a particular form of freedom at that.[7] This is a freedom, for persons and corporations, from interference by government so that they are progressively less encumbered by rules and regulations when it comes to the pursuit of self-interest. The result, it is claimed, is that efficiencies will accrue from the liberation afforded by the market mechanism, and that this will be enabled by a competitive and possessive individualism. This is the very idea that informed Gordon Gecko's 'greed is good' mantra: that the unrelenting pursuit of self-interest and the unbounded drive to fulfil one's personal desires is the foundation not just for economic prosperity, but for morality itself. In place is a simultaneously narrowed and exaggerated vision originally presented by 18th century economist and philosopher Adam Smith. As Smith famously argued back in 1776:

> It is not from the benevolence of the butcher, the brewer, or the baker that we expect our dinner, but from their regard to their own interest. We address ourselves, not to their humanity but to their self-love, and never talk

to them of our own necessities but of their advantages. Nobody but a beggar chooses to depend chiefly upon the benevolence of his fellow-citizens.[8]

Gecko wasn't talking about a simple and hearty meal of meat, beer and bread, and nor did he share Smith's conviction that self-interest would and should always be tempered by compassion and generosity. Enshrined in Gecko's monologue was that idea that the 'self-love' to which Smith avers can be a motivating force for non-economic as well as economic life, especially if it is stripped of any vestiges of care for the well-being of others. This is not just about the division of labour and the mechanics of trade and exchange. It is tantamount to taking the self-oriented values that are derived from the management of the economic, most especially liberal capitalist, sphere and generalising them to all walks of life. It also entails taking the very specific practices and values that have developed in large corporations as a means to pursue self-interest, while claiming them to be both effective and morally righteous across all social and personal activity from education to electricity provision, and from health care to child care. It is here that the cultural meanings of selfishness and narcissistic self-preoccupation are upturned so they come to be regarded as virtues rather than personal shortcomings.

As the influential philosopher and social theorist Michel Foucault elucidated as early as the late 1970s, we need to be careful to ensure that we don't conflate the specific contours and characteristics of neoliberalism with that of classic liberalism. Indeed, Foucault's lectures in 1977 and 1978 showed him to be very much ahead of his time in recognising that, over and above advocating free trade and market-based economic organisation, neoliberalism is a system where:

> the overall exercise of political power can be modelled on the principles of a market economy ... taking the formal principles of a market economy and referring and relating them to, of projecting them onto a general art of government.[9]

The art of government to which Foucault refers is not limited to the government proper; that is, it is not just about those people formally appointed or elected to positions of state authority. He was instead suggesting that neoliberalism extends liberalism's purview from the purely economic realm, into the social, cultural and political practices and discourses that shape our experience of ourselves as subjects. In other words, neoliberalism's defining characteristic is the way that it takes the idea of market-based exchange as a value relevant to economic matters, and applies it to all aspects of life. In one important sense, our book offers a contemporary corollary to Foucault's historical insights as they have subsequently played out. That is, if the neoliberal conviction is that the market is a powerful motif for governing all of life, and CEOs are heroic figures leading the most powerful institutions of the global market, then the CEO too becomes, both actually and metaphorically, a model for success beyond the corporate and economic sphere. Here we see revealed the core idea of the CEO society.

Life exaggerates art

If we fast-forward from the early neoliberalism of the 1980s to the late neoliberalism of today, it appears that the dystopian vision painted in Oliver Stone's movie has grown into a full-blown, yet even more monstrously distorted, reality. This was the very reality that was played out on a massive scale with the election of Donald Trump to the US presidency. In his victory speech on 9 November 2016, Trump took to the stage, and with a look of self-satisfied confidence pledged his allegiance to the American people. In explaining the experience and credentials he would rely on to keep his promise of a returned American greatness, he did not begin with any political, civic or democratic discourse. Instead, he backed himself up with his self-acclaimed business success.

> Working together, we will begin the urgent task of rebuilding our nation and renewing the American dream. I've spent my entire life and business looking at the untapped potential in projects and in people all over the world. That is now what I want to do for our country.[10]

The idea that Trump would run the United States in the same way that he would run a corporation was a refrain that ran throughout his election campaign.[11] Echoed in this chorus was a managerial ideology which maintains that "politics and democracy are simply a hindrance on the way to efficiency and competitive advantages".[12] Democratic values, even those that still have some vestige in neoliberalism, are swept aside in favour of managerial know-how and privilege.

A key episode that exemplifies this happened just weeks before the election in October 2016, when a taped recording was uncovered of Trump making comments about his sexual approaches to women. In what was widely regarded as an admission of sexual assault, the tape had recorded Trump preparing for a meeting with actress Arianne Zucker in 2005. He said to his companion, TV host Billy Bush:

> I've got to use some Tic Tacs, just in case I start kissing her. You know I'm automatically attracted to beautiful – I just start kissing them. It's like a magnet. Just kiss. I don't even wait. And when you're a star, they let you do it, you can do anything … Grab them by the pussy. You can do anything.[13]

The controversy that ensued involved a number of other women coming forward alleging that Trump had also assaulted them. Trump's reported behaviour, as well as his lewd remarks, were condemned in the strongest terms by the mainstream media, his liberal opponents and even members of his own party. The public focus was quite rightly on the problem of violence against women, but what Trump's sexual braggadocio also laid bare was the dangerous culture of authoritarianism that was, and remains, patently present in contemporary American democracy.[14]

What the Trump tape scandal especially highlighted was how the idolisation of executives, as with celebrities, imbues them with dangerous levels of power. Even more perilous is how this adulation can lead a celebrity businessman-cum-politician to ignore accepted social mores and feel he can rise above the laws of the state and the most basic norms of propriety. This is the narcissistic cultural imaginary of the CEO, a person whose sovereignty renders them self-sufficient and beyond reproach. This was of course a central part of Trump's self-credentialism throughout his election campaign. His commitment as a presidential candidate was that he was the person who could single-handedly 'Make America Great Again' by bringing the arrogance of his business persona to bear on the management of corporation USA.[15]

Even when Trump's critics attacked him, it was often based on discrediting the effectiveness and ethics of his management, whether it be his loss-making businesses or his allegedly unscrupulous tax avoidance. Regardless, the idea was that a good CEO would make a good president, and a bad CEO would make a poor one. Even when his democratic opponent Hillary Clinton retaliated against Trump's bragging that he intended to run the United States like one of his corporate building projects, her argument was that "he relied on undocumented workers to make his project cheaper" and had "stiffed American workers".[16] With these remarks Clinton wasn't criticising the idea of business being a prototype for politics. She was just proposing that Trump wouldn't be any good at being a president because of his unscrupulous approach to business. Effectively, she concurred with the idea that liberal democracies such as the United States should be governed as if, in some bizarre metaphorical twist, they were corporations. Nevertheless, in the end the business-man triumphed over the politician-woman.

Throughout the campaign Trump's self-belief never wavered, and for him his own superiority in business and politics went unquestioned. To repeat Trump's own words: 'when you're a star they let you do it. You can do anything'. As we just saw, Trump was referring to a penchant for assaulting women, but his despicable and cavalier views on sexual violence extend also to his exercise of economic and political power. For some, Trump's approach to campaigning was praised for his 'telling-it-like-it-is' approach, but what he said about sexual assault really does get to the heart of contemporary political and social authority more generally. This is a situation where elite power all too often knows no limits, and doesn't take 'no' for an answer. This is a politics and culture that is patently anti-democratic and corporate, as well as one that serves to motivate the imaginary of what we are calling here the CEO society.

The CEO as a hero of our times

The figure of the CEO politician that Trump exemplifies marks the apogee of the executive as an idealised and heroic cultural icon beyond work and business, as well as beyond politics. While politicians like Trump may have campaigned on the basis that a CEO-styled action man was just what American politics needed, the acronym of CEO is, for politics, a repatriated one that did not actually originate in business. The use of the term 'chief executive officer', together with its abbreviation as CEO, as a title for a corporation's most senior official is actually relatively new. According to Merriam-Webster's dictionary the first usage of 'CEO' in business dates to the mid-1970s.[17] By the 1980s it was the de facto standard as a title for heads of corporations, and remains so.

Although today the title CEO is almost exclusively associated with corporate (and corporate-style) leadership, the earlier usage of the term chief executive was in reference to political or military leaders. In his 1876 annual message, United States President Ulysses S. Grant stated that:

> It was my fortune, or misfortune, to be called to the office of Chief Executive without any previous political training. From the age of 17 I had never even witnessed the excitement attending a Presidential campaign but twice antecedent to my own candidacy, and at but one of them was I eligible as a voter.[18]

Around the same time, in his 1850 novel *White Jacket,* Herman Melville referred to the senior lieutenant on a navy ship as a chief executive. The book's protagonist complains: "I have no reason to love the gentleman who filled that post aboard our frigate".[19] Why so? Not because of his lack of seafaring skills, but on account of his lack of concern for the wellbeing of the rank-and-file sailors. In Alexander Peterman's 1891 instructional manual *Elements of Civil Government,* a chief executive is an elected official, a president, governor or mayor whose responsibility was "seeing that the laws are enforced".[20]

By today, the idea of the CEO has outgrown its origins in politics and the military, and has become an established position in corporations as well, more generally, as a symbol of corporate power and leadership. Of all those charged with the power of an executive, that is with the authority and right to supervise, manage and direct, the CEO is chief amongst them. The CEO is the head, the apex of power pointed to the heavens by a triangular hierarchy of offices.[21] There is much more to the cultural meaning of the CEO than a simple association with formal administrative authority. As the person at the very pinnacle of the 'officer class' of corporate employees, it is the CEO who has long been "surrounded by an aura of high achievement, leadership positions, power, huge bank accounts, stretch limousines and luxury".[22] This image of the CEO, by now well established, is akin to that of the celebrity, with all of the accompanying material trappings of wealth and power.

This notion of the CEO celebrity is not metaphorical, and many corporate heads have achieved the status of being heroically appreciated household names. The very idea of the CEO as a celebrity refers to those CEOs who are well known outside of business and financial circles, most commonly through their presence in show business and popular culture.[23] To be a celebrity, a CEO be skilled not just at "being a good manager, but also at projecting a charismatic identity as a leader in the public domain".[24] Donald Trump is an extreme example of a celebrity CEO: a US president who has been the head of his own business empire, who has long been in the media spotlight, and who has also been a major television personality through his show *The Apprentice*. Like 1980s US President Ronald Reagan, he even has his own star on the Hollywood Walk of Fame. As well as this, there are many other CEOs who are household names, but who have never worked in the entertainment industry. Think of old hands like Richard Branson of Virgin and Bill Gates of Microsoft, as well as newer contenders such as Elon Musk of Tesla Motors and Mark Zuckerberg of Facebook. In addition to countless documentaries, the late Steve Jobs, former Apple CEO, has had four feature films made about him, the most recent of which earned Michael Fassbender an Academy award nomination for his portrayal of Apple's CEO hero.

Autobiographies, more often hagiographies, of CEOs litter the shelves of bookshops to the extent that they have become a special sub-genre. Not content with the heroes of not that long ago – whether they be explorers, astronauts, sportspeople or rock stars – contemporary audiences also seem to want to know about the inner working of the minds of senior businesspeople: to pry into their personal lives, learn what makes them tick, and perhaps hope that a bit of that celebrity success might rub off on them. As one might expect, these books are largely written by men. Jack Welch of General Electric, well known for his straight talking, published *Jack: Straight From the Gut*.[25] Louis V. Gerstner Jr. bragged about his extraordinary transformational leadership capabilities in *Who Says Elephants Can't Dance? How I Turned Around IBM*.[26] Founder and former boss of Nike, Phil Knight, portrays himself as a *Shoe Dog* when telling the story of how he built a mega-corporation on the back of a $50 loan.[27] Of course only a truly successful genre would be worthy of a spoof and 2016 saw the publication of *The Autobiography of Donald Trump's Hair*.[28]

In the rapid expansion of neoliberalism's influence since the 1970s and 1980s, it is perhaps unsurprising that the cultural valorisation of business has also resulted in corporate leaders being pitched in heroic terms. Notably, in the era before neoliberalism heads of organisations were largely unknown to the public; imagined to be conservative, conformist and detached figures who had the job of managing a cadre of other men in matching suits and ties. In the 1950s Sloan Wilson, in his novel *The Man in the Grey Flannel Suit*, painted an image of business executives as colourless conformists trapped in cage-like offices, robbed of individuality, and whose work ruined all dimensions of their miserable lives.[29]

In his 1956 book *The Organization Man* William H. Whyte similarly portrayed the executive as an empty and obedient yes-man, lacking in individual character or conviction.[30] Whyte characterised the 'social ethic' of the executives of his time as corporate herd followers, lacking in personal qualities and imprisoned by the beneficence of large organisations. In what he dubbed an 'age of organization', Whyte lamented the uniformity and unquestioned consensus that he saw as defining the collective identity of business executives. Were these executives to be admired and emulated? Certainly not. Whyte wholeheartedly advocated that corporate employees should actively resist the corporate cultures of their time. "For the more power organization has over him", Whyte wrote of the executive, "the more he needs to recognise the area where he must assert himself against it."[31]

Things have changed, and by end of the 1990s what author and business commentator Gideon Haigh called the 'cult of the CEO' was well established, most particularly in the United States but also elsewhere in the capitalist-democratic developed world.[32] No longer shackled by the collective orthodoxy of a previous generation, individual valour appeared to have entered the boardroom; at least as a value that was publicly lauded amongst the business community, its pundits and its acolytes. The new generation of CEOs were glorified as stock market superheroes who, in a single bound, could enable the corporations they led to leap to new heights of achievement and excellence. The new CEOs were imagined as some kind of Moses figures in pin-stripes who could by sheer force of will part the rough seas of the market so as to lead their organisations to the promised land. As Haigh clearly argued, this is a myth that defies the fact that the fortunes of any single large and complex organisation can be attributed to the behaviours of a single individual, especially in the short term. Nevertheless, the 'cult' he referred to was one that held as steadfastly to that idea that it could.

The exorbitant rewards that had started to be given to CEOs by this time reflected their new mythological status. So while Whyte might have bemoaned the waning of individualism in the mid-20th century, by the time the early 2000s had arrived that very same individualism had returned in an extravagant form. This new generation of managers were being entranced by a discourse of adventurous entrepreneur-ialism, told as they were to 'first, break all the rules' and foster individuality in each and every one of their employees.[33] Along with the growth of the cult of the CEO came massive personal rewards, with CEO salaries relative to those of average workers skyrocketing. In the United States in 1983 average CEO pay was 46 times that of ordinary workers. This rose to a multiple of 195 in 1993, 301 in 2003, 331 in 2013 and 335 in 2015.[34] The same pattern is repeated the world over, whether it be in Australia, Chile, France, Hungary, Taiwan or South Korea.[35]

With new cultural credibility, the media-enhanced image of the celebrity CEO was one rendered very much in an individualistic image, with the celebrity status being attached to the heroic assumption that firm performance could be attributed exclusively to the actions of the CEO.[36] If anyone else was involved, workers for example, then it was assumed that the value they created was just an extension of the might and will of their leader. To put it another way, a "CEO acquires celebrity status when media sources attribute a firm's positive performance to the CEO's actions in a way that generates a powerful impression of renown and credibility for that CEO".[37] This is the false promise at the heart of the CEO society.

The media and the culture industries have solidified the image of the CEO not just in terms of heroic status within their own company or industry, but more generally as an imaginary ideal that can guide ordinary citizens in their day-to-day lives. A person so affected might well have no interest in a company other than through a strange new form of fandom for its CEO. The 20th century idea of the executive as a dreary bureaucrat is nowhere to be seen here. Also absent is the image of capitalists as 'fat cat' exploiters, profiteers and personal wealth maximisers. The new celebrity CEO was a 'cool cat' who legitimated neoliberal capitalism and reinforced corporate power and brand image.[38]

As the 21st century dawned, the CEO had become a primary hero for neoliberal times; a kind of global super-leader whose personal charisma, aptitude and determination could single-handedly drive organisations to hitherto unknown levels of success and prosperity. So ubiquitous was the image of excellence that the idea of the CEO has become a metaphor for success in all aspects of life. Weight loss can be achieved by becoming the 'CEO of your own body',[39] men can be romantically successful by getting the 'inside story from the C-suite on leadership that works in life and in business',[40] and the good life can be achieved by becoming the 'CEO of me'.[41]

Corporate values/social values

If the CEO is a hero of our times, the times we are talking of are those we call neoliberal. As we have already canvassed, having developed globally since the 1970s and 1980s, we are now living in an era where on an international level large corporations control more and more aspects of our lives. This has brought with it a dominant doctrine that prizes the free market as the most effective means of organising political, social and economic affairs.[42] By this logic, governments should retreat from interfering with market processes, instead being obliged to ensure their liberated functioning. Like the liberalism from which it takes its name, neoliberalism proffers a belief in the inevitability and desirability of capitalism. Moreover, as political economists Gérard Duménil and Dominique Lévy explain, neoliberalism is based on a particular extension of capitalist inequality as enabled by a reconfiguration of class interests.[43] This emerges through widened structural income and wealth inequalities, and the attendant growth of power being held by a distinct social minority.[44]

With neoliberalism we have a mode of domination exercised in the nexus of capital ownership, executive management and the reach of financial institutions. Central to the emergence of this was a process whereby corporations were liberated by the new freedoms of the global market economy. These economic changes also have significant social dimensions and effects. Neoliberalism entails the modification of economic relations and practices so as to favour what has come to be called 'the 1%' – a phrase popularised by the Occupy Movement from 2011 to demonstrate how global wealth was concentrated amongst the vast minority of the world's population. With their slogan 'we are the 99%', Occupy illustrated both the potential power of the minority and their exploitation by the majority.

Such dissent is not just about the unbalanced facts of economic life, but also about the socio-cultural ideals that it has generated. As Wendy Brown argues, with neoliberal reason:

Both persons and states are construed on the model of the contemporary firm, both persons and firms are expected to comport themselves in ways that maximise their capital value in the present and enhance their future value, and both persons and states do so through practices of entrepreneurialism, self-investment, and/or attracting investors.[45]

It is in the character of the CEO that this construal is personified as a position to be respected and emulated. Having begun to outline this development, it is our task in the rest of this book to fully interrogate the ways that the CEO has become a model not just for business activity, but also across a broad range of social and cultural locations. It is also our task to assess the dangers that this nigh on worship of executives poses for society; that is, for the book's eponymous idea of the 'CEO society'. This is a society where corporate leadership has become the model for transforming not just businesses, but all forms of economic, political, cultural and personal affairs. No longer just managerial administrators, the very idea of a CEO is, for many, a cultural icon. It is the reverence for corporate wealth and power, for example, that fuelled the success of the television programme *The Apprentice*. As well as propelling Donald Trump to stardom in the mid-2000s, the show was replicated the world over from Africa to Vietnam. It is a popular illustration of how CEOs epitomise modern desires for innovation, wealth and success.

The growth of the CEO society has been heralded by the metaphorical adoption of CEO language, practices and values such that everything ranging from fighting for promotions to running democratic campaigns to even looking for love can be seen through the lens of the lionised business executive. This is a dangerous path that we find ourselves on after decades of neoliberal consensus: a path where life itself is reduced to a market analysis of costs and profits, competitive rivalry, functional efficiency and the instrumental pursuit of self-interest. In question here is not only how we got ourselves into this situation, but also what it portends for the future of democracy and society as a whole, and what it means for individual citizens in the contemporary world. What demand investigation are the vicissitudes of how corporate values conventionally associated with business executives are becoming a modern paradigm for modelling social relations as a whole.

Whether it is in business, politics, culture or social life, what is at issue is the late stage of narcissistic corporate neoliberalisation where the boss of a corporation has become established as a perverse ego ideal across so many aspects of existence. There are of course many people who celebrate this idealisation of the business executive, and we will be meeting them in the pages to come, but understanding this phenomenon requires a more critical and nuanced view. In one sense we can account for the undue influence of corporations on politics and culture as linked, for example, to campaign contributions and marketing. Beyond this, what also needs to be emphasised is the reconfiguration of these spheres in conformity to a corporate ethos epitomised by the CEO, revealing how even as financial capitalism is being progressively challenged by some, we find ourselves increasingly living in a CEO society.

In exploring the character and conditions of the CEO society, what we are examining is the impact of corporate values associated with authoritarianism, self-determinism and economic rationality both inside and outside of boardrooms. Politics is one central domain, with Donald Trump being the most severe example of how the CEO society creates a form of corporate pseudo-democracy where politicians are not just influenced by major companies but embody their values in extremis. Beyond politics, in need of interrogation is the influence of this trend on interpersonal relationships, where social bonds become judged as if they were 'market opportunities', education is an investment in future earnings and, along the way, exploitation and profiteering come to be regarded as noble achievements, as, for example, heralded in *Forbes* magazine's homage to the richest of the rich in its annual list of the world's billionaires. Included in *Forbes'* thirtieth anniversary list in 2017 was advice on 'billionaires' secrets building wealth'.[46]

The implications of the CEO society are both significant and dangerous. Traditional values, or even hopes, of social welfare, political democracy, community support and personal compassion fall increasingly by the wayside. Nevertheless, we are at a time where the celebration of the CEO as role model continues unabated in many spheres of life. Tellingly, this is all happening at a time when social and economic inequality are burgeoning around the world. Indeed, with Trump's election in the United States it could even be said that despite the problems and inequality created by corporate neoliberalism, it is still a business executive who is thought by many to be the very person who can solve those problems. While market ideologies remain flashpoints for political and social debate, a defining feature of today's CEO society is that the ideal of the business executive epitomises modern desires for innovation and success economically, politically and culturally.

Executising society

As we have been discussing, the rise of the CEO is inexorably linked to the explosion of neoliberalism, and the relations and distinctions between the two are worthy of elaboration. At its heart, neoliberalism represents the move towards a hyper-capitalist social order, entailing the adoption of market values as the cornerstone for structuring social, political and economic relations. What this neoliberal transformation involves appears on the surface rather straightforward. It is the reduction of the state and expansion of the private sector in all areas of social, political and economic life. It means in principle that traditionally public areas such as health care and education must conform to market logics of competition, efficiency and profitability. It furthermore takes as its foundation the idea that freedom is equated with individualism and capitalism. It also conjures up utopian visions of a market society based on innovation, meritocracy and, ultimately, personal freedom and responsibility.

The reality is obviously quite different. Neoliberalism has led to exploding inequality, the expansion of the power of capital, corporate social domination and the erosion of liberal democracy.[47] Its ideological championing of market freedom has resulted in greater economic anxiety and a systematic attack on public welfare. In its place, what has emerged is social division and a general backlash against the state and much of civil society. In short, it has brought about a society where the majority struggle and elites prosper. Underpinning this reality is the promotion of a market logic claimed to be both objective and desirable. Perhaps the most obvious of these is marketisation. In general terms it entails "adopting the methods and values of the market to guide policy creation and management".[48] Here the enemy is red tape and inefficient bureaucracy, problems that can supposedly only be defeated by letting the market run free. The privatisation of public services is a central way that marketisation has been implemented. Indeed, the big sweep of neoliberal reforms in the 1980s and 1990s in countries like the UK and Australia saw a massive transfer of state-owned organisations into private hands, including energy companies, state-owned banks, trains and telecommunications. The private sector and the 'enterprise' that it was said to harbour was hailed as a model of productivity and innovation. If marketisation is the adoption of neoliberal methods in the public and not-for-profit sectors, then privatisation is their full-scale handover to private interests.[49] As scholars Megginson and Netter observe:

> It is rare for a completely new economic policy to move from novelty to global orthodoxy in the space of two decades. Nonetheless, this has occurred for the political

and economic policy of privatization, defined as the deliberate sale by a government of state-owned enterprises (SOEs) or assets to private economic agents.[50]

Under the logic of privatisation, it is assumed that institutions and services are best placed into private hands. In this respect, the public interest becomes dependent on the spread of private interest.

Neoliberalism is also characterised by the spread of financialisation. This concept refers to "a process whereby financial markets, financial institutions, and financial elites gain greater influence over economic policy and economic outcomes".[51] Everything is judged according to physical metrics, and profitability and value are measured purely in economic terms. As such, the only true consideration is whether something is financially viable – all other goals being superfluous. Importantly, while these values are ubiquitous they are also quite flexible; actually existing neoliberalism is malleable enough to fit a wide range of specific cultural social and economic contexts,[52] even if its explicit meaning can appear tricky to pin down. Despite this inconsistency, however, neoliberalism continues to operate in a manner that respects overriding hyper-capitalist ideals and whose particular instantiation can still be implemented strategically to change the dynamics of a diverse set of organisations and communities.

For an ideology that is so enraptured with the freedom of individuals there has thus far been a profound gap in understanding the forms of power that neoliberalism affords to particular people. What we do know is that since its inception neoliberalism has been accompanied by the presence of charismatic economic and political leaders. In the United States in the 1980s, for example, it was fuelled by a cult of personality for larger than life masculine characters such as President Ronald Reagan, and CEOs including Chrysler's Lee Iacocca and General Electric's Jack Welch. These people were presented as leaders-cum-action heroes who would bring market deliverance to companies, countries and ultimately the world.

This form of capitalist idolisation points to a deeper neoliberal discourse of executive power as it relates to marketisation. Notable is the widespread belief that a business-style leadership is necessary for solving organisational, social and economic problems. The chief executive officer is put forward as the embodiment of the strong, capable and forward-thinking leader who can get things done. The prominence of the CEO therefore is not just economic but ideological. It is the idealisation of the figure who encapsulates capitalist freedom and success; the individual who is able to achieve their goals regardless of what gets in their way. Even more perniciously, the very idea of the CEO serves as the basis for restructuring social and political relations. Capitalism is constantly in a crisis of leadership, plagued by corporate scandal and disaster, economic misfortunes and financial instability, ecological unsustainability and environmental catastrophe, joblessness and poverty, and is in need of someone to solve them. The CEO is one such character, like a wishfully imagined lone ranger, who can be called on to fix what is wrong. Values such as democracy and collective deliberation are dismissed in favour of an all-powerful executive figure who can deliver profits and progress, and solve problems.

Democracy and the CEO way of life

More than eighty years ago, the American philosopher John Dewey wrote an impassioned plea for how democracy was much more than a system of government, and was much better regarded as a 'way of life'.[53] Dewey expressed concern for how the social values and ideals that democracy represented could too easily be reduced to its formal and institutional operations as "a special political form, a method of conducting government, of making laws and carrying on governmental administration by means of popular suffrage and elected officers".[54] As a way of life, democracy was better understood as an approach to human sociality and co-existence based on cooperation, egalitarianism, equality, participation, self-regulation and rule by consent. For Dewey, democratic living was directly opposed to autocracy and authoritarianism, as well as to the oppression and coercion they entailed.

In an up-turned way the CEO society also proffers a 'way of life', though one very much antithetical to Dewey's democratic ideals. It is a way of life because it goes beyond the specific institutions and organisations that CEOs inhabit. The CEO society has, in this sense, transcended the corporate world and come to inform how people behave and interact in society more generally. The CEO lifestyle has a broad ambit, and can be seen in the budding entrepreneurialism foisted on an Uber driver, and the competitive individualism that provokes many parents to want their seven-year-olds to beat the competition in government-sponsored school exams. With this, the values pressed on to our lives in the CEO society rest on inequality, human rivalry, self-interest and exploitation. And while Dewey could not have presaged the society of today, his presentation of democracy as being counter to authoritarian inequality has a direct corollary to present conditions. The CEO society, even though it exists and has been enabled by the formalities of liberal democracy, is in its very essence anti-democratic. At its worst democracy itself is rendered in authoritarian and competitive terms, reduced to a market for votes in a contest for political authority. At risk in this executive approach to life is the very possibility of retaining democracy as a social ideal worthy of upholding.

The rise of this CEO 'way of life' has not gone unchallenged. There is a veritable explosion of attempts to construct a progressive social alternative. Indeed, emerging political movements such as Occupy and Black Lives Matter have eschewed the need for a leader. They have instead experimented with collective decision making, shared power structures and an ethos of democracy rather than executive authority. Consequently, they serve at the forefront of taking power back from CEOs and redistributing it to the rest of society. Emerging is a clash – an existential social choice – between whether we lead a CEO or democratic life as a society.

2

The idolisation
of the CEO

In 2008 the global economy teetered on the edge of total collapse. The financial system was in ruins and its free market values were close to being completely socially devalued. Even the staunchly conservative and neoliberal *Wall Street Journal* proclaimed that the "crisis compels economists to reach for a new paradigm".[1] Not surprisingly, the bankers and corporate executives responsible for causing this crash went from being popular heroes to public enemies. Suddenly the titans of Wall Street were no longer the self-styled 'masters of the universe' that Tom Wolfe had defined some twenty years earlier but were virtual psychopaths whose wily greed led the world to the brink of financial ruin.[2] It appeared, at least for a while, that the vanities of the financial elites might finally burn on the bonfire of hubris. The fire soon fizzled, and even as the cultural stock of individual executives plummeted, the perceived value of the business executive emerged largely unscathed.

Yet where did this corporate hero come from? More importantly, how did it manage to resurrect its heroic status despite evidence that it is not deserved? It is tempting to think of this capitalist idol as timeless, as if there is no difference between the merchant whose entrepreneurial spirit brought goods to all corners of the globe, the top-hatted captain of industry who revolutionised production and with it society, and the tech entrepreneur whose discovery ushers the future into the present. Looking beyond these rosy images, a more complex and unsettling picture emerges. This is not an affirmative impression of the valiant businessperson whose ingenuity should be a role model for one and all. As we began to explore in the previous chapter, it is instead of a society where corporate ideals of rivalry, self-interest and even exploitation are spreading so as to transform all areas of human life in its own image.

Our attention is this chapter turns to how the rise of the CEO society emerged through the history of the chief executive as an increasingly public figure, especially in the West. The 19th century business titans and robber barons evolved into the conservative professional executive technocrat of the post-war era. The free market revolution of the 1980s glamorised the image of businesspeople and simultaneously, CEOs came to symbolise cherished ideals of creativity and enterprise and were publicly perceived as singularly responsible for the success or failure of a company. As the 20th century turned into the new millennium this fetishising of the CEO spread into a broader promotion of CEO values. CEOs had become cherished and admired celebrities as well as role models whose lessons could be applied to all areas of one's existence. We witnessed the birth of the CEO society populated by individuals seeking to deploy business executive principles anytime, anywhere and for any purpose.

Curse of the CEO

The CEO is often presented as a heroic figure. This may sound like hyperbole, but even a quick review of the business and popular media reveals the almost mythic esteem often granted to executives, and their ability in, according to *CEO Magazine*, "doing the right thing" while achieving "success in the global marketplace".[3] When a particular executive fails, or is embroiled in scandal, there is a quick defence that it is the individual who is at fault for not living up to the moral status of the position they hold. So when in 2017 the discredited boss of Turing Pharmaceuticals, Michael Schkreli, was convicted of securities fraud and conspiracy in the United States, it wasn't greed-infused CEO capitalism that prompted him to ruthlessly profit from price-gouging on life-saving medications. Rather, the pharmaceutical industry disowned him as a 'bad apple' whose individual actions had besmirched an industry that describes itself as dedicated to the "increased longevity and improved lives for millions of patients".[4] As one individual is justly punished, the system that created him persists.

The Schkreli case points to the way that moral judgements are passed on CEOs and corporate activity, and how this morality draws on the individualism central to neoliberalism. Accordingly, while individual CEOs can be judged on the morality of their behaviour, from a neoliberal standpoint this morality is entirely a question of personal character rather than being a cultural or systemic phenomenon. Moreover, CEOs should be good, not just for goodness' sake, but because, as reported in the *Harvard Business Review*, there is a 'return on character' whereby:

> CEOs whose employees gave them high marks for character had an average return on assets of 9.35% over a two-year period. That's nearly five times as much as what those with low character ratings had; their ROA averaged only 1.93%.[5]

It is thus posited that the morality of the 'good CEO' is what enables them to be the embodiment of capitalist agency. They are the people who can navigate the brutally competitive modern marketplace and come out on top with their ethical credentials intact. Consequently, they serve as a model for the righteous exercise of freedom itself. Ironically, this personification of freedom is accompanied by a general feeling of unfreedom as experienced by many whose labour is at stake in the free marketplace. The difficulty of finding a job in line with one's skills and potential, the anxiety of constant competition, the fear that one will never achieve one's professional and personal goals all contribute to the affirmation of those CEOs who have somehow managed to succeed on the back of their own character, talent and initiative.

In practical terms, the individualisation of corporate success leads to a desire to uncover what type of personality is needed to reach such capitalist status. In short, how can I too be a winner in a market system full of losers? If it is accepted that executives, who it is assumed have pulled themselves up by their proverbial bootstraps, deserve all their success, then for the rest of us to be successful, we need to know how they got there and what we can do to be just like them. By this logic, it matters little that empirical evidence clearly shows that those with wealth have a built-in advantage over those without it.[6]

The fact remains that many, if not most, executives are successful due more due to social advantage than to any particular personal traits or hard work.[7] Empirically, there is a disturbing lack of diversity among top executives, and even when women and minorities succeed in management they most commonly are better educated than their white male counterparts, adopt perspectives and values associated with traditional elitism, and come from privileged family backgrounds. Effectively, to be accepted amongst the elite, they cannot differ too much from other people in power.[8] This contradiction between public perception and actually existing reality of executives can lead executives themselves to exaggerate their prowess to shareholders and the wider public over and above their class- and race-based privilege.

Renowned academic and present Dean of Harvard College Rakesh Khurana has written about what he calls the curse of the superstar CEO.[9] He observes that the defining characteristic of CEOs is not business acumen or a visionary understanding of the social, economic and political context. Rather it is charisma, the ability to convince others of the CEO's own value and worth. In his words:

The secret to being a successful CEO today, it's almost universally assumed, is leadership. Such qualities as strategic thinking, industry knowledge, and political persuasiveness, though desirable, no longer seem essential. Particularly when a company is struggling, directors in the market for a new CEO – as well as the investors, analysts, and business journalists who are watching their every move – will not be satisfied with an executive who is merely talented and experienced. Companies now want leaders. But what makes a successful leader? When people describe the qualities that enable a CEO to lead, the word they use most often is 'charisma'.[10]

Khurana refers to this as a curse since this means that the basis for corporate leadership is worryingly insubstantial. It is about perception rather than sustainable long-term innovation and growth. Moreover, it undermines the development of new skills and organisational models that could actually deliver these desirable outcomes. Charisma plays dangerously into desires by organisations for a 'corporate saviour'.[11]

This executive curse transcends the boardroom, putting on a cultural pedestal those whose main attribute is charisma and the ability to talk their way into power in the manner, for example, that Donald Trump used the stage of the political rally to convince large numbers of Americans to vote for him. Such mythologising puts at risk sustainable economic growth and genuine innovation, instead reinforcing an ethos of impressive but ultimately hollow promises. Short-term gains are prioritised over long-term thinking. Charismatic authoritarianism is promoted at the expense of cooperation and democracy. Hence, the curse of the CEO is not only bad for business; it is a drain on society as whole. The question, then, is no longer can executives save us but can we be saved from them?

Executive history

As highlighted above, CEOs are amongst the most revered members of modern society. Khurana describes them in quasi-religious terms, as self-identified saviours who seek to be worshipped. They stride across boardrooms and through corridors of power around the world, supposedly wielding their influence and driving forward innovation and job creation. The fates of these individual captains of industry of course can ebb and flow, as can their popular esteem. However, the trajectory is one where the ideal of the CEO grows ever stronger, extending beyond the corporate boardroom into all spheres of society. Yet this modern role model has a complicated and evolving history. Tellingly, its beginnings had little to do with conventional economics, especially in relation to the conflation of the idea of the CEO with the spirit of entrepreneurship. The roots of the meaning of the term entrepreneurship itself can be found on the battlefield of war. This is a term that was "borrowed from the French in the 15th Century to describe a military commander leading troops into battle".[12] Such military foundations point to the deeper ideology at the heart of this heroic figure, one premised on power, competition and conquest. The rising dominance of the free market only entrenched these values further.

This can be linked to the origin of liberal economics in the formative works of Adam Smith.[13] The (in)famous concept of the 'invisible hand' first proposed by Smith in passing became important for promoting an early vision of the liberal capitalist economy. This was an economy seen to be moved collectively by the unknowing pursuit of individual self-interest by a multitude of economic actors. It was an economy where individuals, each one employing their abilities for their own benefit, are moved by this unseen force to promote the collective good even though they harbour no intention to do so. As we saw in chapter 1, Smith's work, or at least a narrowed version of it, was a forerunner in advancing competition as the foundation for society generally, and beyond the economic realm. To this end, the historical importance of Smith was largely based on his role in the "elevation of competition to the level of a general organizing principle of economic society".[14]

A century later, English political philosopher John Stewart Mill would declare that "only through the principle of competition has political economy any pretension to the character of a science".[15] Mill was implying that competition alone could be claimed to have causal validity in explaining the machinations of the economy. Everything else is, in the language of economics, *ceteris paribus*: effectively, nothing else matters. Not just a question of scientific inquiry, Mill also suggested that self-interest, executed through competition, was a matter of public morality as much as private advantage,

in that more than organised government it served to "recon-
cile public benefit with private pursuit of personal gain".[16]
By implication, to contribute to this moral project, the ideal
citizen of the political economy was one who embraced an
entrepreneurial competitive spirit for his or her own maximal
economic benefit.

This ethos was reflected in the increasing social and
economic significance of companies and corporations from
the 18th century onwards. The corporation, as a legal body,
was popularised, in a nascent form, in the late Middle Ages
as a means of constituting guilds, towns, universities and
religious institutions. However, the proliferation of the
corporate company, first to meet mercantilist needs and
then transforming into the industrial juggernauts in the
1800s, was a significant change that spurred the creation of
the 'modern' executive.[17] This also saw the beginning of the
expansion of private business interests into the public realm,
with the industrial revolution in the West giving birth to a
'gilded age' of wealthy industrialists who controlled not only
the economy but also had significant political influence, especially in the United States.[18] Liberalism provided a convenient
moral justification for the amassing of great personal wealth
by the few.

The promotion of profit maximisation as the highest
social and economic value also brought forward an idealised vision of business executives as the main progenitors of
progress. In the early 20th century these were the scientific
managers who were forging more efficient and productive
organisations, and spreading prosperity in some *avant la*

lettre version of trickle-down economics. Engineers like Frederick Winslow Taylor and industrialists like Henry Ford were lionised for revolutionising production in the factory and on the assembly line. Many felt that what they were doing for manufacturing heralded the prospect of a better, more modern world filled with prosperity for all.[19] In 1908, when the inaugural Dean of Harvard Business School, Edwin Gay, was looking for someone to teach industrial organisation, he brought Taylor on board. He was hugely popular because, as a member of Harvard's faculty at the time said, "it seemed to provide something of a formula for management". By 1914, a course dedicated to 'The Taylor System of Management' had become a mainstay at the school.[20]

Although some may have seen them as heroes, this view was not universal. Elsewhere, business leaders were being portrayed in much less sanguine terms as capitalist exploiters. Karl Marx famously declared that "capital is dead labour, which, vampire-like, lives only by sucking living labour, and lives the more, the more labour it sucks".[21] Similarly, he proclaimed that the bourgeoisie "has become a vampire that sucks [the smallholders'] blood and brains and throws them into the alchemist's cauldron of capital".[22] Somewhat more prosaically, and on the opposite end of the political spectrum, Frederick Taylor was called to give testimony to a US congressional hearing of the House Committee to Investigate Taylor and Other Systems of Shop Management in 1912. Why? His approach to management was questioned for being authoritarian, abusive and even un-American.[23]

The entrepreneur as personified in the CEO, and the entrepreneurial spirit as a value at the heart of capitalism, has long been caught between being seen on the one had as a central figure of economic hope and prosperity, while on the other hand being challenged as economically and even socially undesirable. The evolution of the CEO to this day reflects something of this ultimately productive tension. Business commentator Jerry Useem explores this in his consideration of the '100 years of evolution' of the chief executive.[24] Specifically, he highlights the transition of the public persona of the CEO over this century, oscillating from tyrant to statesman to destroyer. By Useem's account the tyrannical business executive characteristic of the late 19th and early 20th century robber baron era had, from the 1920s on been metamorphosed into something of bland administrator, a corporate yes-man. It wasn't until the later 20th century, after Ronald Reagan and Margaret Thatcher's neoliberal reforms in the 1980s, that CEOs came to occupy the twin personas of culturally valorised celebrities and single-minded 'destroyers' obsessed with maximising shareholder value at all costs. These different characterisations signified not only the changing nature of economic relations but also of its perceptions of leadership.

Amidst the vicissitudes of the value judgements made against CEOs, there have been constant efforts to prop up the image of the business executive as a legitimate public figure who contributes to the public good and is worthy of emulation and respect. Reflected in such heroisation is a central dimension of capitalist ideology: namely that the rich and powerful members of the capitalist class are deserving of their elevated position on account of merit rather than by mere dint of circumstance. In play is the Janus-faced history of capitalism itself. On one side, a market economy must continually innovate and evolve in order to briefly satisfy, but never finally satiate, its seemingly unquenchable thirst for profit. On the other side, it must recreate itself as a positive force for social progress and economic justice. This dynamic is akin to economist Joseph Schumpeter's highly influential notion of creative destruction.[25] With this term Schumpeter identifies what he sees as a defining feature of industrial capitalism: it "incessantly revolutionizes the economic structure *from within*, incessantly destroying the old one".[26] In parallel, it would seem, the social meaning of that structure requires a similar cycle of destruction and innovation. Along these lines, anthropologist David Harvey has drawn on this idea to describe the internal dynamics of neoliberalism itself:

> [Neoliberalism] has become incorporated into the common sense way many of us interpret, live in, and understand the world. The creation of this neoliberal system has entailed much 'creative destruction', not only of prior institutional frameworks and powers ... but also of divisions of labour, social relations, welfare provisions, technological mixes, ways of life and thought, reproductive activities, attachments to the land and habits of the heart.[27]

Neoliberalism, and the form of capitalism it is attached to, must, by this account, confront all crises with new discourses to justify its reason for being, yet must do so without altering its defining features.[28]

The evolution of the business leader reflects this social history of capitalism and of capitalists. What we now call a CEO, as a cultural figure, is a running personification of capitalist progress emerging from the industrial revolution onwards, all the way from the robber baron, to the company man and to the celebrity CEO. Across these different personifications we can see how the very idea of the CEO represents the current instantiation of a broad and evolving imagining of the meaning of both capitalists and capitalism. Most affirmatively, the CEO has been symbolised through a romantic vision of leadership that would trickle down so as to shape social wellbeing overall. In the contemporary era, such capitalist veneration has reached new heights through the creation of the idealised figure of the CEO celebrity hero.

The paradox of authority

The CEO is a profoundly contradictory figure within contemporary capitalism. As we have explained, CEOs can be worshipped or despised; they can be cast as heroes or villains; they can be portrayed as the drivers of progress or the ones most responsible for dragging it down. This duality points to the more fundamental tension: that the CEO must at once be economically exploitative and socially legitimate. An irony of the free market is revealed: for its profiteers to prosper they must also seek to be culturally beloved, or at the very least accepted, while doing whatever it takes to achieve that prosperity.

Culturally, CEOs live a type of double life. They are required to act like utterly ruthless businesspeople whose unnervingly singular focus is on the bottom line and the financial growth of the corporations they lead. This could and often does mean sacrificing their employees' wellbeing and even their livelihoods on the altar of profit maximisation and staying globally competitive. If necessary, this can ultimately entail overseeing the demise of the firm itself at the hands of its chief executive, liquidating it for the greater financial good of its owners (of which the contemporary CEO is inevitably one, given remuneration structures). Yet the CEO must match this cold commercial prowess with the perception that the outcomes of their actions serve valuable social functions. This is especially so when this success comes at the individual and collective expense of the majority of the population. Clearly, to be effective, a CEO must be publicly shown to be pursuing a purpose that is loftier than mere economic exploitation and lusty profiteering. There is simply no long-term mileage in having the reputation of Al 'Chainsaw' Dunlap, the 1990s CEO of Sunbeam whose cavalier management practices of merciless downsizing, focus on short-term profit and accounting creativity saw him both rise to fame and fall from grace. Dunlap was renowned as a ruthless downsizer who was, at least for a time, revered by the stock market for his unremitting pursuit of profits at any cost; that is, until a shareholder class-action suit was filed against him for accounting fraud.[29]

To avoid this public fate and to ensure the social reproduction of a market economy, and the value of the CEOs who drive it, a process of cultural moralisation is required.[30] In relation to this, sociologists Marion Fourcade and Kieran Healy identify a longstanding convention in economics of expounding the morality of markets.[31] This can come in a number of forms, as they explain:

> the *doux commerce* tradition is carried forward by arguments that the market nourishes personal virtues of honest behavior, civility, and cooperation. Others have seen markets as a necessary condition for freedom in other aspects of life, most prominently in politics and in the cultural realm. A final tradition, represented today by the bulk of prescriptive macroeconomics, emphasizes economic growth as a condition for human progress.[32]

Related to this moralisation of the market is a moralisation of chief executives themselves; they are often promoted as the key to human progress *tout court*. It was common for business leaders in the late 19th and early 20th century to be portrayed as being ethically gilded with ideals of paternalism. They were responsible for morally and economically 'taking care' of their employees; guiding them to a more righteous (and profitable) way of life. This moralistic form of top management evolved, from the early 20th century, into the professional administrator. Administrators were meant to faithfully oversee the workings of a good business and in doing so reveal the way to best organise and oversee a more efficient and progressive society. They were depicted as, quite literally, the personification of the perfect functionary in sociologist Max Weber's notion of the bureaucratic ideal type.[33] In the post-Second World War era this developed into the responsible company executive: the dutiful and forward-thinking caretaker whose ideas and authority would ensure that the company was profitable and sustainable. Managers of that time were thought of as somewhat drab characters, conformists who faithfully executed the requirements of the corporations they served until they graciously accepted the gift of a gold watch marking their retirement.

The development of the idea of the CEO to this day reveals a more general paradox of authority, one that transcends capitalism itself. Notably, the less socially useful those in power actually are, the more socially useful they must present themselves to be. More precisely, there is often an inverse relationship between the actual benefit of a culturally sanctioned authority figure and the benefit that they claim to have made. This paradox manifests itself in two distinct but intimately associated ways. It is both personal and systematic in character. Authority, hence, must be justified equally to the individuals who are granted and who exercise power and privilege as well as to the underlying system that permits them to do so.

The modern-day chief executive is a prime example of this contradiction of capitalist authority. However, this is by no means a historical exception. Market-driven chattel slavery in the 18th and 19th centuries operated according to a similarly legitimising paradoxical logic.[34] Slave owners were supposedly no mere exploiters and brutalisers of indentured men, women and children. Rather, they were officially put forward as their rightful guardians, their protectors and providers. Ideologically, this bitter cultural fiction was maintained through a discourse of racial superiority. By the mere fact of their 'whiteness', slave owners were seen as deserving of being a master of human bondage. Entrenched contemporary racism owes a debt to this sad legacy. As writer, lecturer and broadcaster Kenan Malik explains:

> the persistence of differences of rank, class and peoples in a society that had accepted the concept of equality ... the discourse of race did not arise out of the categories of Enlightenment discourse but out of the relationship between Enlightenment thought and the social organisation of capitalism.[35]

It is not surprising to learn that such justifications of authority were also adopted by early industrialists in relation to their employment of wage labour. Wage labour was propagated based on an idealisation of business owners as having the knowledge and experience to know how to best manage their firm and its employees. Their expressed innovativeness, commercial acumen and financial savvy were perceived to be proof positive that they were fundamental to keeping the corporation, and more broadly the economy, afloat. The managerial class was thus born. Their privilege was underwritten by the belief in the inherent superiority of certain types or classes of people in comparison to others. This could be understood either through a racehorse theory of good breeding or as a function of an individualised meritocracy. Either way, business was positioned as an environment where only the fittest survived, and where those survivors were the ones most capable of ensuring the evolution and progress of society.

The legitimate authority of contemporary CEOs is an extension of this genealogy. They are justified as the rightful leaders of a society whose extreme financial rewards, elevated social status and heightened political power are authorised based on their perceived individual merit as businesspeople and the broader contributions they make to the economy. In a world of economic competition it is the CEOs, so the story goes, who rose to the top and as such are deserving of our full respect, devotion and deference. Capitalism thus continues to be portrayed by its acolytes as a natural order where those who enjoy power, privilege and prestige are those who morally deserve it.

CEO idol

Throughout human history people have turned to idols for salvation, be they heavenly or secular. Coming from above or walking amongst us mere mortals, idols help make sense of the existing world, calm our existential anxieties and promise guidance that will sweep us away from woe. History is also littered with a collection of false idols, brilliantly glittering but ultimately hollow figures that lead individuals and communities astray. In modern times, CEOs have been raised up to idol status. They stand as the most exalted golden calves of our times – superhuman figures to be followed and emulated by the masses.

So exalted, citizens, customers and workers are cajoled into looking at managers as paragons of virtue and professionalism. Business owners and entrepreneurs are offered up as the epitome of a vital and necessary entrepreneurial spirit. Company presidents, as much as being positioned as creative entrepreneurs, must also exude the sober ethics required for making profits and being responsible fiscal and social citizens. Central to the everyday economic reproduction of the market has been this idolisation of its most prominent leaders. Once upon a time it was John F. Kennedy who said to the nation, "we choose to go to the moon". Today the honour goes to Amazon boss Jeff Bezos, who in 2017 announced, "It's time for America to go back to the Moon, this time to stay ... We should build a permanent settlement on one of the poles of the Moon".[36]

Despite the accolades and pronouncements, however, it can appear strange to publicly highlight successful businesspeople in light of their morally questionable responsibility to prioritise profits over all else. Yet the admiration of businesspeople is couched in an appealing promise of individual advancement and social progress. The trick is to promote the idea that the free market can make society better for everyone. This idea was infamously lauded in Ronald Reagan's 'trickle-down economics' whereby it was presumed that prosperity for those at the top of the economic tree would filter down to prosperity for the rest of us. Despite all the evidence suggesting its crude falsity, this is a theory that still animates many politicians even today, with free markets promising to eliminate wasteful spending and lower taxes, in the process creating burgeoning employment and productivity. If you believe this, then you can also easily accept the related myth that CEOs can independently spur new growth and propel innovation.

In today's world the idolisation of the CEO is extending to new heights, far beyond just holding commercial savvy in high esteem. CEOs are exciting market visionaries and social movers. Just a few decades ago tech entrepreneurs like Microsoft boss Bill Gates and Apple supremo Steve Jobs started to be propounded as possessing the thinking that would push us toward a bright future. Today that same mantle has been passed on to the likes of Facebook's Mark Zuckerberg and Google's Larry Page. Such figures represent a key competitive advantage that transcends mere technical intelligence. In the United States in particular this CEO worship has exuded a particular flavour of American exceptionalism. Steve Jobs was an illustrative and special example, with his genius often heralded on the public stage. Writing in the *New York Times*, Walter Isaacson portrayed this view in vaguely racist terms:

China and India are likely to produce many rigorous analytical thinkers and knowledgeable technologists. But smart and educated people don't always spawn innovation. America's advantage, if it continues to have one, will be that it can produce people who are also more creative and imaginative, those who know how to stand at the intersection of the humanities and the sciences. That is the formula for true innovation, as Steve Jobs' career showed.[37]

Such genius is often portrayed as ineffable and wide-ranging in its manifestations. In one instance it could be seen in brilliant braggart dealmakers like Donald Trump negotiating and winning the competitive race to a level where business is imagined as a creative art. In another it might be the non-conformist forward thinking of Richard Branson whose ideas would save the world from business as usual.

This idolisation reveals the over-arching celestial quality at the heart of the CEO society. It has long been noted that the belief in the free market is as much, if not more, religious as scientific in character. It revolves around the faithful devotion to a dogmatic view of humanity and the world; what economist Joseph Stiglitz refers to as a pervasive 'market fundamentalism'.[38] Yet there is an arguably even greater spirit of religiosity permeating this hyper-capitalist system. It represents a celestial order on earth, where the CEO is the all-knowing, powerful, secular god rightfully worshipped by their less talented but devoted followers.[39] Such idolisation reaffirms the righteousness of this present-day divine capitalist universe, fending off any facts about corporate misconduct, the merciless pursuit of corporate self-interest, an industrially devastated ecology, or out of control global inequality.

Becoming master of the universe

The mass exaltation of the supposedly all-powerful CEO, increasingly seen from the 1980s as an innovative generator of shareholder value, is especially interesting in light of how depersonalised and technical modern financial capitalism has become. The new reign of capital is built, in this regard, not by the entrenched free market values of human pluck and initiative but on complex algorithms and financial reporting. In this sense, neoliberalism represents "an effort to elevate 'unconscious' processes over 'conscious' ones, which in practice means elevating cybernetic, non-human systems and processes over discursive spheres of politics and judgement".[40] The use of big data and people analytics are all the rage, promising to precisely determine how employees can best maximise their productivity, and how customers can best be targeted. Some employers have even gone so far as to hire health care analytics companies to figure out if female workers are trying to become pregnant. This is done by data mining their medical insurance claims, drug prescriptions and internet search queries. Large US corporations such as Walmart and Time Warner, for example, both employ companies who specialise in gathering employee medical information.[41]

The social currency of the CEO is, in no small part, a response to a growing fear of economic dehumanisation. There is little room for personhood in modern capitalism: people, whether customers, voters or employees, are required only to be data points to be profitably analysed and engineered. The big data industry, backed by the likes of Google, Facebook, Amazon, Intel, Microsoft and IBM, is expected to be valued at over $200 billion by 2020.[42] The appeal of this industry is that it offers the fantasy of being able to predict the future, and to use that knowledge for one's own benefit. The particular cultural attractiveness of the highflying business executive is also grounded in a shared desire to feel in control, rather than being at the mercy of the contemporary market-place and its technical wizardry. In this spirit, the investment one might put in the power of the CEO is a furtive belief in our own existence as a unique and self-determining person, who is able, like our idols, to fully realise our independence and potential.

In the CEO society, the idea of a strong leader has only become more affectively powerful in the public conscious-ness. This reflects a contemporary 'sovereign fantasy' in which people strive to feel free from manipulation by an impersonal system by affectively investing in an external figure of authority whose power and agency they can imagine themselves being capable of.[43] CEOs epitomise this fantas-tical figure of the empowered sovereign. Their vaunted decisiveness, guiding vision and ability to proverbially 'get things done' speak to this deeper aspiration being the master of capitalism rather than its mere slave or apparatchik. While the idea of serving or being under the rule of another person may be a less than appealing proposition, it is far better than having to bow down to an automated server. Specifically, even in subjugation, serving a powerful leader offers the possibility that one day you personally can attain such power and even lord it over others. This reading puts a new perspec-tive on the rather conventional discussions of mastery as they relate to the modern free market. Perhaps the most evocative, if not foretelling, in this regard, was Tom Wolfe's portrayal of stockbrokers and financiers as the new 'masters of the universe'.[44] Describing one of these fortunate few in his book *Bonfire of the Vanities* he observes:

There it was, the Rome, the Paris, the London of the twentieth century, the city of ambition, the dense magnetic rock, the irresistible destination of all those who insist on being where things are happening – and he was among the victors! He lived on Park Avenue, the street of dreams! He worked on Wall Street, fifty floors up, for the legendary Pierce and Pierce, overlooking the world! He was at the wheel of a $48,000 roadster with one of the most beautiful women in New York – no Comp. Lit. scholar, perhaps, but gorgeous – beside him! A frisky young animal! He was of that breed whose natural destiny it was ... to have what they wanted![45]

The masters of the universe Wolfe depicted were the pin-striped victors of the new free market order; the buyers and sellers of money and influence. They were at the top of the pyramid looking down from their thrones on Wall Street at a fresh hyper-capitalist world they were remaking in their image.

In the decades since Wolfe's era-defining novel, the business executive has become the stuff of dreams on a much broader scale than his novel could have imagined. This is a dream of the penthouse life, a different world of luxury and power, with the influence to steer companies and exist above the everyday moralities of mere mortals. The 2013 movie *Wolf of Wall Street* epitomises this potent mixture of wealth, agency and romanticised debauchery. Ostensibly a critique of the sins and excess of finance, it was also a cinematic celebration of all its transgressions. This was not make-believe; it was based on the autobiography that Jordan Belfort wrote when he has in jail after being found guilty of money laundering and securities fraud. It tells a story of how he was able to make millions of dollars while leading a rock-and-roll Wall Street lifestyle of sex, drugs and white-collar crime. It depicts a bacchanal vision of modern existence, a gluttonous orgy of profiteering while fulfilling your wildest fantasies.

These feverish visions of extravagance, while crossing any and all conventional lines of ethical and social propriety, are also a manifestation of the larger longing to feel in control. The forces of the free market and globalisation produce a general sense of anxiety and powerlessness. There is nothing that can be done about loss of secure jobs, boarded up shops, closed factories, outsourcing and mass environmental degradation. The list of modern cultural ills appears almost endless. They are unfortunately, though, simply part of an inevitable process of marketisation, one that seems to have no end and is leading all of us on a long march to nowhere. The dream of being like a CEO – wealthy, influential, empowered and in control – is a glittery antidote to this pronounced alienation. The existence of CEOs tells us that the dream can come true, even when the reality of lived experience tells us that it cannot.

This consideration of the CEO as a cultural ideal points to a popular modern fixation with the 'anti-hero'. CEOs are the passionate reaction against a capitalist system that seems to have ever more total governance of our existence.[46] Figures like the mafia boss, gang leader and the drug kingpin, for example, challenge technocratic visions of a free market based on objective economic laws. The capacity to break the rules and beat the game is an understandable fantasy in an age where it is the system, not the people, that appears most in control. Anti-heroes offer a subtle but nonetheless potent attack on the hardening power relations surrounding this emerging neoliberal world. The transference of wealth to the top 1%, the entrenchment of mass inequality as an apparently unchangeable 'fact of life', reflects a growing unease with the assumption of capitalist meritocracy.

The CEO, at first glance, may also seem to be the complete personification of this unfair privilege. Yet they are still exemplars, not so much of fairness, but of the existence of the dynamism and alterability of this system. On the one hand, the image of a visionary and hardworking executive plays into a myth that capitalism may be unequal in its ultimate rewards but it gives everyone an equal chance to attain them. Thus CEOs don't just represent our servitude but also our desire for mastery; or to be more precise, the still existing possibility for us to be one of the masters of the universe – to be in charge of our environment and shape events rather than merely be shaped by them. Even if becoming an actual business titan is largely impossible for all but the few, everyone can use their wisdom and knowledge to gain mastery of their own world and reap the benefits. Thus, for example, when in 2017 Australia's LaTrobe University advertised its MBA, it did so by appealing to students' desire for comforts that supposedly come with money and power. Never mind wanting a good education and an opportunity to contribute to society, the ultimate purpose of education was something quite different. As LaTrobe put it:

If you're not in seat 1A read this
Business leaders fly business class …
We'll connect you with people who already sit is seat 1A,
so you can network your little socks off.

Trickle-down empowerment

The CEO is the ultimate contemporary figure of power. CEOs, in their ideal form, have the ability to thrive in the market, save companies and spread their influence across the world. They are part of a global elite: those chosen few who actually can make decisions that matter. Politicians may sometimes get more attention and the hope of democracy still flares up (especially during election season), yet it is little secret that it is the business executives who hold the real sway over society. The contemporary attraction of the CEO is based on how this power can be passed on to those of us languishing in the masses. Indeed, within the CEO society it is not wealth that is ultimately prophesied to trickle down to the everyday person, but empowerment.

It is no surprise that many people seeking to become more powerful themselves would look to CEOs as heroes and role models. President and CEO of Campbell's Soup, Denise Morrison, is on record as saying: "If you want a CEO role, you have to prepare for it with a vengeance".[47] But these captains of industry are the living embodiment of the modern era's class privilege and inequality. They peer down from the heights of their unearned wealth and luxury to pass judgement on the people they profit from. Indeed, while they certainly have sometimes earned the ire of 21st century people, they have also retained the abiding admiration of many. They are popularly imbued with having discovered the secret to modern success. The shelves of modern bookshops and pages of magazines are filled with CEO advice promising to help people from all walks of life achieve their goals, whatever they may be. The business success books, whether they are by Donald Trump or Jack Welch, are the most obvious, but it doesn't end there. Eric Shiffer, CEO and chairman of the Patriarch Group, can teach you how to keep fit at fifty,[48] and former Clif Bar CEO Sheryl McLoughlin offers sage advice on how successful businesspeople can have happy marriages.[49]

The formula for such success is, obviously, quite diverse and cannot be identified as any one single thing. It is a veritable potpourri of advice for how to boost productivity and efficiency. This can range from the rather banal idea of cultivating good habits to the more mystical proposition that there is a 'secret' that will unlock the door to you realising your most cherished desires. The actual content of such sage guidance is rather beside the point. More significant is the idea that they contain real wisdom to see through the matrix of the present-day free market and enable the reader to mould it to their will.

There is an underlying egalitarian assumption in CEO idolisation. As mentioned, only the very few can scale the capitalist mountain to become one of its VIPs, but the knowledge for doing so is accessible to all who are willing to pay and listen. The tyranny of the executive is transformed into an empowering self-help culture, where the only obstacle to power and success is oneself. While individual execu-tives may be self-interested and exploitative, and the system they collectively represent may be responsible for society's economic problems, their 'wisdom' cannot be denied. It would be foolish to ignore it, as it provides a clear path to a better, more fulfilling existence. At least that's the story of a CEO society characterised by the market values of instru-mentality and productivity, which in turn have become a dominant source of what it means to be the type of person who gets things done.

The CEO tantalises us as the purveyor of mystical techniques for conquering this seemingly increasingly impenetrable free market world. But, like a corporate Wizard of Oz, the projected, but ultimately false, image of greatness hides an all-too-human reality unable to fulfil the wishes as so spectacularly promised. This promise, however, does not just arise from the hubris of CEOs themselves, but has emerged as part of a new form of government. Tradition-ally, neoliberalism has been understood as being dedicated to 'small government', as characterised by the retreat of the public sector and the slow death of the welfare state. It trumpets the inherent and all-encompassing values of marketisation, privatisation and financialisation. Although convincing, such a reading risks missing the important role of government for perpetuating the CEO society's hyper-capitalist order. Specifically, government functions as a source for expanding market knowledge to the general population. As cultural and political theorist Jeremy Gilbert presciently observes,

[Neoliberalism] advocates a programme of deliberate intervention by government in order to encourage particular types of entrepreneurial, competitive and commercial behaviour in its citizens, ultimately arguing for the management of populations with the aim of cultivating the type of individualistic, competitive, acquisitive and entrepreneurial behaviour which the liberal tradition has historically assumed to be the natural condition of civilized humanity, undistorted by government intervention.[50]

In the current sense, neoliberalism also plays a crucial part in the production of the person who longs for CEO-style empowerment. This reveals the dramatically colonising aspect of the present-day free market. A key critique of capitalism is its unquestionable thirst to find new markets to exploit. It is committed to an infinite and constant expansion to discovering ways to profit from fresh places, people and products. This expansion, especially in the modern era, is also being driven inward toward shaping the very subjectivity of subjects in all areas of their existence. The CEO is now not only conquering the external world but the internal one as well. Increasingly, they must spread their ideology to all corners of existence, waking up the successful executive latent inside every single one of us With the right advice you can find the 'CEO in you' and "uncover your hidden goals, face your fears, summon your strengths, and propel yourself to a wonderful future".[51]

The importance of the CEO today extends beyond any one charismatic figure. It is an entire way of making sense and acting in the world. In this regard, it is a veritable way of being. The overarching and increasingly dominant idea that every problem, no matter what it is, can be solved simply by being decisive and instrumental. When Kevin Plank, CEO of sports clothing company Under Armour, wanted to sing the praises of Donald Trump's approach to the presidency, for example, he did not focus on his statesmanship, diplomatic skills or political experience. Instead, he opined that "to have such a pro-business President is something that is a real asset for the country … he wants to build things. He wants to make bold decisions and be really decisive".[52]

Beneath Plank's flattering comments lies the idea that decisiveness can provide individuals with a sense of security in an otherwise fragmented and rapidly changing cultural environment. The growing prominence of the CEO rationality is a constant for grounding and maintaining identity. In this respect, in the CEO society we are continually involved in "a never-ending process of incorporation where people 'figure' and 'refigure' themselves across the spectrum of social relations".[53] We are not attaching ourselves directly to each other but interacting with one another as part of the general, though forever changing and messy, moral order of things via the moment-to-moment incorporation of the 'materials of our culture'.[54] Through this vaunted and sage CEO wisdom we might just think we are given the substantive tools to tailor reality to our own specific circumstances and aspirations.

Despite its power and prevalence, the idolisation of the CEO is by no means universal. Movies like 2015's *The Big Short* explicitly satirise the idea of the all-knowing, all-powerful financial executive, presenting them instead as mostly inept bosses with little understanding of the complex financial world they rule over, or the economic catastrophe they were largely responsible for causing. Even worse, they are portrayed as greedy and parasitic – a class of people who would bring about the apocalypse if it added to their wealth in the short term. In real life, figures such as Martin Shkreli who, in 2015, raised the price of life-saving drugs by 5000% overnight, present the personification of placing profits over people.

Despite an awareness of the more nefarious dimensions of CEO behaviour, the desire to be a CEO can be still be traced across various economic, cultural, political and personal relations, not least by the explosion of global demand for business and management education over the past decades. More generally, managerialism continues to be perpetuated as an applied ideology – a set of 'empowering' techniques recasting social relations as an opportunity to put into practice a CEO mentality. Anything can and should be made more competitive, productive and efficient, whether it be parenting, getting an education, or running a government. Regardless of where one finds oneself in life, the CEO society tells us that it is always good to be more focused, definite and instrumental; to be a winner. Each moment, each encounter, each obstacle can be seen as an opportunity for being a better CEO in our own existence. Amidst its global wars, ideological extremism and crises, the new millennium has transformed society such that the idea of the CEO has become a vital social force; one where, even if the individual business titan may be condemned, the general CEO wisdom continues to hold power. We all can be winners if we are willing to embrace the executive way of life.

3

Competing in the executive economy

The dominance of the CEO as a central figure in the economy has become so socially entrenched that for many it goes unquestioned. The cultural image of the innovative, decisive and when necessary ruthless chief executive is the primary, if not increasingly exclusive, view of modern organisational leadership. However, this shared public image is not an innocuous or straightforward description of the way things are, and more than anything it gains its credence through that which it evades and obscures. Most especially, the cultural ideal of the contemporary CEO excludes from the public imagination values, now rendered as old-fashioned, associated with industrial democracy and employer–employee power sharing. Indeed, even if one finds the authoritarian image of the CEO to be morally distasteful, such leadership is still commonly accepted as necessary in what is characterised as a brutal dog-eat-dog business world. Business is, by this way of thinking, akin to armed combat, with the aspiring manager advised to "create a threatening presence" as you "declare war on your enemies".[1]

The CEO society presents itself through an economic fantasy of executive power. This fantasy champions the agency of CEOs who can single-handedly lead companies and nations to a financial promised land. CEOs are heralded as the captains of modern finance and industry whose mission is to steer organisations through rough and choppy market waters. At stake is a vision of the contemporary economy as shaped by extraordinary and strong individuals, such that all other economic actors (for example workers and consumers) are reduced to being bit players in someone else's story. Here the liberty, potential and value of all people risks being invested in the power of singular individuals who are able to take control of complex business realities.

While it is the case that the CEO is a pre-eminent economic figure of our times, as we explored in the previous chapter it is also true that they represent a strange combination of idolisation and revulsion, and the existence of the CEO society does not mean that it is accepted by everyone on its own terms. CEOs attract esteem for their abilities to reach the apex of business success, but they also generate righteous anger at their unearned privilege. Either way, they reflect a form of market empowerment positioned as being available to all but achieved only by a select few. This is why, for many, the CEO does stand as an ideal to strive toward, the epitome of influence and power in an otherwise dispiriting neoliberal order. It is in this way that, at least for its advocates, the flipside of the CEO society is an executive economy where all agency and leverage is invested at the top, such that the rest of us languish at the mercy of the CEOs. The focus of this chapter is on the character of this executive economy, with special attention to the contradictions that it encapsulates when the fantasy of CEO power meets the reality of economic life.

The small world of the CEO economy

CEOs personify the ideological assumptions of capitalist meritocracy, supporting an individualist logic that the market fairly rewards those who most deserve it, even if they face obstacles. When Alan Joyce, CEO of the Australian national airline Qantas and son of working class Irish parents, received the prestigious Queen's birthday honour in 2017, he declared:

> It's a great credit to Australia because it shows this country is a true meritocracy; that an Irish immigrant who came here 21 years ago can run an iconic brand like Qantas and receive one of the highest awards in the honours list shows you how welcoming and open and fantastic a country this is.[2]

Underpinning this survival of the fittest fantasy is a conviction that even amidst gross inequality and undue privilege, competition ensures that only the very best and most hard working are successful. It is fairly reasonably assumed that a major corporation or a large university would never survive, let alone prosper, unless it paid the going rate for the world's best individuals. This is the very excuse trotted out when runaway executive salaries are publicly questioned. As popularised by

McKinsey and Company's Ed Michaels, Helen Handfield-Jones and Beth Axelrod, chief amongst the weaponry of this war is that in order to succeed, corporations need to fight a 'war for talent' with their competitors, with disproportionate salaries for those at the top.[3] Since the idea was introduced in the late 1990s, an elite global labour market has emerged, with its operators able to define who can (and who cannot) get access to the most senior positions. Equitable for all? No, rather it has led to the creation of a 'new boys' network' that empowers the few while disempowering the many.[4]

The assumption that those who rise to the top do so because they are the most talented is challenged by the reality of how CEOs acquire and maintain their elite status. The present economic system has been convincingly criticised for being oligarchic rather than meritocratic, and it is widely held that power is in the hands of a very few. In a much cited 2014 study on contemporary American politics, professors Martin Gilens and Benjamin Page note that:

> Americans do enjoy many features central to democratic governance, such as regular elections, freedom of speech and association and a widespread (if still contested) franchise. But we believe that if policymaking is dominated by powerful business organisations and a small number of affluent Americans, then America's claims to being a democratic society are seriously threatened.[5]

CEOs are a core part of this elitism, their hands pulling and pushing at our economy and politics, even as their position at the top makes them as much a target for political derision as it makes them role models.

Longstanding criticism of CEOs and their elitism is testament to its power and prevalence.[6] The counter-argument relies on an individualised market logic: CEOs must be valuable otherwise the marketplace would not pay them so highly. This follows the still prevailing neoliberal axiom that while the free market may be unequal, it is not necessarily unfairly so. It is further assumed that organisations simply cannot afford to continue employing those not adding significant value to their bottom line. In other words, inequality is a necessity if we are to have a meritocratic market system.

Upon closer examination, this mirage of perceived competitive advantage disappears. In particular, acquiring the position of CEO has been shown to have as much to do with who you know as with what you have done. The sociologist Gerald Davis has described the 'small world of corporate elites' in which existing relationships across top corporations allow executives to retain their privileged positions.[7] In short, those doing the hiring end up employing people like themselves.

Rather than such collusion casting a negative light on the vaunted position of the CEO, it has instead been popularly transformed into a highly marketable skill, with the ability to use your networks to forge profitable partnerships considered an essential part of any leader's resume. As the president of the New York Stock Exchange Tom Farley declared in 2015 in *Fortune* Magazine, "When I think about my own career, I owe every job I've ever had to networking".[8] It would appear that in the age of oligarchy the most valuable commodity one can have is oligarchic status and oligarchic friends. What this reveals is a fundamentally non-competitive marketplace based on social ties, cultural capital and patronage.

Executive power

Central to the neoliberal competitive myth is the idea that inequality is justified by a public ethos of meritocracy. If one sees the world as a form of competition between self-interested individuals, then the result is that there will be some winners and some losers; in economic terms, the rich and the poor. Competition is seen as a natural order, and what matters, ethically, is not the outcome but rather whether the game was played fairly such that the spoils of victory could be positioned as legitimate. Far from something to bemoan or eradicate, in the CEO society the gap between the 'haves' and 'have nots' is deemed socially necessary to motivate individuals to better themselves and, by default, to contribute to society and to the economy.

The idea that life is a competitive game and that those who play can be considered winners or losers, is deeply implicated in the growing power of corporations in social, political and economic life. Modern capitalism glorifies individual enterprise, conjuring up images of the hard-working self-made person pulling themselves up by their own bootstraps all the way to the top. The reality is of course dramatically different. It is dominated by huge corporations, faceless puppet masters shaping our choices and economic fates. This has been the case for some time and, as political scientist Benjamin Barber, explained:

By many measures, corporations are more central players in global affairs than nations. We call them multinational but they are more accurately understood as postnational, transnational or even anti-national. For they abjure the very idea of nations or any other parochialism that limits them in time or space.[9]

This is a condition that has been described as 'corporate sovereignty', in that corporations themselves have by now achieved a level of power equal to if not greater that sovereign nation states, so as to be less and less beholden to the laws of any given state.[10] Corporations as diverse as JP Morgan Chase, Toyota, Walmart and ExxonMobil reign supreme on the world stage, existing as complex Leviathan-like institutions whose sheer power is only matched by their utter complexity. The individual thrown into this complexity enters a life of competition where one must set out to win, at least as best as one can, in the context of a world where corporations more and more determine both the rules of the game and the spoils that are awarded to its winners.

The values of individual competition that drive neoliberalism and the CEO society it has spawned are directly opposed to the collective community values promoted and enshrined in the welfare state. The result is a situation, as described by renowned sociologist Zygmunt Bauman, where "citizens are now abandoned to their own cunning and guts while held solely responsible for the results of their struggles against adversities not of their own making".[11] At the core of this corporate-competitive existence is a rather profound tension. In one sense this is a form of humanism in that it prizes the individual as a locus of self-control, always striving to achieve its own interests. This is so whether that individual is an economic entrepreneur, a consumer or an employee. As well as this, the individual is constructed as a unique information point to be personally collected, analysed and exploited amidst the morass of big data. Individuals are the customers whose preferences can be predicted and fulfilled. Career progression is tracked and planned for using people analytics. Our capitalist self is determined not on a financial ledger but through a big data algorithm. It reflects what sociologist and philosopher Maurizio Lazzarato refers to as the shift from conscious subjection to unconscious "machinic enslavement" where people exist as a "gear, a cog, a component part in the 'business' and 'financial' assemblage".[12] To this effect Lazzarato argues that being a person located in this economic system is less about being a rational subject who makes informed choices, but rather that one's choices are defined by a system that it is almost impossible to comprehend. The irony that this leads us to is how, under current neoliberal conditions, the individual person is at once seen as a self-contained vessel of rational agency, while simultaneously abstracted to being passively controllable through technologies of surveillance and computation.

What this reveals is a critical experience of dehumanisation, like the workers at Amazon's Scottish warehouse where excessive monitoring left them feeling like they had to "work like robots" while experiencing "paranoia with job security" and being penalised for taking sick days.[13] Concurrently, social media filters our details through algorithms, enabling targeted advertising to cajole us into pursuing tailor-made, mathematically determined, lives. This situates people in a virtual world defined through surveillance technologies, social media and an ever-updating series of data sets. Following Lazzarato, political economist Will Davies suggests that neoliberalism acts to "simulate and pre-produce a reality that does not yet exist, a reality that is only virtually present", yet presents itself as concrete and unassailable. As Davies evocatively describes, the vision of the 21st century economy is one where:

> Traders surrounded by screens of price data are not, therefore, subjects viewing signifiers of some absent reality, but agents within a reality of telecommunications and information processors. Decisions are taken along the way, but they are not taken at some 'objective' distance on the basis of conscious reflection or deliberation. They are effects of the system, which now includes the behaviors, bodies, brains of those employed by it.[14]

The existential fear of the modern age has evolved from big brother to big data.

As we began to explore in chapter 2, the rise of CEOs as idealised cultural figures has, in no small part, been a reaction to the evisceration of humanity predicated by the use of contemporary information and communication technology. The CEO is a figure associated with extreme and exclusive

agency, hence positioned as the antithesis of digital dehumanisation. Facebook might be gathering intimate details about
your age, relationship history, or political views in order that
you can be pigeonholed as a 'type' for the purpose of targeted
advertising, but Mark Zuckerberg still comes across as a self-
styled authentic individual. As a hero to emulate, the CEO
embodies individual freedom delivered from both economic
oppression and amorphous digitised institutional control.
The executive is the charismatic exception to these dehumanising realities. What we have here is the living embodiment
of a human being who still appears to have the power of self-
determination. The CEO is a person who can cut through
institutional red tape and the 'machinic enslavement' of
life, to wield real power and influence. This executive power
symbolises the possibility that, however remote, we can still
consciously forge our own destinies in an economy and world
where this feels increasingly impossible.

The rise of corporate influence and domination is also
implicated in the role of government, with nation states
now widely viewed as mere puppets to corporate interests
and desires. More formally, this manifests in good political
governance being associated with the implementation of
policies that are conducive to big business. The effect of this is
entrenchment of corporate interest and a neutering of political innovation, as international studies researchers Morten
Bøås and Desmond McNeill explain:

Powerful states (notably the USA), powerful organisations (such as the IMF) and even, perhaps, powerful

disciplines (economics) exercise their power largely by 'framing': which serves to limit the power of potentially radical ideas to achieve change.[15]

This framing renders values that represent dominant corporate interests – such as competitiveness, individuality, self-reliance, independence, greed and self-interest – as normal and natural. Moreover, it is within a CEO society that government and other political institutions have normalised the ascension of corporate power, while at the same time restricting their own power through a mantra of small government. Political sovereignty, in this respect, is being eroded and to some extent transferred to corporate conglomerates and the economic elites who run them.[16] As such,

> From the early 1990s onwards, the call for less state has gradually been substituted by a call for a better state. This new approach should not be confused with a plea for a return to the strong (Keynesian or socialist) state. Rather it implies better and transparent governance of what is left of the state after neoliberal restructuring has been implemented.[17]

Perhaps not surprisingly, this has, on occasion, cast corporations in the modern role of international villains. While they are officially promoted across the world as the drivers of economic growth and prosperity, they have also been put forward as the main enemy of progress. Indeed, corporations in industries as diverse as agribusiness, energy, finance

and technology have all been singled out for their detri-
mental impact on society and the environment. Collectively,
corporations have also been held responsible for the global
'race to the bottom' that pits countries against each other
to attract corporate investment at the expense of the health
and wellbeing of their broader populations.[18] Far from being
the engine for material prosperity, in such instances corporations are widely lamented as the deliverer of oligarchy,
inequality and environmental devastation. Consequently,
a 2008 UN Global Compact paper proclaimed that "[t]he
global crisis in financial markets raises a range of important
and urgent questions regarding corporate sustainability
generally ... For this reason it is more important than ever
to build market legitimacy and political support based
on sound ethical frameworks".[19] Even with such critique,
however, it is not the system of market capitalism, which
sustains corporations, that is being questioned, but rather
some particularities of its operation. In the end it is still
'market legitimacy' that is posited as a realistic and desirable goal.

Ideal fantasies and anxious realities

Although corporations, the markets they operate in and
the CEOs who lead them are often publicly positioned as the
unequivocal locus of power and harbingers of prosperity,
the internal discourse of corporations is often characterised by a particular neoliberal anxiety. With this, individual
corporations are seen to be constantly under threat and

having to reinvent themselves in order to be successful. International competition has never been so intense or pervasive, and even the most successful companies in the past run the risk of present extinction. Indeed, there are many once-successful corporations that faded suddenly into oblivion. If you don't change with the times you might just end up like Nokia, Blockbuster or Eastman Kodak, all of which suffered by not keeping up with technological change. Taking Blockbuster as a specific example, in the early 21st century the success of its home video and video game rental business propelled it to being valued at US$5 billion. Unable to adapt to the new technologies of online and on-demand video propagated by companies like Netflix and Rebox, however, Blockbuster suffered a rapid decline towards bankruptcy in 2010.[20]

Not the least, the performance anxiety raised by the threat of competitive failure can lead to a crisis culture replete with endemic problems of burnout and breakdown among top management. As the *Wall Street Journal* recently reported, "job fatigue catches up to some executives amid mounting expectations; no more forced smiles".[21] This is not a new phenomenon, and even as early as the 1990s psychologist Harry Levison observed that:

> Fifteen years ago, executive burnout was a new phenom-enon. Not so anymore. Today extreme feelings of stress are pervasive and growing worse. Reengineering, downsizing, and increased competition have multiplied pressures in the workplace. At the same time, dual-earner

couples suffer time and energy famines at home. In the 1990s, it is hard to find peace anywhere.[22]

It might just be that the cultural fantasies of executive heroism are less likely to translate into experiential realities for those on the rise to the top. Businesses are under constant pressure to remain competitive and build profitability. There are few if any opportunities to pursue any strategy other than maximising short-term gains at all costs, including the personal costs to those in charge.

The existence of executive burnout, a condition brought on not just by long working hours and intense work pressure but also by over-identification with work, reflects the broader character of the 21st century free market.[23] The widely held picture of corporations as conquerors of the globe runs parallel to an acute sense of paranoia about our own sense of disempowerment and bondage, manifested in symptoms such as cynicism, exhaustion, insomnia, loss of self-esteem and depression. This has only been exacerbated in recent years, not just amongst executives, but for all workers. Prevalent in today's workplaces are workaholic cultures where you might earn a salary working from 9 am to 5 pm, but if you want promotion you've got to be at work from 5 pm to 9 pm as well, and seven days a week at that. The pressures can be constant, and they press down on working people. This is exemplified by a former Uber employee who explained that working for the technology company meant that "I felt like I was on call all the time … I got texts on the weekends. Emails at 11 at night. And if you didn't respond within 30 minutes, there'd be a chain of like 20 people".[24]

As we discussed in chapter 2, there is a traditional portrayal of capitalism and capitalist as vampiric with an unquenchable thirst for economic exploitation of workers and new markets. Marx tellingly described capital as a vampire sucking on the blood of labour, where each victim "only slightly quenches the vampire thirst for the living blood of labour".[25] Yet what may be more accurate in the present context is corporate globalisation as a type of Frankenstein's monster. Corporations may well have become hideous and deformed creatures that society can no longer control, and that have little regard for the wellbeing of their human creators. For all of their influence, monstrous corporations have little apparent agency. They are caught in the same trap as the mass of individuals and communities they so ruthlessly use to their advantage: profit or die. Even more troubling, the bondage to the market that characterises the CEO society is presented as being inevitable. It can appear that we can no longer fight or reform this monster as it recklessly pursues share value and profit maximisation at all costs, including, of course, human costs. Instead, everyone from the top of the economy all the way down must equally accept its demands and serve its desires.

In their study of the introduction of competitive market-driven practices into Australia's national public broadcaster, organisational theorists André Spicer and Peter Fleming observed:

senior management made strategic use of globalization discourse to legitimate managerial initiatives such as the introduction of competitive contracting and commercialization. The discourse of globalization around which these practices were couched relied upon a trope of inevitability, external pressure and organizational survival.[26]

This characterisation of the free market has taken on a life of its own. It is has been a means to authorise organisational change by being cast as an unavoidable and unalterable fact of modern existence. No corporation, whether or not they would even want to, can stop the tide of hyper-marketisation and ceaseless competition – they must simply respond. Lost, in turn, has been the human element of these broader geo-political shifts. The myth of the CEO is very much entangled by the assumed powerlessness to the market that is imbued in neoliberal culture. In this scene, the CEO rises above the realities of organisational life so as to arrive as the one figure who simultaneously responds to and controls this dispiriting reality.

CEOs, at least in their idealised form, are hired and promoted as the sole individuals able effectively to tame and shape the market for the benefit of the corporations they lead. In the boardroom they stand up as masterminds who can bring the necessary changes to maximise a company's competitiveness. Crucial to their perceived economic function is the presumption that they play a primary role in shaping a corporation's vision and being a catalyst for their necessary innovation. CEOs are like comic book superheroes. They are portrayed as the ultimate change makers, cutting through unpredictability of the market and the uncertainty of shareholders as they leap over the tall buildings of global cities' central business districts. They are also the chief promoters of the 'economic correctness' necessary for firms to survive in a hyper-competitive modern capitalist business environment.[27]

In this spirit, the executive is positioned not just as a leader but as a veritable corporate saviour,[28] touted as having the wisdom and wherewithal to turn the company around. It is this very logic that led Donald Trump to declare on the topic of America's lost greatness that "I alone can fix it".[29] This is the type of strong image that prevails even when faced with realities that do not, and cannot, live up to the fantasy. Writing in *The Atlantic*, business journalist Megan McArdle clarifies:

> CEOs are too often empire builders, squandering retained earnings and diluting share values in order to make dubious corporate acquisitions. Or they become enamored of visionary projects which have a low probability of success – but which could, if all the stars align and the moon goes into half eclipse and Glinda the Good arrives with her magic wand, cement the CEO's reputation as a genius of inestimable proportions.[30]

The very likelihood of CEO mediocrity is decreased by a dedication to perpetual change, often less as a means of overcoming real market threats and more to play up the importance of an incoming top executive. This is especially so in light of the huge salaries now invested in these leaders and the need to justify those expenses to shareholders and employees. Despite all this, the CEO is still portrayed as a heroic figure, the captain of the corporate ship, fearlessly guiding it through the rough seas of a stormy global capitalism, always wary of possible attack from nefarious competing vessels in a never-ending race to the treasure.

All of this points to the cultural foundations for championing CEOs as contemporary heroes. They are much more than rich, exciting celebrities; they are imagined as the very people who can shape the world to their desires. They promise the power of seeing clearly through the fog of an increasingly disconnected and complicated market reality in order to make change happen and get what they want. In a time of economic powerlessness, they represent a compelling vision of economic power. No doubt even the burned-out executive can fantasise about living up to the exaggerated image of the CEO.

The CEO fantasy

The appeal of the CEO runs profoundly deeper than just being exalted because of their wealth or higher status. As we have been exploring, they are the symbol of continued human agency and influence in the face of a dehumanising market and technological rule. Their potency is found in their supposed singular ability to navigate towards their vision, in the process moulding this seemingly arbitrary and anarchic capitalist reality to their own desires. They are positioned culturally as the only real people who are empowered enough to still have free will.

CEOs are the public face of what is an otherwise extraordinarily depersonalised modern system of corporate authority.

Every day across the world people are confronted with large businesses over which they have relatively little control. Examples are myriad and range from the annoyance of being put on hold for hours while trying to lodge a complaint on the telephone, to coping with feelings of powerlessness while trying to negotiate for improved wages or conditions, to a sense of failure at being unable to stop the ways that corporate business practices are leading to environmental degradation in your community, or simply to being bombarded by advertisements across every possible channel of communication. It is more than justifiable to feel that corporations hold all of the power and people almost none. This frustration is even more pronounced in the daily interpersonal interactions with those working in corporations. Your line manager is sorry that you have to work this weekend but there is a pressing deadline that has to be met; the operator sincerely apologises for the delay and not being able to help you but there are procedures that must be followed; and the politician is sorry that there cannot be greater environmental and labour protection but that's just the way to attract corporate investment.

For good or bad, the CEO stands out as a person who can effectively alter the present situation if they so choose, signifying a distinct fantasy of 21st century empowerment. The attractiveness of the CEO therefore largely rests on their overwhelming appeal as having power and freedom. As commentator Ruth Sunderland observed in *The Guardian*:

On the one hand, businessmen are idolized out of proportion to their real achievements; on the other, they are disproportionately blamed for the failures of the companies they lead. It taps into atavistic human urges to search for strong leaders, and to conduct witch-hunts against individuals seen to embody threats to the community.[31]

What this also means is that if a particular CEO fails, the myth lives on; it is just that one person wasn't good enough to live up to it. Whether it be WorldCom's Bernard Ebbers being sent to prison for conspiracy and fraud, or Kmart's Chuck Conaway being convicted of misleading investors in 2009, faith in the idea of the CEO appears able to withstand any scandal. This plays into the fantastical character of the CEO. In this sense, a fantasy is an ideal that people strive toward as well as an anchor for their idealised identity. The idolised CEO builds upon a broader modern economic fantasy of market rationality. Here the 'sky is the limit' for all those willing to be strategic and ruthless enough to succeed.[32] Moreover, the presence of this idealised possibility prompts people to more readily accept their lived realities of inequality, exploitation and domination, as the belief lives on that things will be different at some unknown point in the future. The existence of actual CEO 'winners' is required to sustain this fantasy, and as such casts the CEO not as an undeserving or entitled player in a rigged capitalist game, but as an especially rational, effective, driven, and therefore most rightfully rewarded, member of society.

Popular television programmes like the international reality TV franchise *The Apprentice* that has been on air since 2004 only reinforce this affective vision. Accordingly, in such 'reality' television programmes contestants compete for the opportunity to rub shoulders with successful CEOs in the hope that they can become like them after touching the hems of their metaphorical garments. The organising logic for the contestant, as much as for the once-removed viewers, is that:

> 'if I work with Donald Trump [former host of the US version of *The Apprentice*], I am closer to one day being like him.' Thus, organizations use envy to affectively 'seize' employees with promises of future individual freedom and respect as it extols the virtue of the person who envies today through hard work will be the person envied tomorrow.[33]

Bill Rancic, the winner of the very first season of *The Apprentice* in the United States, stated years later: "Donald Trump was obviously someone who changed my life … He was great to me. He negotiates great deals, he understands business and he understands how the world works. He's someone I am forever grateful to".[34]

Moving beyond mere material wealth and social status, the CEO also becomes a figure who can ideally represent that best of present-day morality and justice. This may sound strange amidst a history of financial crises and corporate scandals, yet there remains a cultural fixation with the desire for a 'good boss', one who is reasonable, just and wise. Commenting on the 'cult of the CEO', David Prosser, former business editor of *The Independent* newspaper in the UK, writes:

We have always identified with the people behind large companies more than with the companies themselves. The human instinct is to look for the story about another human, rather than a faceless corporation ... Yet the need to personalize seems to have become more acute in the 21st century. There are good reasons for this. First, while the standards required may not yet be being met, it is fair to say that responsibility and accountability are more important themes than ever before in the world of business – and it takes human beings to accept these mantles.[35]

The actual misbehaviour of executives plays into this fantasy, bringing about feelings of mass disappointment that need to be assuaged by a revitalised desire for a 'good' economic sovereign.[36] Just think back to 2014 when the chairman of the Co-Op Bank in the UK, Paul Flowers, was filmed in what looked like a cocaine and methamphetamine drug deal. This, together with accusations linking his financial incompetence to his dalliances with male prostitutes, led to his downfall. This did not, of course, tarnish the reputation of business executives more generally. Rather, Flowers was disparaged because he was not executive material and shouldn't have been hired in the first place. The ideal of the CEO was left unblemished – rather, here was a man who didn't have what it takes to live up to it. As then British Prime Minister David Cameron stated, the first question to be asked should be "why was Rev Flowers judged suitable to be chairman of a bank?"[37]

The CEO exemplifies the potential to be self-determining in an increasingly technical, cutthroat and complex economic environment, with any failure to live up to that image being a personal failure rather than a crack in the fantasy. CEOs are those who appear to have escaped the chains of a dangerous and labyrinthine financial regime to forge their own path forward. They are the masters of the universe as much as they are masters of their own fate. They have risen above the brutal competition of the neoliberal marketplace to conquer all before them, reap their earned rewards and wield justice as they see fit. In the world of the CEOs, only the fittest survive.

The freedom to execute

There is an appealing modern vision of the CEO as all-powerful; a figure publicly embraced for their wisdom and business acumen. Of course, as we have been exploring, the reality of the CEO and their public reception is not as straightforward as the more singular representation of an idealised fantasy. It is also crosscut with popular anger at the privilege they enjoy and condemnations of their often discovered wrongdoing. Yet this dual public persona, being both loved and hated in different ways, raises a rather more fundamental question. In light of how despicably top managers can act in practice, what makes them still so attractive to some members of the wider population, many of whom they actively exploit? This was, for example, the question many asked in relation to why working class people voted for a self-admiring, brash and entitled billionaire tycoon like Donald Trump.

To understand this apparent contradiction, it is necessary to move beyond rather simple explanations of material envy. The idea that people jealously aspire to be like their economic and social 'betters' misses the fundamental appeal of the CEO. On closer examination, this appeal can be traced to the original promise of economic liberalism itself. In the contemporary period, the free market is often put forward as inherently good. It is seen as unquestionably the best and most realistic economic model, the one to which 'there is no alternative'. In its original justification in the latter part of the 20th century, popularised and promulgated in particular by Ronald Reagan in the United States and Margaret Thatcher in Britain, the free market and its supposed spirit of enterprise was promoted as a means of breaking through bureaucracy and 'getting things done' in a way that was seemingly natural rather than pre-planned. Indeed, this is the heart of the liberalism that Friedrich Hayek proposed back in 1944, and which was taken up with such gusto by conservative politicians in the 1970s and 1980s.

Hayek's belief that prosperity can only result from a market economy, and that state economic planning would lead to tyranny, was echoed in the cold war logic that pitted Soviet central planning against a putatively superior as well as inevitable free enterprise=based economic organisation. Social democracies and their support of the welfare state were tarred with the same brush, portrayed as inefficient and stagnant bureaucracies in need of market reform. The introduction of marketisation, it was heralded, would streamline these cumbersome institutions and create a more responsive and effective social system. In turn, this translated organisationally into a prizing of 'post-bureaucracy' as a more agile and responsive way for corporations themselves to adapt to the demands of increased competition under neoliberalism. Post-bureaucracy, as it was widely embraced from the 1980s on, was meant to produce new organisations "structured to increase flexibility, with less formalization and more decentralization than in the traditional bureaucratic organization".[38]

Post-bureaucracy was positioned as a full transformation that would radically improve the operations of corporate and public organisations alike, even if the reality of this transformation could never live up to its revolutionary rhetoric.[39] What is important, in this regard, was that from its very inception this new economic order had a deep and abiding sense of morality. The advancement of post-bureaucracy would bring organisations not simply greater efficiency but an increased capacity to allow people to perform effectively and productively do their jobs. As business school professor Christian Maravelias clarifies, post-bureaucracy was presented as:

> a form of organization that has made a distinct break with the bureaucratic legacy. For the sake of flexibility post-bureaucracy is alleged to emancipate individuals from the formalistic constraints of bureaucracy, arranging them instead in organic and fluid networks.[40]

Post-bureaucracy appealed not merely to purveyors of market rationality of wealth and promotion, it also spoke to mass longings for institutions that did not feel so weighed down by red tape and rules, unresponsive as they appeared to individual desires. The promise was nothing less than freedom!

The CEO is the personal embodiment of this original post-bureaucratic neoliberal promise. Contemporary CEOs personify the creation of organisations that would be flexible and effective rather than unbending and ultimately futile. Jack Welch, former head of General Electric, very much a 1990s prototype of today's ideal CEO, said it plainly: "People say that now that the Soviet Union is out of business, we have no more truly dangerous enemies. They're wrong. The Soviets couldn't beat us; but economically, the bureaucracy and bureaucrats still can".[41] CEOs such as Welch emerged as figures to be celebrated for their decisiveness and capacity to execute. What better an enemy to pit themselves against than a bureaucracy imagined as a soulless system, where rules and procedures get in the way of the exercise of human ingenuity and sovereign will? CEOs are imagined as forward-thinking, 'visionary', always looking outside the proverbial 'box' for answers, and never beholden to blind tradition or fair processes. They are conjured up in an image of the natural rule breaker, subversive in their willingness to go against the 'way things are done around here' that stops them and others from 'getting things done'. This fiercely independent and anti-bureaucratic image of the CEO presents an agency and freedom that plays up to executive-type values of determination, productivity and ultimately the power and ability to exercise free will.

It is worth noting at this point that different cultures, at different historical junctures, celebrate certain forms of freedom over others. According to cultural anthropologist Sherry Ortner, "every culture, every subculture, every historic moment, constructs its own forms of agency, its own modes of enacting the process of reflecting on the self and the world and of acting simultaneously within and upon what one finds there".[42] In the CEO society, the forms of agency that are trumpeted the loudest are ones that involve being able to find novel ways to compete and win, as well as to be more efficient and effective. What is most revered is the ability to conceive and execute a strategy in a way that productively challenges conventions, streamlines processes and transforms one's visions into realities.

Such executive agency, obviously, complements a deeper capitalist view of the world. It is the obsessions with the new and the encouragement of the freedom to innovate for the purpose of maximising profit that is a contemporary manifestation of a long-standing 'myth of progress': a neophiliac fixation that establishes novelty as a virtue and tradition as a weakness.[43] The purpose of striving for this increased agency and newness is simply the accumulation of more and more power, status and wealth. This neoliberal desire for power is both objective and relative. It is an unquenchable thirst for riches and luxury as well as enhanced influence. Yet it is also pathologically competitive, an eternal game to be won against rivals, with success measured as much by your opponent's losses as your own victory. It includes the perverse thrill of being able to say to people 'you're fired' while moving onward and upward to greater economic and social power.

The CEO society is completely saturated by free market values. These values insist that the highest good is to be the most exploitive, the most cunning, the most innovative and the most profitable, all while maintaining an aura of respectability and morality. Forget justice, democracy and due process, it's all about the 'art of the deal'.[44] Crucial for the achievement of these goals are corporate friendly attributes of decisiveness, firm yet charismatic leadership, and ruthlessness. Almost completely marginalised, by contrast, are virtues associated with community, power sharing, collective deliberation, equality and true diversity. The executive world is portrayed as an epic man-on-man battle, where only the strong thrive. Accordingly, the weak must accept their fate submissively and deservedly.

Executive agency, as we have described it, is completely confined to a capitalist worldview. No matter how politely it may present itself, this is not agency to change the system or the rules of the game. The 'game' (that of market-based competition) is positioned as an inevitable, inherent and desirable part of human nature and evolution. Any freedom enjoyed by our heroic CEO is one where they are bound inextricably to excel in the permanent market order. CEOs may be the bosses of other employees, but they are certainly not the masters of capitalism itself. Suddenly their freedom looks very false, given ultimately that they must obey the mercurial needs of capital and markets. Freedom therefore is found solely, in being decisive in executing their will as an executive. To do otherwise is simply not an available alternative.

From rags to CEO riches

21st century capitalism has been convincingly criticised for its role in dramatically increasing economic inequality.[45] The result is a global society composed of winners and losers, with the latter far outnumbering the former. The CEO is the epitome of this injustice; the executive at the top of an exceedingly narrow socio-economic pyramid of wealth and success. Such disparity is not an unfortunate by-product or unintended consequence of the hyper-capitalist order in which we live; instead it is fundamental to its concrete operation and social legitimisation. For such levels of profit to be made, economic elites must be able to maximise their advantage over the vast majority of society while culturally being given license to do so. The senior executive personifies how neoliberalism attempts to overcome this fundamental, and at face value unresolvable, tension.

The CEO stands as a popular force for bridging the widening equality gap that is fundamental to the CEO society. More precisely, while only a select few can ever match the accomplishments and wealth of corporate CEOs, everyone has the ostensible opportunity to do so. Here structural privilege is ideologically masked by an alluring figure of the corporate titan whose business guile, forward thinking, determination and sheer will potentially allow anyone to become a social and economic success. Despite their wealth and success, we can still identify with CEOs, and because they appear to us as 'real people', it is just possible we might one day be like them. When the marriage of Spotify CEO Daniel Ek to Sofia Levander was reported in *Hello Magazine*, they talked about all the celebrities and other CEOs there to wish the happy couple well. Comedian Chris Rock ran the service and Bruno Mars was the wedding singer. Mark Zuckerberg, who was also there, posted on Facebook: "We're at Lake Como in Northern Italy to celebrate the wedding of our good friends, Sofia and Daniel Ek ... Many people know Daniel as one of the great European entrepreneurs – the founder of Spotify. I know him as a great friend and dedicated father". Even the most vaunted CEOs are real, down-to-earth human beings after all!

On a quite literal level, within an often byzantine modern corporate reality, CEOs reveal a clear path to upward career promotion. They are the epitome of the agency associated with employability, where "each worker is more aware and a more independent organiser of the succession of activities and commitments that, combined, constitute his/her working life".[46] While it may be all but impossible to reach the peak of the neoliberal mountaintop, we are told we can all make use of executive-type skills to climb up our own mountain of success, no matter how small it might be. This is rendered even more plausible if we believe that deep down people like Mark Zuckerberg are no different to us.

It is important to acknowledge that CEOs, as business-people, are very much distinguished from other social and economic elites. Their lofty position is generally put down to their own hard work and talents rather than any rigged fiscal system or inbuilt cultural privilege. Obviously, reality commonly shows that equal opportunity is at best a mirage and at worst an utter deception. Nevertheless, we still have the cultural images of Bill Gates as the college drop-out who founded Microsoft, Richard Branson starting his empire as a schoolboy running a record business out of the back room of a church, or Starbucks chief Howard Schultz upbringing on the mean streets of Brooklyn. Even Donald Trump is in on this, once telling his own rags-to-riches story when he proudly (albeit falsely) claimed that he started his own empire with a 'small loan' from his father of \$1 million![47] Whether one believes the stories or not, the dream on which they rest is potent. What seeks to be unquestioned is the assumption that CEOs are the proverbial cream of the economic crop, having risen on the back of their own acumen and merit alone. Even in cases where a CEO's privileged background gives them greater access to money, skills, social networks and knowledge, the fantasy is maintained that their lofty positions are well deserved and necessary – in Trump's simple terms: "I have a very good brain".[48] What this promotes is that success is a possibility open to everyone of merit, and can be aspired to universally.

The rise of the CEO's social status and its place in the CEO society more generally has turned what could be a distinct point of criticism into a profound source of economic attraction. According to its logic, one's relative share of the economic pie is no longer a function of structural inequality or individual greed, but is a valid scorecard on which to judge a person's moral worth. This is similar to what human geographer Nigel Thrift called a 'fast subject': a person who is forever trying to collect 'material' to ensure that they can present themselves as a 'success'.[49] It also echoes a broader desire for individuals to use their marketability in accordance with the business credo 'control your own destiny or someone else will'.[50] Consequently, experience is merely a pretext for ordering and adding to one's employment biography, one's existence reduced to a living process of updating one's CV to get ever more economically ahead.[51]

In the CEO society there is an attempt to reverse the principal class contradiction of the capitalist system. In this putative order, those at the bottom of the fiscal heap are to be scorned and castigated, taking personal responsibility for their 'failure'. Their lot in life would be improved if they simply embraced the executive knowledge and lifestyle, and became the self-made people that they should and could be, if only they tried harder. As motivational speaker Zig Ziglar used to say: "You were born to win, but to be a winner, you must plan to win, prepare to win, and expect to win".[52] A failure to win, by this logic, is completely of one's own making, emerging as it does from an unwillingness to do what it takes. Inequality thus transforms from being a malaise of the current order into a golden opportunity that can be taken by individuals to better themselves. In the end, being on the bottom of the economic ladder, if it persists, is a clear indication that a person is not worthy. Any disparities in wealth and career advancement are cast as signs that the 'have-nots' just need to work harder and smarter in order to get ahead.

In the CEO society, an unrelenting desire for corporate profit has transformed and become personalised into an inextinguishable need for people to win. No victory is assured, no position is ever stable, no promotion is ever good enough, and no success is guaranteed for long. There will always be a new challenge to overcome, another rival to best, a new goal to strive for. And even in triumph, one can always reflect on the ways it could have been done better, more efficiently and more productively. If there is a failure, it's a learning experience, and every win is a doorway to greater success. The changes that mark the advent of the CEO society have gone so far as to reconfigure the theological foundations of corporate capitalism. These foundations are no longer found merely, or primarily, in the divinely enshrined hierarchy of the company. They are discovered in the salvation made possible by embodying, in one's own earthly existence, the heavenly promise and moral worth of the CEO.[53] This executive faith is only strengthened more in failure, as loss sets the stage for one's redemption; to use one's hard-earned executive wisdom to climb back up and strive again.[54] Life risks being reduced to a constant effort, always necessary but almost inevitably futile, to realise the new millennium dream of going from rags to CEO riches.

Celebrating the executive economy

The free market is supposedly the ultimate celebration of individual liberty. It trumpets the ability of people to develop their talents, pursue their own vision of happiness, and earn their just rewards. In reality it is dominated by monolithic corporations, mass conformity and undeserved economic privilege. The CEO is both the most obvious symptom of this state of affairs, as well as being perceived as its greatest antidote. CEOs represent a world of ill-gained luxury and simultaneously serve as symbols that demonstrate the ability for anyone to achieve such fiscal glory. Moreover, they provide neoliberalism with a perverse but nonetheless profound sense of moral justification. The very cultural ideal of the CEO captures a desire for there to be some meaning to this system, a clear rational explanation for why some people have advanced beyond the lowly masses, and a promise that the success of those 'winners' can also be achieved by those economically less fortunate. Such is the CEO society.

At the core of neoliberalism lies an ethos of competition where constant struggle between rivals for supremacy will spur innovation and progress. Morality is defined, in this system, as winning, maximising one's ability to compete, and ever finding new ways to gain an edge over one's opponents. A critical element of the CEO society is an ongoing mystification of its chief executive. More precisely, as we have elaborated in this chapter, this requires a justification for the elevation of the CEO within the public consciousness, even when endemic corporate scandals and a global financial crisis should have brought them careering back to earth from their lofty economic perches once and for all.

While it is reasonable to feel that CEOs and corporations are in the process of dominating so many dimensions of our social and economic life, the corporate model is not the only form of organisation available. Its top-down paradigm is being progressively challenged by desire for greater collaboration in the workplace and daily life. Disliking one's boss of course is as old as work itself. Yet this has now led to forms of resistance where people have a growing aspiration to eliminate bosses altogether. The resurgence of cooperatives speaks to these radical desires to fire CEOs and replace them with democratic values and practices. There is also a growth in participatory community budgeting as well as open-source information and problem solving. While still at the peripheries, these forms of organizing reveal the potential to go beyond the narrow and destructive limits of the current CEO society.

In part, what these types of organisation are resisting is the very idea that cooperative human behaviour in the economics sphere needs to rest on the presumption of CEOs' perceived competitive advantage as people. The mystical aura of entre-preneurship that CEOs are imbued with can be challenged, no matter how deep it runs. What the CEO represents above all else is hope in an increasingly hopeless economic situation, and we must turn to other sources of communal hope in order to resist the CEO society. When asked what leadership is, American Express CEO Ken Chenault referenced Napoleon and said, "the role of a leader is to define reality and give hope". As a result, Chenault claimed that he constantly asked himself "how do I construct a vision to engender hope and motivate people to reach challenging objectives?"[55] The Waterloo for the CEO might only be possible once we find hope other than in figures of elite authority.

4

The CEO politician

The election of Donald Trump to the presidency of the United States would appear to be the clearest testament yet to the idea that, in the CEO society, chief executives are now recognised not just effective heads of corporations, but also as viable and desirable political leaders. Trump is an extreme intense case in many ways, being the only businessperson ever to become US president without having held any other form of political office. For Trump, it is his self-proclaimed genius at business that has given him all the necessary credentials. The idea of the CEO politician, however, did not start with Trump, even if his political success marks the zenith of its possibilities. This was evident even before Trump was a serious contender as the Republican Party's candidate in the long campaign trail leading up to his election in 2016. Indeed, while we have discussed Trump at some length earlier in the book, in this chapter we want to chart the development of the CEO politician prior to Trump's arrival on the electoral scene so as to establish the CEO politician as a central manifestation of the CEO society in so many corners of the world. Our purpose, in a sense, is to explore how the wave of adulation for CEOs on which politicians such Trump surfed to victory grew to tidal proportions.

Trump wasn't the only business executive on the 2015–16 campaign trail. On Monday 4 May 2015 former Hewlett-Packard CEO Carly Fiorina launched her short-lived run as a candidate for the United States presidency. Even though her candidature was path-breaking as the first female ever to run as a Republican for this position, her campaign publicity focused first and foremost on her experience as a business leader. The previous February she declared: "HP requires executive decision-making, and the presidency is all about executive decision-making".[1] Echoed in her statement was the abiding theme that she believed would resonate with voters: the message that "what she did for HP, she can do for America".[2] Despite this bragging, Fiorina's record as CEO was far from perfect. At the time it was said that hers was a tenure "marked by layoffs, outsourcing, conflict, and controversy – so much so that several prominent former HP colleagues recoil at the idea of Fiorina managing any enterprise again, let alone the executive branch".[3] While such criticisms spoke to Fiorina's competency as a business leader, it perhaps missed the more fundamental question that Trump finally brought home: does having been a CEO, even a successful one, serve as a good and proper background for political leadership? The answer to this question, as we address it in this chapter, speaks directly to how the CEO society embodies a changing, some would say dangerous, relation between leadership, corporations and democracy.

The convergence of political and corporate leadership

Leadership remains a pre-eminent concern of 21st century life. The turn of the century brought with it renewed discussions of what it means to be a proper leader as well as a consideration of the social values that leadership demands. Underpinning these debates are shifting notions of political and social responsibility. Conventional assumptions of the public and private are quickly evaporating as the power and influence of the state has receded in response to the growth of neoliberalism and globalisation. Prompted by a political consensus of the value of markets to hitherto non-commercial realms, and by a more general economisation of ever-broadening aspects of life, economics has eclipsed politics as the central governing discourse. By now everything from education, to health care, to prisons, and even to one's personal social relationships are conceived of in terms of competition, exchange, financial self-interest and personal advantage.[4] Corporations, in turn, have taken on, at least rhetorically, a more active role in providing for social welfare and public goods, as well as for being direct players in global politics.[5] In light of these changed practices, perceptions of what it means to lead both public and private institutions are being dramatically transformed.

The changes to leadership heralded through neoliberalism are witnessed in the evolving image of elected politicians in relation to that of corporate managers. The ideal politician is increasingly one who embodies the business values of efficiency, agility and profitability. Popularly referred to at times as the 'CEO president', this model of political authority reflects a government's perceived role in maximising a country's economic competiveness within a volatile global market. There is a strange contrast, however, in that while politicians are acting like hardnosed tycoons, corporate authority figures are progressively touting their social responsibility as well as freely advising politicians on how they should go about governing the nation-cum-economy. Chief executives present their businesses as not simply profit-driven but as providing larger public goods such as environmental sustainability, social justice linked to diversity, and helping prepare workers for today's job market. Even the Volkswagen Group, shaken in 2015 by a scandal over rigging millions of vehicles to falsely pass fuel emissions tests, could proudly claim that: "as far as Volkswagen Group is concerned, bearing its social responsibility has long been at the heart of our corporate culture".[6]

The convergence of corporate and political leadership is indeed ironic in that it tends to reversal. The private has become public and vice versa. On one level, this paradoxical condition of the way leadership is represented simply reflects existing socio-political realities. However, popular discourses are also influential in constituting and reinforcing such ideological shifts. These dynamic changes are where, in the CEO society, corporate leadership has come to infuse the meaning and practice of political leadership. In proffering that politicians should emulate the styles of corporate executives, this new leadership strengthens the marketed perceptions of the state's function heralded by neoliberalism.

This is a trend that takes the well-established practice of new public management as a means through which public services and non-profit organisations are managed like corporations[7] and extends the dominance and ubiquity of corporate models to the 'management' of nations themselves.

The changes we outline are not benign; they mark the further embedding of the triumph of neoliberalism over democracy. The rise of the CEO politician is part of the broader cultural changes in the expected social role of government as being both modelled on, and in service of, corporations. Rather than being accountable servants of the electorate, in the CEO society politicians are expected to be active decision makers in pursuit of efficiency and competitiveness. This represents the deeper transformation in the functions of public leadership, with politicians progressively expected to maintain a country's economic solvency in a competitive capitalist global economy. Centrally important is how the extension of corporate models of leadership to politics is helping to strengthen neoliberalism ideologically, and to weaken democracy practically. Moreover, questioning these leadership discourses can create new opportunities for challenging this emerging neoliberal status quo

Even though in contemporary times it is politicians who are increasingly emulating CEOs, the story starts in a manner quite opposite to this. Historically, the popular perceptions of the virtues associated with CEOs saw the forms of charismatic authority previously associated with political leaders become translated into the business domain. As sociologist Max Weber defined it long ago:

The term 'charisma' [is] applied to a certain quality of an individual personality by virtue of which he is set apart from ordinary men and treated as endowed with supernatural, superhuman, or at least specifically exceptional powers or qualities. These are such as are not accessible to the ordinary person, but are regarded as of divine origin or as exemplary, and on the basis of them, the individual concerned is treated as a leader.[8]

Political leaders have conventionally been judged, at least within liberal democracies, according to political values of consensus building and policy acumen. The ideal leader was one who could craft and implement effective policies and garner the support of the citizenry. Moreover, their success was linked to their capacity to maintain ruling coalitions as well as foster inclusiveness. They did so commonly, or at least ideally, through inspiring mass sections of the population with the very charisma that Weber identified, acting as 'spellbinders' for pursuing specific ideologies and policy goals.[9] Their success hinged, furthermore, on the delicate balance of presenting a clear alternative to rivals while maintaining a close affinity to the voter's existing political positions.[10]

At a more prosaic level, politicians were deemed successful based on their continued electoral viability. Outside of normative concerns of ideology or judgements of effectiveness, there lay a general view that a political leader was only as strong as their ability to win power. While not always ethically esteemed, in this regard there is a certain respect granted to the political actor who can navigate the cutthroat world of modern democratic politics. This reflects the traditional 'great man' view of political leadership, whereby politicians are rendered publicly into 'heroes', inspiring individuals to follow them with reverence and awe.[11] The image of the modern-day CEO draws heavily on this epic tradition, transforming the business manager from an effective administrator to a transformational business hero.

As charismatic leadership became a catchphrase for corporate management in the 1980s and 1990s, it was also infused into the 'new' politics. During that time, traditional political values of inspirational consensus building took on a new life, particularly within much of the West, and especially in the United States and Great Britain. President Bill Clinton and Prime Minister Tony Blair exemplified this potent mixture of seemingly charismatic appeal, effective policy making and electoral success. Clinton's leadership style was described, in this regard, as connecting with voters personally through his charisma. Political commentator Mike McArdle proselytises as follows:

> Bill Clinton was a political genius in a lot of ways. But his brilliance was not in framing issues or governing or formulating policy; he had advisors for those things. Bill's genius was in positioning himself in the public's eye. His dazzling personal skills gave him the ability to make a member of any audience feel that he speaking directly to them, that he was one of them.[12]

The ideology of the 'third way' was positioned politically as both novel and centrist, but it was driven through tried and tested ideals of political leadership.[13] These ideals reflected a desire both to win and to achieve tangible social results, linked to an inclusive and widespread coalition politics. Just as importantly, they connected this rather moderate pro-market agenda with established political tropes of individual and collective uplift. Famous chronicler of political leadership, Fred Greenstein, observed a passionate appeal made by Clinton to an African-American audience in support of his centrist agenda:

> In March, I happened on a telecast of Clinton addressing an African American church congregation that could scarcely have been more responsive if Martin Luther King had been in the pulpit. Speaking with ease and self-assurance, Clinton issued a call for policies that would enable citizens to lift themselves by their bootstraps rather than relying on government handouts. Explaining that he was making the same proposal to audiences of whites, Clinton called on all Americans to put aside their differences and recognize their common bonds.[14]

Thus even as the political class increased their commitment to economic management and development, political authority remained predominantly wedded to the established paradigms of the charismatic and effective 'political leader'; the very paradigm that business leaders themselves were being urged to emulate.

The political leader as CEO

The popular perception of political leaders has undergone a profound shift in the 21st century. At a time when business managers were trying to be charismatic and transformational, political leaders had started to emulate traditional business qualities of efficiency, productivity and profitability, conventionally associated with corporate executives. In the CEO society there has thus been a direct shift away from charismatic authority towards hardnosed economic management. This has occurred through political leaders trying to be more like CEOs – the very same CEOs who were striving to emulate charismatic political leadership a short time before. The difference is, however, that the dimensions of CEO leadership that were repatriated into politics did not include charisma and popular appeal, focusing instead on business management acumen.

What happened was the rise of what can be called the 'CEO Model of Political Leadership'.[15] The view of Rajeev Gowda, Chair of the Centre for Public Policy at IIM-Bangalore, exemplified this new business model of political leadership:

As democracies mature, you need different types of people. You go from wanting people who can lead political agitations and write constitutions, to people who can manage a budget and improve the efficiency of programmes. That's where an MBA training comes in useful.[16]

By the dawn of the 21st century CEOs had become celebrities and politicians now sought to imitate them, just as the CEOs had previously emulated an idealised image of the charismatic political leader. What politics took from the 'cult of the CEO',[17] however, was not the image of a leader with a captivating persona who was capable of unleashing people's talent, but rather the CEO as an effective manager whose single-handed determination could get things done. In many cases politicians were expected to be a type of business 'man' who managed for commercial and financial success.

If neoliberalism is taken to involve "converting the distinctly *political* character, meaning, and operation of democracy's constituent elements into *economic* ones", the political leader became more a leader of the economy than a leader of the populace.[18] What was taking shape with the dawn of the new millennium was a fresh vision of the ideal politician as constituted in a particular image of the CEO. Importantly, this is not just a metaphoric shift. Contemporary times have seen numerous examples where former corporate leaders have taken on political careers, for better or for worse. Italy's Silvio Berlusconi came from Finivest, founder of Hyundai Chung Yu Jung was a South Korean statesman, and former UN Secretary General Kofi Annan has a management degree from MIT and headed up the Ghana Tourist Development Company.[19]

The election of George W. Bush to the US presidency in 2001 was perhaps the biggest signal of the CEO values being brought to bear on the presidency of the United States. In his initial campaign Bush heralded his business-based education and experience, specifically his MBA from Harvard Business School. Voicing an opinion that seemed at the time common to many, a former classmate of Bush's at Harvard asked pointedly: "The lawyers and the generals have had their chance. Why not give an M.B.A. a shot?"[20] Bush was explicit in describing his proposed leadership style as akin to that of a top corporate executive. He maintained that as president "[m]y job is to set the agenda and tone and framework, to lay out the principles by which we operate and make decisions, and then delegate much of the process to them".[21] Bush's administration followed suit with an impeccable business pedigree. Vice President Dick Cheney, Secretary of Defence Donald Rumsfeld, Commerce Secretary Don Evans, Labour Secretary Elaine Chao, Chief of Staff Andrew Card Jr. and Treasury Secretary John Snow were all former corporate CEOs.[22]

Bush's presidency prioritised values of decisiveness, efficiency and productivity (even if it often didn't deliver them). He was hailed as "the very model of an MBA president".[23] He was also singled out for being the embodiment of a novel type of 'CEO president'.[24] These qualities were not confined to, or discredited by, the presidency of George W. Bush. Indeed, in his campaign for the presidency in 2012 Mitt Romney followed suit and was similarly valorised by his campaign promoters for his business background, experience that it was assumed would translate well to politics. As public policy expert James Pfiffner observed:

Voters like to think that business people are efficient and that they can bring good practices to government. But they only think about the best run companies and the worst run agencies. They forget about the thousands of start-ups that go broke every year.[25]

The entry of the CEO president into the political arena marked a pronounced change in how the presidency was being popularly framed. Whereas once a business approach might be judged critically in terms of its advantages and disadvantages for political leadership, by the early 2000s the new CEO style of political leadership was being portrayed in a much more uncritical way. To this end, political and business leadership traits were increasingly conflated as one and the same.

In one sense it has been argued that politicians and CEOs need to display similar leadership qualities, such as "vision", "getting followers", "execution", "emotional intelligence", "listen[ing]" and "confidence".[26] Despite this, as we have been arguing, the new CEO political leadership focused less on these charismatic qualities, and more on practical matters of economic management. The now exiled former Prime Minister of Thailand, Thaksin Shinawatra, was perhaps the most explicit in identifying his leadership role with that of a corporate executive. Prior to his entry into politics Shinawatra's business activities, especially in the Thai telecommunications industry, had made him one of the country's wealthiest people. Moreover, he sought to transfer this success directly to political governance. Elected in 2001, he stated that:

A company is a country. A country is a company. They are the same. The management is the same. It is management by economics. From now onwards, this is the era of management by economics, not management by other means. Economics is the deciding factor.[27]

Shinawatra did not dilute his view: the analogousness of country with company brought with it the idea that citizens were employees, and other countries were market rivals. Most tellingly, the head of government was declared the 'CEO leader' whose primary goal was to foster economic growth.[28] Shinawatra was a popular politician, winning elections with landslide victories; victories that were achieved at least partly on account of "his image as a decisive 'CEO' leader who would act quickly to solve problems".[29] What we have here is no longer a matter of just bringing leadership skills and attributes to bear on politics, but rather the wholesale economisation of society such that it is regarded as a business.

Leading the economy

The idea that corporate leadership embodies a more decisive, unilateral and effective means to govern than traditional political leadership, while explicit in Shinawatra's rhetoric, reflects more general tendencies in the changing discourse of politics in the CEO society. Symbolising this change, corporate leaders have been hailed as having the leadership skills necessary for steering the economy; a view especially resonant in the wake of the 2008 financial crisis. In the United States, 2010 was labelled as the "high water mark for the CEO as candidate"; more than forty business magnates ran for seats that year, many of whom won convincingly.[30] Reflected in this was a deeper shift in what was expected of politicians. They were meant to embody the skills thought to be the property of the successful businessperson. According to political scientist Susan MacManus, voters were "looking for financial acumen, and they associate that with CEOs. They can talk with credibility when they talk about real financial issues".[31]

Similar indicators can be found with the former Prime Minister of Australia Tony Abbott. Elected to office in 2013, Abbott epitomised the contemporary neoliberal politician to the point of virtual caricature. Upon being elected he quickly set about implementing a series of pro-business policies including removing the carbon tax on corporations, negotiating international trade agreements, repealing laws that protect workers, and privatising the last of the government-owned corporations. In signalling this agenda, on the night of his election he announced: "Australia is under new management and is once more open for business".[32] Again, here we see political leadership being recast as a form of business management, coupled with commercial and economic issues taking precedence as the primary function of government. Such changes echo not just in political pronunciations, but also in terms of electoral expectations; the CEO politicians were winning.

With his popularity falling in 2015, the news media not only questioned Abbott's political understanding, but also asked the pointed question: "if Tony Abbott was CEO, would he be sacked for his performance?" In considering this, Richard Dennis, Executive Director of the left-leaning think tank the Australia Institute, suggested that we might "think of government in terms of a business structure", with the prime minister being the CEO, the party room being the board of directors and the voters being the shareholders. By implication, Dennis opined:

> any CEO who does a poor job of keeping their board informed and aligning their agenda with that of their board is sailing into dangerous waters. Tony Abbott has made much of his right to make 'captain's calls' on key decisions, but no prime minister should forget that their party room has the right to replace a PM whose judgment they don't support.[33]

The 'captain's calls' that Dennis referred to concern a phrase Abbott used to defend unilateral decisions that he was prone to making without consulting his cabinet ministers. Examples ranged broadly from delisting Tasmanian forests as world heritage areas, rendering them open for logging, to awarding an Australian knighthood to Britain's Prince Philip. This directorial approach reflects one key difference in political leadership conceived as managerial rather than democratic. It suggests that the advent of the CEO politician is in fact a retreat from democracy towards more single-handed forms of decision making. This is a similar criticism that was faced by Thailand's Thaksin Shinawatra, in that the CEO style is seen to be one based on authoritarianism and a centralisation of power around the leader.

In late 2015 Malcolm Turnbull replaced Abbott as prime minister and leader of the Liberal Party of Australia. While Abbott was a conspicuously pro-business neoliberal, Turnbull came to the job with a CV of impeccable business credentials. A self-made dot.com millionaire from the late 1990s, he is former partner and managing director of Goldman Sachs in Australia. He was even featured in *Fortune Magazine* as "one of the richest politicians in Australia".[34] Turnbull drew on this business experience very early in his leadership. In his first extended press interview of 2016, he stated unequivocally that "Australians expect, me as Prime Minister to manage the budget responsibly, to get the most bang for their taxpayer buck, to manage the government efficiently". He also condemned spending on education as "reckless" and made industrial relations and tax reform his chief areas of focus.[35]

National leaders must obviously be fiscally responsible, however, and Turnbull showed from the start that this was his primary priority. As the scuffle for power started in 2015, Turnbull damned Abbott as having "not been capable of providing the economic leadership our nation needs". Then, after he took power, when asked whether Abbott would be seen on his frontbench, he responded: "It's very important in government, as it is in business, to ensure that there is renewal".[36] The comparison is unequivocal. Moreover, Turnbull has been steadfast in describing politics explicitly in business terms. Agility, innovation, creativity and disruptive change are the future for Australia, according to him. No talk here of equality, freedom or social justice. That would be bad for business. This 'leadership' talk reads more as though it has been lifted from the type of management books sold at the airport bookshop than from a serious political manifesto. And in true managerial form, behind the rhetoric of progress lies an agenda of grassroots cost cutting. Education and health, two areas of government spending most closely linked to social equality, were at the top of Turnbull's first budget hit list.[37] Cutting penalty and overtime rates for workers was, from the outset, also firmly on the economic agenda.[38]

As we have seen, in the CEO society politics has become increasingly more business-like not merely in its priorities but also in its personnel. The ideal politician increasingly mirrors the image of the hardnosed business executive with business and economy at the top of the CEO politician's agenda. This tendency, albeit not as crude as in some other cases, can be seen also in the recent presidency of Barack Obama. As political theorist Wendy Brown elucidates, Obama came to power in 2008 on the back of a campaign driven by a 'hope and change' rhetoric that promised he would be the transformational leader that could unite the people of the United States, guiding them out of a war-torn recent past towards a new era of justice, opportunity and progress.[39]

By the time of Obama's second term in office, however, things had changed. In his State of the Union address in 2013 he was still calling for political change associated with tax reform, health care, clean energy, home ownership, education, increases to the minimum wage and various forms of social justice, but this time "each of these issues was framed in terms of its contribution to economic growth and American competitiveness".[40] "The North Star that guides our efforts",

Obama claimed, is "a growing economy that creates good, middle class jobs".[41] The focus was primarily economic, directed towards job creation from foreign investors, training people to do those jobs, and ensuring adequate reward for doing them. The situation, as Brown describes it, is such that "attracting investors and developing an adequately remunerated workforce – these are the goals of the world's oldest democracy led by a justice-minded president in the 21st century".[42] The situation is one where all forms of change can only be justified politically if they can be seen to drive economic growth. The president is there not to ensure freedom, equality and justice, but rather to formulate "social justice, government investment, and environmental protection as fuel for economic growth ... competitive positioning, and capital enhancement" such that "the conduct of government and the conduct of firms are now fundamentally identical".[43]

The CEO politician and the executisation of democratic leadership

The intimate association of political and business leadership in the CEO society reflects a more fundamental shift within representations of democracy. Traditionally, elected politicians are meant, at least ideally, to serve and respond to the needs of their constituency. Their main priority was to ensure the present and future welfare of those they represented. Democratic leadership was viewed as being simultaneously populist (i.e. attuned to popular opinions and desires) and courageously forward thinking (i.e. willing to go against short-term political gains in the name of ensuring voters' long-term interests). These ideals are far from ever having been fully realised in practice, but they did set out the broad coordinates for what 'good' democratic leadership was and should be. The dominance of the CEO politician has, however, reconfigured this ideal, giving primacy to the demands of the market over people.

This evolution can be termed the neoliberalisation of democratic leadership, and is a central feature of the CEO society. In general terms, a key dimension of neoliberalism has been the transferring of power from the public to private sphere. The function of the government in this transition is to promote "a programme of deliberate intervention ... in order to encourage particular types of entrepreneurial, competitive and commercial behaviour in its citizens".[44] Not surprisingly, such a change has potentially dramatic consequences for democratic norms and practices. Wendy Brown speaks of the neoliberal political transformation of humanity as increasingly characterised by "an image of man as an entrepreneur of himself".[45] This embrace of the 'economic man' extends to what is expected of the ideal political leader as well, emphasising the necessity of entrepreneurialism and good business sense.

This process of neoliberalisation is exemplified in the merging of fiscal and political responsibility. The image championed is of a responsible democratic leader who is able to act decisively to guarantee a robust market and economic growth. Such responsibility is directly and strategically connected to neoliberal austerity policies and expanded financialisation.[46]

The dangers of such ideologies are not only that they uniformly don't work but also, according to Blythe, that:

> Ideologically, it is the intuitive appeal of the idea of austerity – of not spending more than you have – that really casts its spell. Understanding how austerity came to be the standard policy in liberal economic thought when states get into trouble can reveal why it is so seductive and so dangerous.[47]

The CEO leader is similarly dangerous and seductive to present-day voters in their promise to lead the country in accordance with established corporate values.

CEO politicians are meant first and foremost to serve the market rather than citizens. Their popular accountability is therefore largely indirect: to meet the needs of voters by attending to the market and its needs. For this reason, neoliberal fiscal regulations are cast as a form of 'anti-politics'.[48] This signals the advent of a novel type of ideal democratic leader, one able to impose market reforms on an often unwilling population, seemingly for their own good. Here politicians can heroically resist popular but 'irresponsible' demands by citizens. In particular, they must be politically resilient and tactical in order to justify reforms. In this neoliberal era, governance experts Paul Posner and Jón Blöndal suggest that:

> savvy political leaders have proved adept at framing deficit reduction as an economic growth program. They are able to lay economic problems such as high interest

rates and inflation at the doorstep of high deficits. The sacrifices involved in fiscal consolidation must be justified by pointing to prospective economic gains in the near term, whether it be easing credit market pressures or staving off the potential for a full-scale exogenous debt crisis.[49]

What is present is less a democratic deliberation over values and policies and more a popularity contest over who is sufficiently strong and self-controlled to responsibly manage the economy. It is this that has given rise to a new political 'hero' willing to do what is economically necessary to preserve neoliberalism.[50] Literal manifestations of this in the United States are organisations such as the Council for Citizens Against Government and Fix the Debt, which give politicians actual 'hero awards' based on the degree of their fiscal conservatism. Undoubtedly, the wake of the 2008 financial crisis put this practice into question, especially as austerity seemed to cause greater economic problems than it solved. Nevertheless, democratic discourse still plays on the ability of a strong leader to enact 'responsible reforms' that will 'cure' capitalism and restore it to health. In this way, the CEO society espouses a desire for a leader who can steer a nation through an economic downturn in a way similar to a change of the management executive at a corporation.

This neoliberalisation of leadership also affects how voters are understood. The popularity of the CEO politician has been accompanied by and helped to produce the 'shareholder citizen'. This type of citizen stands as the inverse of the so-called "citizen shareholders" who "don't have a direct voice in governance but who are intimately affected by it", therefore highlighting "the relationship between economic interests in corporate actions and social and political interests of investors as members/citizens of society".[51] By contrast, the shareholder citizen is expected to understand the market effects of their political decisions and vote accordingly. It mirrors how sociologists Lynne Philips and Suzan Ilcan describe neoliberalism as expecting individuals to "become self-regulating … and market-knowledgeable".[52] As such, in this new era it is not only that the CEO politician is democratically desirable, but also that it is the democratic obligation of each shareholder citizen to vote for such business-like leadership.

The new business of political leadership

In this chapter we have highlighted the relationship between public and private sector leadership as they have changed through the development of neoliberalism from the late 20th century to the present day. This shows how political leadership is increasingly linked to conventional business values of efficiency, effectiveness, profitability, productivity and success against rivals. As we suggested at the outset, this trend towards the CEO politician was a significant part of Donald Trump's appeal as a presidential candidate. Never afraid of hyperbole, Donald Trump epitomised a particular form of CEO competitive ethos. In one of his campaign rallies he proclaimed:

We're going to win. We're going to win so much. We're going to win at trade, we're going to win at the border. We're going to win so much, you're going to be so sick and tired of winning, you're going to come to me and go "Please, please, we can't win anymore." You've heard this one. You'll say "'Please, Mr. President, we beg you sir, we don't want to win anymore. It's too much. It's not fair to everybody else." […] And I'm going to say "I'm sorry, but we're going to keep winning, winning, winning, We're going to make America great again."[53]

This focus on competitive victory exemplifies a particular neoliberal view of the value of markets, their applicability to all walks of life, and the rivalry which they assume. This is part and parcel of the changing images of leadership brought on by the CEO politician, as well as reflective broader shifts in the 21st century configuration of socio-political power as privileging the values of capitalism over those of democracy. In the CEO society, democracy is reduced to being at best a tool to achieve economic and competitive goals. Politicians, in this vein, still retain their status in the public imagination, at least in part, as the main drivers of social change; it is just that the social change that is demanded is largely directed to financial, economic and market-related matters.

Of course, the association of political rule with business values is not necessarily new. As early as the 1920s, scholars were complaining of the dangers of the politician as a 'personnel manager', akin to a business tycoon, who used their power to bestow favours and influence on their friends.[54] Even more presciently, there is a tradition of theorising and advocating for what political scientist Eugene Lewis called 'the political leaders as entrepreneur'.[55] Here, an ideal political leader was one who "creates or profoundly elaborates a public organisation so as to alter greatly the existing pattern of allocation of scarce resources".[56] Neoliberalism has provided the ideological scaffolding for these ideas to both expand and take hold as a central part of politico-economic discourse. At a structural level, politicians are expected to mirror the traits and behaviour of their business counterparts in order to ensure that private markets maximise their efficiency and profitability.[57]

In a CEO society where it can often seem impossible to distinguish between a CEO and a president, one might question, as does Wendy Brown, "what happens to the constituent elements of democracy – its culture, subjects, principles and institutions – when neoliberal rationality saturates political life" up to a point where that saturation reaches the very top.[58] Significantly, changes in both the practice and cultural expectations of private and public leadership reinforce neoliberalism at the expense of democracy. Indeed, this is part of the defining character of the CEO society. This revision to political leadership does more than reflect neoliberal dogma, however; it also helps to facilitate and constitute it. Political scientist Neil Brenner has argued that discourses of globalisation facilitated what he referred to as a 'normative re-ordering' of international politics such that they have come to reflect neoliberal ideologies.[59] Analogously, witnessed in these emerging popular representations of leadership is the facilitation and expansion of market values.

In creating the CEO society, neoliberalism, as a political and economic doctrine, has normatively reordered the cultural landscape related to leadership. The dominant portrayal of politicians as having to be like businesspeople strengthens this reconfiguration of power. The election of Trump exemplified corporate democracy's maturation – a potent mix of executive authority working on behalf of pro-business special interests. The executisation of politics, however, is far from complete and recent years also bring optimism that there is growing resistance to it, and support for a different and more truly democratic politics. Responses to Trump's presidency are a clear indication of this, with politicised citizens having turned out in large numbers to show dissent. The Women's Marches in the United States, held in January 2017 to protest against Trump's election, for example, marked the largest protest in US history and, to Trump's apparent chagrin, they were supported in solidarity across the globe.[60] By the best estimate the Women's March in Washington attracted three times as many people as the Trump inauguration.[61]

The insurgent campaigns of Bernie Sanders and Jeremy Corbyn in the US and UK, respectively, have revealed a growing strain of progressive anti-CEO politics. Momentum in Britain and the Sanders-inspired organisation Our Revolution embody this spirit, both pointing in the possible direction of a post-CEO politics and society. Momentum was established in 2015 specifically to support Jeremy Corbyn's leadership; and with more than 200,000 supporters, it campaigns to increase citizen participation in politics, as well as to reverse "the privatisation of railways, the energy sector and public services" and "redistribute wealth and power from the few to the many".[62] Similarly, Our Revolution's mission includes a pledge to revitalise American politics in an age of corporate media control and corrupt political financing, so as to "reclaim democracy for the working people of our country".[63] This commitment to reversing the corporate encroachment on government combines a dedication to ending the gross inequality fuelled by neoliberalism and replacing it with a politics that is bottom up, collectivist and committed to democratising social relations.

To a significant degree, both these movements have been created to actively resist the way that political leadership has become yoked to business interests. They make visible liberal democracy's pro-corporate priorities as well as pushing back on the limits of political action within this broader neoliberal environment. This enhanced visibility creates the potential basis for questioning the marketisation of politics and changing the dominant view that the ideal democratic political leader is analogous to a particular image of the CEO. At stake is whether democracy and public rule will be replaced by the private control that is a central dimension of the CEO society.

5

The CEO as a model for living

While the power of the CEO dominates both the economic and political spheres it also transcends them, extending broadly into culture more generally. It is with this extension that the CEO society works to mould how individuals and communities can navigate the contemporary world. At play is the further evolution of a particular idea of what it means to be human, as encapsulated in the so-called 'homo economicus'. Homo economicus was originally formulated to indicate a basic unit of economic theory: the rational individual who is fully aware of their own economic self-interest, and who is driven to single-mindedly pursue it. In practice, economic behaviour has been found not always to be motivated by such a narrow and selfish set of concerns,[1] but it is the presumption that people acted as if each were the self-serving homo economicus that lay at the foundations of the liberalism that neoliberalism extended. In some sense it can be said that with neoliberalism the position of homo economicus was less descriptive of a present reality, and more prescriptive of a normatively preferred way of being.[2] In today's terms this translates as a human existence defined by maximising one's gains and minimising losses, economically or otherwise, through being ruthlessly productive and efficient.

In this chapter we examine the CEO as a special manifestation of homo economicus, as well as a figure whose cultural dominance cements it as a model for others both inside and outside of economic life. In so doing we trace the CEO through their fall from grace following the 2008 global financial crisis, to their subsequent phoenix-like resurrection as a model for what it means to live a valuable and productive life. We note that the idea of homo economicus that is intimately tied up in the imaginary of the CEO is not without cultural contradictions, at least on the face of it. One might legitimately question, for example, how a way of life based on economic maximisation can appear to directly contradict the concurrent normative emphasis on good living. Indeed, today there is a veritable obsession with being healthy, fit and well balanced.[3] As part of this, there is a clear cultural desire that suggests people should live life to the fullest and resist being a slave to their job or career. This is hardly a straightforward reflection of the transfusion of the image of the workaholic, profit-driven top manager into everyday life. Such a straightforward reading, however, belies the complexity of the CEO ideal and its ability to contain ironies and contradictions. Scratching beneath the surface reveals that the CEO also symbolises the ultimate ability to work hard and play hard in such a way that it incorporates homo economicus and a broader conception of the 'good life' without needing to compromise on either.

Celebrity CEOs in particular are often renowned as much for their varied forms of thrill seeking and lavish lifestyles as they are for their business ingenuity. One only has to think of Virgin's Richard Branson's hot air ballooning escapades, or Oracle's Larry Ellison's adventures in championship regatta. Sandy Lerner, co-founder of CISCO systems, is an especially fascinating case, given his penchant for donning medieval armour, climbing on a shire horse and fighting it out in jousting competitions.[4] CEOs present an image of the contemporary business titan as someone for whom the normal rules of work and life simply do not apply, with Lerner taking this to an almost comical level. For the CEO, anything is considered possible, whether it is skydiving in the morning, making a multi-billion dollar deal in the afternoon, having cocktails with movie stars in the evening, or solving the world's problem in Davos at the weekend.

As we explore in this chapter, the idolisation of the CEO runs deep in contemporary society. In this context the CEO offers a blueprint to all of us for effectively organ ising our existence in what is presented as a fulfilling and self-actualising manner. Executive values proffer the neces- sary wisdom for people to both define and achieve their hopes and dreams across the full spectrum of life's possibil- ities. This is a vaunted vision of the 'good life' that celebrates executising your very way of being in the world. Everyone owes it to themselves, in this respect, to be a successful CEO of their own life, just as in corporations themselves it is touted that happiness, engagement and wellness are the new return on investment.[5]

The executive existence

Being a contemporary CEO means so much more than just being a top-level businessperson. CEOs personify what can appear as an entirely better type of existence than the one led by the majority of the population. This promises an existence where life is lived to the fullest, and power, wealth and connections are used to satisfy every whim in ways mere employee (and even less so unemployed) mortals could never do. These modern-day heroes do not just think on the cutting edge but supposedly live that way too. One of the most interesting developments, in this respect, is the adventurous CEO just introduced. The staid company president has been largely replaced in the popular imagination with one who is likened to an action hero. Moving beyond the conservative confines of the boardroom, the modern chief executive is renowned for having the latest technology before anyone else – once it was the chunky 1980s mobile phone, now it is home automations systems and robotics.[6]

Many CEOs are celebrated for their thrill-seeking spirit, where instead of wearing a suit and tie they are flying in aeroplanes, running marathons, or even breaking world records. Richard Branson, who has made a number of attempts to be the first person to circumnavigate the globe in a hot air balloon, suggests that: "Being and adventurer and an entrepreneur are similar. You're willing to go where most people won't dare".[7] If that's not enough, in 2014, at the age of sixty-three, he broke the Guinness world record for 'most people riding a kitesurf board', when he and three bikini-clad young women rode the waves in the British Virgin Islands.[8] According to one recent study 'sensation seekers', understood as active risk takers who chase unusual experiences, are better CEOs than their unsensational counterparts.[9] Such types of people, it is claimed, are more likely to push companies towards success, especially when that success is driven by innovation.

As we have been discussing throughout this book, it is with the CEO society that we have witnessed the rise of the CEO as a role model not just in matters of business, but in relation to life generally. The CEO as a risk taking and adventurous innovator is a key dimension of this. Indeed, it is in light of this especially masculine-heroic persona that CEOs can be viewed not just as social and economic winners, but as having the character traits and personalities that we might also wish to emulate outside of business as well. Central to the personal appeal of the CEO is the idea that they are figures who follow their own rules and are not beholden to the same norms as the rest of us. CEOs are cast in the image of masculine western individualism, limited only by their own sheer will and potency. One just needs to think of stories of Mark Zuckerberg building a billion-dollar Facebook empire in his jeans and t-shirt, or Steve Jobs 'revolutionising' society after a youth spent expanding his consciousness through hallucinogenic drugs. The attractiveness of such images is rooted in much more than their wealth; it is in CEO's mooted ability to forge their own path free from social interference or regulations.

A telling example comes in the form of GoPro CEO Nick Woodman. As one of his former college classmate recalls, Woodman would:

spend hours painstakingly putting together a model glider, which crashed on its first flight. Woodman was unfazed and went right back to work building another model. The lesson … is that Woodman was never frightened by the threat of failure. Now it's these same qualities – passion, determination and innovation – that GoPro investors have to believe Woodman will bring to his role as CEO.[10]

This observation illustrates how the neoliberal promise of individual freedom embodied in heroic individualistic values is given human form in the CEO. While many of us, as workers and employees, remain more deeply regulated by a repressive corporate existence, these economic elites appear to act as they please, their potential always realised in the here and now. Success, so the story goes, has given CEOs the right to a unique freedom from having to conform to normal cultural, or even physical, constraints. This reflects the so-called 'upper echelon theory' of executives, a theory which proposes that it is the traits, values and abilities of top managers that are deemed to be the drivers of organisational outcomes.[11] Never mind the complex interactions and skills of workers and middle managers, top executives alone are the sole organisational agents, singularly responsible for collective outcomes. The qualities associated with exclusive talent are positioned as allowing CEOs to break through any frustrating bureaucratic roadblocks on their way to corporate performance. In this 21st century corporate class system, CEOs are treated as modern royalty not just by their companies, but also by the world. The story goes that getting what they want is their hard-earned and well-deserved reward for reaching the top of the business mountaintop, leaving the rest of us to look up to them in awe and envy.

Even though such individual freedom may be positioned as an elite privilege unavailable to everyday people, there is still a profound basis for the popular appeal of the CEO. It is their apparently singular capacity to successfully 'navigate' an increasingly complex and cutthroat world. Even CEOs who are not renowned for adventurous endeavours outside the office can be revered for their supposed ability to take charge of their lives. They are imagined as the ultimate path breakers; people who have found the secret to determining their own destiny rather than having it 'trickle down' on them in ways they neither chose nor desired. CEOs are appointed as gurus for the modern age; corporate spirit guides to living an effective and successful existence. Within such an imaginary they are also a kind of superhuman mental coach who can help everyone 'win' in all areas of their lives, and they have developed the habits to make you, too, more effective and productive. CEOs are 'exemplary' in that they provide an attractive standard for others to aspire to.[12] When accepted as an exemplar, they have the knowledge to allow each and every one of us to rise to the top. For those who believe, emulating CEO perfection is the way that you can become the person you always wanted to be.

CEOs represent a type of all-encompassing 'executive life-style' that can be imagined as being applicable to all of us. It is not simply or even primarily about making profit or earning a gigantic salary. The modern CEO is symbolic instead of how people are supposed to be able to achieve personal goals of maximising individual desires, and of fulfilling their wildest dreams both inside and outside the workplace. Self-help books are a telling barometer of the cultural power of the idea of the CEO. One book that reflects the CEO spirit is promisingly entitled *Going from Homeless to CEO: The No Excuse Handbook*.[13] What will you learn in the pages of such a volume? Nothing less than "how to overcome adversity, anger and jealousy to create a successful and happy life".[14] This draws on the assumption that one of the greatest strengths of the CEO is in teaching others through their words and examples how to live their lives well. If that doesn't work for you then you'd better read Robin Sharma's *The Saint, the Surfer, and the CEO: A Remarkable Story about Living Your Heart's Desires*.[15] If the title isn't tantalising enough, with it comes the promise of awakening "our highest selves to the miracle our lives were meant to be". The CEO is the miracle worker!

A defining feature of the 21st century is that the very real wealth and power of CEOs epitomises the arrival of a new gilded age.[16] Their influence extends beyond mere economic power and political influence into guiding contemporary knowledge and identity. They act as powerful role models, combining long-term vision with short-term rationality. In this regard, they play a similar role in the public imagination to entrepreneurs. The latter are held up as paragons of capitalist virtue, personifying the ideals of creativity, disruption and innovation, and playing into a cultural fantasy whereby economic improvement can be easily attained through hard work and ingenuity. Tellingly, their influence is not confined to those who decide to start new businesses.

Entrepreneurship is a multi-purpose ideal that can be deployed to motivate and judge the actions of modern individuals more generally, and while not all entrepreneurs make good CEOs, all CEOs can be entrepreneurial by being ready to take advantage of new opportunities. Popular reality TV shows like Britain's *Dragon's Den* (airing on the BBC since 2005) and the United States' version *Shark Tank* (on ABC since 2009), where wannabe entrepreneurs try to convince a panel of investors to back their ideas, feed into this myth. In this case it is successful businesspeople-cum-investors who are positioned as the ultimate judges as to what is valuable and how such value can be maximised. These 'sharks' are not inventors but exploiters, tasked with spotting the latest trend and ruthlessly maximising their economic gain from this foresight. They are also viewed as applying the rationality, devoid of sentiment or traditional beliefs, necessary to the prosperity of organisations.

It is Steve Jobs, widely accepted as the singular creative genius behind the success of the Apple Corporation, who is for many the ultimate example of the successful entrepreneur. Perhaps the most famous line in the 2015 film biopic, named simply *Steve Jobs*, is uttered by the character of real-life technological innovator Steve Wozniak. He pointedly asks Jobs:

What do you do? You're not an engineer. You're not a designer. You can't put a hammer to a nail. I built the circuit board! The graphical interface was stolen! So how come ten times in a day I read Steve Jobs is a genius? What do you do?[17]

In question here is the somewhat mysterious and immaterial nature of entrepreneurship – it is less about creating anything tangible than about taking advantage of the realities others create. It is this form of entrepreneurship that CEOs engage in, leveraging the materially productive and inventive capacity of others. Entrepreneurial CEOs, albeit at the heads of already well-established businesses, are entrepreneurial to the extent they are focused on identifying opportunities for others to realise, while maximising the yield from each opportunity. Every experience represents the potential for a new business venture, while in the social world, each moment represents another chance to take charge of your life and maximise your overall value.

Facing an executive crisis

As we have been exploring, the contemporary CEO symbolises something much deeper and dramatically more significant than corporate management. At stake is the ability to control one's own destiny and sense of self. CEO heroes cannot only purportedly shape the market; they can also shape their own lives rather than them being shaped by society. In considering this, one needs to examine not just the contours and characteristics of the idealised CEO, but also investigate how and why this idealisation can maintain and reinvent itself through time. The most telling example of this comes in the form of how the CEO, as a cultural ideal, survived the 2008 financial crisis, a crisis that directly challenged the idyllic vision of CEO heroics. One only need think back to December 2008 when President Barack Obama scolded the heads of the largest US auto firms for flying to Washington in private jets to ask for financial bailouts. As one Democratic Party representative added: "Couldn't you all have downgraded to first class or jet-pooled, or something, to get here? It would have at least sent a message that you do get it."[18]

This is just one example of how, for a short time after the crash, those on the top of the corporate ladder seemed as powerless as those on the bottom. As well as that, the failure seemed to indicate that neither CEOs nor their financial advisors had any greater idea of how the market worked, or any greater ability to control it, than anyone else. As much as people feared a complete global financial meltdown, they felt more broadly that the 21st century economy was marked by the blind leading the blind. In the words of president and chief executive operating office at Goldman Sachs, Gary Cohn:

> When you go through these situations you either just throw yourself in the middle of them and try to deal with everything coming at you 24 hours a day, seven days a week, or you sort of get in a position where you withdraw and you try and just reason and try to understand exactly what's going on.[19]

There was no clear direction forward and no visionaries who could the lead the way to a better future, just a bunch of apparent amateurs trying to figure things out for the first time. All that was left for modern citizens was to try to brace themselves as a runaway global free market fell off the proverbial cliff. Moreover, the CEO suddenly appeared like a fall guy for the crash rather than as a hero. As even the chairman and CEO of JP Morgan Chase lamented:

> If management ruined their companies, their boards should have been fired, management should have been fired [...] If you said to me, how do I feel about some of these C.E.O.'s who walked away with $50, $100, $150 million and their company blew up? Terrible. It's outrageous. I agree with them. Everyone says that's bad. If this company went bankrupt, we should all give back the money we earned in the last five years or more. You wouldn't have to ask me.[20]

What, for a time, became apparent was a serious capitalist existential crisis as well as a derailing on the path to the CEO society. What was the purpose of the market? Did it have any identity besides representing merely a race to the historical bottom? Was there any future for capitalism that was not apocalyptic? This sense of pervading crisis also infected CEOs as the hubris of the mythology met with the humility of the realities. CEOs had turned into the global bogeyman, ruining things for all of us. Their once vaunted freedom was now reviled as symbolising excess and exploitative privilege.

As well as a global financial crisis, what was going on was a full-blown executive crisis. The masters of the universe, the ultimate winners, were now considered the lowest of the low. They had failed to win a rigged game and even worse made the whole world, including ironically themselves, into what neoliberalism hates the very most: losers. Suicide rates spiked, with the risk factors identified as home foreclosure, debt and job loss. 'Economic suicides' was the name they were given.[21] As economist Andrew Farlow critically notes in his book *Crash and Beyond: Causes and Consequences of the Great Financial Crisis:*

> As we picked our way through the causes and conse-
> quences of such explosive events, a range of deeper and
> more troubling questions left their trails across our
> minds. Why did public policy have so little to say about
> the dangers as they were growing? The costs turned out
> to be astronomic ... Perhaps the fundamental question
> is not why the crash happened, but why it was allowed
> to happen.[22]

While people clamoured for CEOs to be held accountable and be prosecuted, serious questions about the present and future were emerging. This was not least a practical matter. As people saw jobs being lost, shop fronts being boarded up, and politicians crying austerity, what they wanted above all else was economic recovery. Yet with the world's top executives in disgrace, who could lead such a dramatic economic revival?

What arose was a novel fantasy of executive-led recovery that allowed the shattered reputation of the CEO not only to be miraculously resurrected but to come back stronger and more broadly influential than ever. This played into an appealing affective crisis narrative. With such a narrative, all faith must be invested in the recuperation of a golden past that existed before the upheaval.[23] In the case of the 2008 global financial crash, there was a strong shared longing to go back to a time when prosperity seemed assured and the market was manageable. To this effect, all that was supposedly needed was some 'common sense' regulations to curtail corporate risk taking, and business as usual could resume. In the United States President Obama confidently proclaimed in 2009 that:

> I think that we just went through a couple of decades where there was an artificial complacency about the dangers of markets going off the rails. And a crisis like this reminds us that we just have to put in some common-sense rules of the road, without throwing out the enormous benefits that globalization had brought in terms of improving living standards, reducing the cost of goods, and bringing the world closer together.[24]

These desires for recovery were of course perfectly understandable, and they clearly shed light on why ideologies of the free market survived, and even thrived, in the wake of having caused an international economic meltdown. But this still only scratches the surface of why CEOs continue to be idolised by so many. Whereas individual executives may be reviled for their greed and corruption, as an ideal they have retained a solid gold allure. The financial crisis pointed to a deep insecurity resting on the fear that it was futile for humans to influence the economy, and this reverberated with a more general fear that we lack agency more widely. Suddenly people were pushed into facing the possibility that their lives were lost to the whims and unpredictable fate of a supernatural market. Where since the advent of the 20th century it had been righteously condemned that "money is the secular God of the world",[25] now it was feared that finance had become an even more reckless god, one that cared little for the humans who worshipped at its gilded altar. This was the deeper ontological insecurity afflicting humanity at the beginning of the new millennium; it was the terror caused by realising that humanity was in a system that had spiralled out of control and beyond human jurisdiction.

The popular rehabilitation of the image of the CEO was not, as Obama suggested, just a practical matter of wanting to hold on to the material benefits afforded by neoliberalism. It was a psychic measure needed to counteract the fear of dehumanisation at the hands of a runaway Frankenstein economy. In other words, we just wanted to pretend that someone was in control, even if all the facts and evidence were telling us that that wasn't the case. The recovery of the myth of the CEO was a reassertion of the power of individuals to shape events and control their destiny. To achieve this meant establishing again an identification with the heroic character of the CEO such that ordinary people too might regain a sense of control over their own lives. To work, and to put people at ease, this required the CEO to be re-deified as the only force that could tame the depersonalised force of the market. Restoring faith in the CEO was less a matter of empirical fact and more a symptom of a human need to find something to believe in at the end of a hard day; with the reality too hard to bear, the fantasy had to return. The promise was held out that everyone could receive grace if only they accepted the modern CEO gospel.

Increasing the value of your life

Nearly a decade after 2008's near total economic crash there appears to be a growing division over perceptions of the social and moral benefits of capitalism. For its supporters, capitalism remains the best and only system for creating wealth, as well as being a natural partner to liberal democracy. For its legion of modern critics, it is an engine for inequality, poverty and repression. CEOs are evaluated in a parallel set of competing standards and assessments. For some they are the popular personification of all that is unfair and wrong with the current order. For others they are the epitome of present-day autonomy, representative of a quasi-spiritual state of self-determination that everyone should strive to achieve.

At the heart of this contradiction is the central question of whether capitalism is liberating or exploitive. Much of the recent condemnations of the free market have centred on its wider macro-level problems, whether they be found in the Occupy movement's reference to 'the 99%', or the UK Labour leader Jeremy Corbyn's 2016 campaign slogan 'for the many, not the few'. For many, the everyday realities of life in the free market economy leaves much to be desired. Its vaunted freedom can feel to most like a highly pressurised form of daily drudgery, where anxiety and fear rule and your boss has the final say over your wellbeing. Expanding on this anxiety, sociologist David Beer observes:

> What makes neoliberalism so powerful as an art of governance is its ability to provoke uncertainty, to play with emotional and physical experience and to demarcate visions of what is worthwhile. Neoliberalism is founded on the production of uncertainty and anxiety through metrics ... These feelings will only be exacerbated if we continue to try to measure everything. The intensification of the measurement of our lives could well intensify the production of our uncertainty and anxiety.[26]

Meanwhile, executives appear to many to be living a life of unearned luxury, their success and riches a by-product of both the consuming citizens from whom they reap profits and a suffering workforce struggling to make ends meet. Of course, apologists for capitalism would paint a very different picture. In their rosy worldview, executives are vital to an organisation and to society's continued existence and growth. They act as captains, a leading force for innovation and regeneration. And this requires an intensive amount of labour for which they deserve to be well paid. In any case, the argument would go, the best way to determine prices is the market, and it is the market that has dictated the massive salaries that CEOs take home.[27] The efforts of CEOs are presented as monumental, and so too should be their rewards! Believe that and you will also believe the story that CEOs suffer for the good of the company, never stopping in their mission to increase its worth. Such martyrdom is hardly present, for example, when senior executives who are 'asked to leave' their companies pocket gargantuan severance packages. In 2017, for example, after three years of service and a 37% fall in share prices, CEO Mark Fields left the Ford Motor Company with an estimated payout of more than US$54 million.[28]

This image of the CEO as somewhere between a martyr and meritocrat raises its own pressing questions. If even its winners are burned out and exploited, is capitalism really worth it? It may produce massive profits and economic growth, but is anyone actually enjoying it? These concerns point, in turn, to the free market's most salient modern selling point: the scandalous proposition that exploitation is actually empowering as well as being fundamental to achieving a happy and fulfilling existence. The logic at play is that exploitation – understood as full advantage being taken of your talents and hard work – is paramount to one's personal development. Critical theorist Colin Cremin has referred to this as 'reflexive exploitation' where "a person reflects on herself as an object of exchange in order to access a wage and social status, to choose a life that is compatible with the injunctions of liberal capitalism".[29] This extends to a fetishising of employability that is also present in the CEO society. Reflexive exploitation manifests, for example, in self-investing in one's CV, regarding it as the ultimate force for one's economic safety and salvation. This is, perhaps, the most perfect contemporary example of capitalism refashioning the actuality of exploitation into the promise of empowerment.

Central to this self-improvement process is also channelling the spirit of the executive into everyday life. It is not just about working hard but about adopting entrepreneurial ethics into all dimensions of one's life. This marks a contemporary extension and reformulation of what sociologist Max Weber famously identified as the protestant ethic as being key to the advancement of early capitalism.[30] Today, however, more is required than the conventional morals of sobriety, thrift and hard work that Weber identified. The CEO work ethic relies more on being opportunistic, cunning and ruthless in the pursuit of one's own value and divinely granted right to wealth and happiness.

Taking to heart the executive mindset is, according to the ethos of the CEO society, fundamental to discovering your own self-worth. Quite literally! It is a continual exploration of a person's perceived strengths and weaknesses in comparison to, and in competition with, others. Self-proclaimed 'dating coach' Neely Steinberg exemplifies this spirit, as it relates to the domains outside of work, in her book *Skin in the Game: Unleashing Your Inner Entrepreneur to Find Love*.[31] Targeted at women and with a glaring pink cover, the book advises the lovelorn to adopt top executive techniques such as being able to "see possibilities in your setbacks and disappointments" and to "plug your knowledge gap". Women are advised to pursue their romantic dreams unabashedly. How? "Think of your entrepreneurial venture to find love as your love start-up. And you are the CEO."[32]

In the present era, books such as *Skin in the Game* push the idea that maturity is less about discovering your moral values and more about discovering your market value in all areas of your life. Thus if someone wants to make a life worthwhile they must cultivate and tap into their inner CEO. By this logic, a failure to do so will lead only to stagnation, personal bankruptcy and a loveless life. Crucially, to adopt the values of the CEO society it is imperative to constantly discover new ways to increase your worth, to find the most efficient and cost-effective way to achieve your goals and to take advantage of the opportunities offered by society, especially before others discover them first and reap their profit at your expense. In the end, it is all down to everyone taking responsibility for their own success. As Starbucks CEO Howard Schultz put it: "I am convinced that most people can achieve their dreams and beyond if they have the determination to keep trying".[33] As a corollary, according the ethos of the CEO society, if you fail to achieve your dreams it means you just didn't try hard enough.

Achieving an executive balance

The importance of CEOs transcends the corporate bottom line. It exceeds a mere individual and encapsulates a whole model for life. To live like an executive means finding one's true value and profiting from it. Digging even deeper, this extension of business to the practices of everyday life exists as a contemporary worldview. It shapes how individuals make sense of and seek to act within their present-day social reality. More so, it is put forward as essential to achieving a healthy 'balanced' existence. The modern era has been marked by calls for work–life balance and the general pursuit of wellness.[34] As previously discussed, this is viewed as imperative to attain both personal and professional fulfilment. Yet in the face of the economic insecurity seemingly inherent in neoliberalism, such dreams can appear to be more of a mirage than a realistic goal. When you are worried about your job and the future of your income in a world where capitalism never sleeps, it is hard to focus on your own wellbeing. Physical burnout and mental anxiety associated with employment (or the lack thereof) are a constant threat, and whereas the ideal of 'balance' might have been meant to show that working could and should be a fundamental part of a fulfilling overall existence, in practice it often highlights just how bad capitalism is for your health.

The CEO does not at first glance offer a compelling example. For all their supposed good qualities, a strong commitment to life outside of their career does not appear to be one of them; the exception being endeavours that replicate the competitive individualism that they pursue at work, whether it be on the golf course or behind the wheel of a racing car. Indeed, executives can serve, to this effect, more as a warning than a role model. They highlight the almost single-minded dedication one must have to reach the top. Unfortunately, in practice this may mean that other areas of one's existence fall by the wayside and are sacrificed on the altar of professional success. Nevertheless, the fantasy defies mundane reality, with executives serving as living proof that one can win at both career and life, so long as both are directed at work. In place of the common despair that achieving balance is impossible, executives are here to share their 'killer tips' for realising professional and personal happiness. For example, as corporate manager Elizabeth Dukes proselytises:

> Richard Branson, well-known CEO of Virgin Group, suggests treating family time like any other important scheduled event. "When you're facing an avalanche of appointments, book time to spend with your family," Branson says. "Put it in your work diary."[35]

Similarly, in a recent *Wall Street Journal* article, male CEOs tell us their work–life rules. Business journalist Rachel Feintzeig writes:

> These business titans are not just the best exemplars of realizing such a delicate and seemingly impossible balance, their skills and even mentality are put forward as crucial to its realization. Increasingly, the responsibility for being healthy inside and outside of work is given to the individual themselves. Whereas nominally companies should strive to create a nourishing culture for such pursuits, in real fact it is employees who must find a way to negotiate their professional obligations and aspirations with their personal duties and desires.[36]

With such pronouncements, life becomes something not just to be lived but to be managed. As part of this, personal health and wellbeing are meant to be 'self-managed'. The CEO is promoted, explicitly and implicitly, as the perfect exemplar for the successful achievement of such personal governance. Individuals must constantly negotiate their time effectively, discovering the most efficient and productive way to profitably balance work and play, career and family. In the CEO society, the wisdom and habits of top executives hold the secret key to this wider vision of success.

The new ideal for life is lived by one who has mastered their personal and professional tensions and who had become the most effective manager of their own existence. The popular self-help book *CEO of Me*, by Ellen Kossek and Barbara Lautch,[37] epitomises this perspective. It promises to help people in their attempt at 'creating life that works'. To do so it explores essential 'work patterns' that can make the difficult personal and professional balancing act a reality. As they describe it:

> Perhaps you have never thought about your personal life as something you need to actively lead and manage like a CEO does, but to make significant life change, you should! In the business world, a CEO is the chief executive officer who is in charge of the management of the entire corporation. The CEO makes strategic choices that deeply affect the organization's current and future health. As CEO of your own life, you constantly make choices about how to manage your work and life … After you accept that you are the master or mistress of your working life and fate, you will be able to make better choices.[38]

Clearly exemplified here is the idea that if people want to be happy in life and work then they must follow the lead of CEOs, with that lead being about assuming agency and control. To live life well, the advice is that it is crucial that we adopt an executive mentality for doing so: we must be ruthless in managing our professional and personal existence effectively, we should strive to discover the rules and methods that work for our lives, and we must at all costs seek to achieve an executive balance. Like a boss!

Unleashing the executive within

As we have been exploring, in the CEO society the importance of the CEO is no longer purely or even primarily economic. Rather it extends into and increasingly dominates non-work existence. Adopting an executive mindset is seen not only to be essential to achieving professional and personal goals; it is aligned with the very idea of leading the good life. Happiness and fulfilment, it is proffered, revolve around thinking and acting like a CEO. All you have to do, according to self-proclaimed bestselling author and CEO coach Allan Cox, is experience the exhilaration that happens when you "unleash the executive within".[39]

At its heart, capitalism, despite all its other ideological and historical complexities, is based on a rather straightforward transaction. Individuals are paid a wage that guarantees, at the very least, their material survival. Any remaining value that the worker creates is profit for the employer. This is obviously still the case in the 21st century. A pay cheque provides a person the ability to buy food, shelter and other life necessities – in some cases only just. As well as this, however, capitalism, as it is practised in the CEO society, exceeds simple material reproduction. It is now centred just as much on the reproduction of life. For the contemporary worker, the workplace is meant to provide "increased physical and mental health" including their "advanced spiritual growth and enhanced sense of self-worth".[40] In this respect, one does not so much live to work or work to live but rather work so that one can live as one wants to.

In the CEO society, labour relations have evolved an image from the struggle for life to the struggle for lifestyle. People, particularly those in the developed world and in more privileged economic positions, are demanding the right to have a job that allows them better control over how and where they spend their time. Consequently, "jobs are increasingly expected to contribute to personal wellbeing, as success is re-defined toward a more comprehensive desire for 'personal fulfilment' outside of work".[41] In concrete terms, this means supporting people's non-work aspirations and obligations, whether that is being a good parent or even just getting into better physical shape.

The CEO society is characterised by a merging of life and work. Corporations now promote a culture that fosters not just their professional but also their personal growth. Fitness centres, sports facilities, massage rooms, spa services, health treatments and nap pods are all part of the benefit packages that modern workers increasingly expect. This question of employees' personal wellbeing as being within managerial purview is commonly presented as empowering. Despite this, the way it is practised is easily interpreted as a mode of corporate discipline that demands workers' bodies and minds be healthy for purposes both inside and outside of work. This creates a new set of pressures for people to lead fulfilling all-round lives and to use their career as a springboard not just for balancing work and life but also for maximising its overall value.

This new ethos is epitomised by the recent appeal to ideas of 'leaning in'. Based on the 'corporate feminist' book by Sheryl Sandberg,[42] the Chief Operating Officer of Facebook, leaning in is a concept that advocates confidently and fearlessly capitalising on business opportunities while encouraging women not to sacrifice their careers for other roles such as wife and mother. Aimed principally at women, Sandberg champions executive-style techniques such as risk taking, applying for jobs in growing fields and assertiveness.

On a similar, although non-gender-specific note, a 2014 *Time* magazine article featured advice from male CEOs on how to prioritise between work and other aspects of life.[43] Executives were encouraged to distinguish between family 'rubber moments' (which your family can bounce back from if you miss them) and 'crystal moments' (which cannot be sacrificed for your career). For example, graduations, weddings and births are crystal, while the occasional football game or school assembly are rubber. To manage this means, of course, investing in the crystal moments, while staying at the office instead of participating in too many rubber moments. The CEO society tells you that you can have it all, if you just manage it the right way. At the core of these lessons is the promise that women and men alike can achieve all their goals, both at home and in the workplace. Significantly, this is not about simply making sure that you achieve balance. Rather it is a set of techniques for calculating instrumentally how you make life compatible with your career so that neither is sacrificed at the expense of the other. In a corporate setting they call this a win–win.

The simultaneous professional and personal bliss that is the crucial promise of the CEO society rests on the ability to treat life situations as if they were business ventures. Doing so means approaching these situations with the acumen and wisdom of an executive. Concretely, it entails constantly assessing the rewards and risks of any life enterprise. One must know not merely what life opportunities are available but their opportunity costs as well. Calculating this through a work–life break-even analysis will yield the optimum outcome. Hence life activities must always be questioned and assessed as to whether they are 'worth it'. This is summed up by executive coach and former senior manager Gary Cohen in *The Washington Post*:

> Yes, you are in fact the CEO of your life. A chief executive sets the strategy and vision for a corporation and it is up to each of us to set the strategy and vision for our lives. It is difficult for a corporation to experience resounding success without a sound strategy or vision, so it will also be difficult for each of us to reach our full potential without a well thought-out strategy and vision for our future. I find it interesting that so many people spend more time thinking about and planning their wedding or even their summer vacation than they do creating the strategy and vision for their lives.[44]

To be valued citizens in the CEO society it is imperative for individuals to adopt a proper entrepreneurial attitude to their lives. Each of us is implored to develop and hone our executive skills to fully take advantage of life's opportunities. Just as we should seek to exploit ever-new capitalist markets and possibilities, so too should we act cunningly to profit from the fresh prospects that life makes available to us. This requires us as individuals, whether we are CEOs or not, to abide by the imperative to discover our own 'CEO brand' as a means to maximise our individual leadership capacity.[45] Essential for this purpose, according to 'professional high-fiver' Sean Kelly, is finding "surefire ways to maximize your life, starting this morning". How might one do this? The advice is to "choose not to snooze", "read your affirmations", "exercise to thrive" and "refuel to feel optimal".[46]

In the present age, a once prevalent criticism of the corporation as being the enemy of a fulfilling and happy life has been turned on its head. It is now the CEO who can show the way for people to find purpose and prosperity both in and outside their careers. By embracing an executive mentality we are told we can do much more than simply find a professional and personal balance. By taking charge and becoming our own CEO it is promised that we can in fact maximise our lives tout court.

Executive duty

The call to maximise one's life by being one's own CEO is by no means just the optimistic rhetoric of an entrepreneurial age. It is perhaps tempting to think such matters are innocuous, a collection of simple pieces of advice for people searching for direction and guidance. Yet such executive knowledge represents a new disciplining morality for organising existence inside and outside of work. It is a normative demand whose much trumpeted empowerment brings with it guilt and self-condemnation. Specifically, it not so subtly proclaims that one must take full responsibility for one's own personal successes and failures. So, for example, despite the rule of patriarchy and prevalence of sexism in contemporary life, it is still assumed that any woman, through the power of her own will, can overcome such structural impediments and have the career and life she wants simply by 'leaning in' like a boss.[47] Sure, austerity and globalisation combine to exacerbate economic insecurity, making it progressively impossible for many people to have the time or resources to lead the life they truly long for. Who cares! If one simply acted like a CEO these structural barriers would magically disappear. The same goes for racial discrimination, and economic inequality generally; the only one responsible for it is you!

The CEO society embodies and dramatically expands dominant discourses of neoliberalism associated with 'responsibilisation'. This is, by sociologist Ronen Shamir's account:

> fundamentally premised on the construction of moral agency as the necessary ontological condition for ensuring an entrepreneurial disposition. Neo-liberal responsibilisation is unique in that it assumes a moral agency which is congruent with the attributed

tendencies of economic-rational actors: autonomous, self-determined and self-sustaining subjects.[48]

So responsibilised, it is expected that individuals and communities will be accountable for their own welfare. This is a particularly demanding form of modern self-discipline. People, whatever their circumstances and backgrounds, are liable for, and are thus deserving of, their own social outcomes; win, lose or draw. The desire to embrace a CEO mentality is therefore viewed as a tried and true path to taking charge of one's own life.

Despite its demands and promises, in practice top-level executive imprimaturs usually end up being more disempowering than empowering; they symbolise an impossible demand for subjects of the CEO society to be ultra-efficient, productive, confident and opportunistic in all facets of their lives. Just as one can never be employable enough, one can likewise never be too executive-like. It is precisely this impossibility that is critical to the survival of this CEO morality. It produces a constant blame cycle where people never feel as if they have fulfilled their potential, either as a person or as an employee. There can be a profound feeling of personal guilt for failing to be the idealised CEO of your life, for being a self-labelled 'loser' or a 'victim' who, regardless of circumstances, should have been able to take responsibility for their own success. Such disappointment serves to motivate people to continually strive harder to embody these executive values in their own existence. It is a fantasy whose real-life disappointment can act to drive people to invest even more passionately and completely in these ideals. It is by making people feel worthless that they then seek to become worthy through embodying the compelling vision of the all-powerful CEO.

This guilt-inducing relationship speaks to the ethos of debt that pervades contemporary existence. Indeed, neoliberalism is built economically on massive personal and collective liability associated with the growth of easy credit, threats to the value of real wages, and the necessity of taking out loans to pay for fundamental services such as higher education and health care. More fundamentally, this reflects philosopher and sociologist Maurizio Lazzarato's notion of the modern 'indebted man'.[49] He notes that:

> The series of financial crises has revealed a subjective figure that, while already present, now occupies the entirety of the public space: the 'indebted man'. The subjective achievements neoliberalism had promised ('everyone a shareholder, everyone an owner, everyone an entrepreneur') have plunged us into the existential condition of the indebted man, at once responsible and guilty for his particular fate.[50]

To this effect, people owe it to themselves to be more CEO-like so they can service a personal debt in order to make the most of their life opportunities. Crucial for doing so is adopting a proper executive attitude. The unwillingness to embrace this CEO life wisdom is to perform a disservice to your present and more importantly your future self.[51]

Beyond one's own self-interest, the CEO society also proffers a moral obligation to become CEO-like for your family and friends. If work keeps you from your partner and children, then the fault lies with your inability to use executive techniques for managing your time better. The moral is that we morally owe it to ourselves, to others and to our community to executise our lives. The ideals of the CEO have spread far beyond the corporate boardroom; they infect all areas of human existence, from the political to the personal. Nothing, not even a global financial crisis whose blame was laid at the feet of the CEO class, could derail the dominant social force that demands that the ideal of the executive should inform how we approach the management of our own lives. The strengthened CEO society that emerged does not just seek to determine our desires, it also tells us how we should pursue and seek to realise them. More precisely, present-day people, regardless of their overall preferences or passions, are cajoled to model themselves after the executive in trying to run their lives profitably and efficiently.

Personal development

The mooted duty to effectively executise our lives also has profound social implications. Notably, it points to how the use of market skills should now extend to achieving environmental, social and economic justice. Beyond a mere desire to maximise economic profit, it is also about creating social value. To this end, the market in practice takes on a certain agnostic quality; it can be used for social good or ill. CEO values of efficiency, forward thinking and innovation are, however, absolutely essential to the success of any human enterprise. In this sense, there is a clear break between market means and capitalist ends. Executive values are universal in their application, and in fact are required for any and all activities, whatever their aims.

The increasingly prevalent notion of the 'social entrepreneur' exemplifies this moralisation of the CEO existence.[52] Represented is a romantic vision of a businessperson who uses their market wisdom and talents for a wider public good. Think for example of the band of CEOs (including Tesla's Elon Musk, General Electric's Jeff Immelt and Apple's Tim Cook) who condemned President Donald Trump in 2017 for pulling the United States out of the Paris climate accord. In such a spirit, criticisms of the environmental devastation caused by capitalism can be remedied by demands for 'green capitalism'.[53] Fears over the recklessness of a finance-driven economy can be supplanted by appeals to the possibility of an 'ethical capitalism'.[54] All that is needed is for committed people to channel their executive spirit in a more moral and sustainable direction.

The very idea of social entrepreneurship reflects the paradoxical, not to say insidious, morality of neoliberalism. This is a morality where personal responsibility is placed above all else. Specifically, individuals and communities are held solely accountable for the state of both their life and broader society.[55] This ethos of responsibilisation plays directly into an embrace of an executive existence, even if ironically it is coupled with a partial rejection of the free market values that gave it birth. It is imperative, in this respect, for everyone to use these market-based CEO principles and skills to make the world a better place for oneself and everyone else.

In an ironic twist it has suddenly become a social duty to accept the social value of entrepreneurial authority. Along these lines, Whole Foods Markets CEO John Mackey and his co-author Professor Raj Sisodia promise that the 'heroic spirit of business' can be liberated through a 'conscious capitalism' that will not only build strong and profitable businesses but also create a better world for everyone.[56] Within such thinking, to refuse to succumb to this entrepreneurial spirit, to reject the wisdom of the CEO, is to hold back the survival and advancement of all. With this, capitalism's reach is not restricted in its outcomes to the promise of economic wellbeing for all, but encompasses ensuring the entirety of humanity's political, social and environmental aspirations.

This moral duty to embrace and emulate the virtues of the CEO that is embedded in the CEO society is not reserved, either, for the privileged few living in developed economies. It is an expectation and demand of all people regardless of their national location, social circumstances or personal background. The use of microfinance as a development tool through which the poor in developing countries are given very small loans so as to turn them into small-scale entrepreneurs and businesspeople perfectly embodies this perverse moral logic.[57] Structural issues associated with geopolitical inequalities are put aside in the promise that economic malaise can be eradicated with greater 'indigenous entrepreneurship'. According to Shahid Khandker, a supporter of microfinance, writing on the official website of the World Bank:

> This innovative banking program ... has created the option for millions of poor people, especially women, to become self-employed entrepreneurs. By empowering women, microcredit has created opportunities to lift countless families out of abject poverty.[58]

The modest gains of these initiatives are far outweighed by the justification they provide for not fully addressing head-on the issues of global capitalism and poverty. They are also suspect in their perpetuation of a false dream that the market is a cure for all of society's ills, a rising up of the executive mentality and lifestyle as the ultimate source of knowledge for solving the world's problems. With such initiatives, the burden of salvation from a poverty caused by a historically instituted system of global inequality that is out of any individual's control is placed squarely on the backs of those most oppressed by that very system. It is not enough for CEOs to simply exploit labour in a global race to the bottom, destroying all labour and environmental protections that they can; they have also cynically tried to remake those they take the most advantage of in their own image, selling them a false bill of goods about the value of executive power for lifting them out of their desperate condition.

As we have seen, the CEO approach is encroaching on more and more dimensions of life. It is worth noting, however, that it is not completely ubiquitous. New ecologically friendly ways of living are emerging into the relative mainstream. These eschew the exploitative and ostentatious values of executives in favour of ones that emphasise care for nature and for others. There is also the rise of so-called 'slow living'.[59] Here the fast pace of the modern capitalist world is forsaken in favour of taking time to take pleasure in life. Value is found in the joy that experiences can provide rather than the profit they can bring. These are of course minor examples, but they do reveal the growing dissatisfaction with having to think and act like a CEO. While these are principally reserved for those who are already economically advantaged, it shows how escaping from the CEO lifestyle is an increasingly privileged form of existence in these hyper-capitalist times.

6

The generous CEO?

In February 2017 Facebook's founder and CEO Mark Zuckerberg was in the headlines again for his charitable activities. This time the Chan Zuckerberg Initiative founded by the tech billionaire and his wife Dr Priscilla Chan handed out over $3 million in grants to aid the housing crisis in the Silicon Valley area. David Plouffe, the Initiative's President of Policy and Advocacy, stated that the grants were intended to "support those working to help families in immediate crisis while supporting research into new ideas to find a long-term solution – a two-step strategy that will guide much of our policy and advocacy work moving forward".[1] This is but one small part of Zuckerberg's charity empire, with the Initiative having committed billions of dollars to philanthropic projects designed to address social problems, with a special focus on solutions driven by science, medical research and education. This all took off in December 2015 when Zuckerberg and Chan wrote and published a letter to their new baby Max. The letter made a commitment that over the course of their lives they would donate 99% of their shares in Facebook (at the time valued at $45 billion) to the 'mission' of "advancing human potential and promoting equality".[2]

The housing intervention is of course much closer to home, dealing with issues literally at the front door of Facebook's Menlo Park head office. This is an area where the median house prices almost doubled to over $1.9 million in the five years between 2012 and 2017.[3] More generally, San Francisco is a city with massive income equality, while having earned the reputation of having the most expensive housing in the entire United States. Chan Zuckerberg's intervention was clearly designed to offset social and economic problems caused by rents and house prices having skyrocketed to such a level that even those tech workers on six-figure salaries find it hard to get by. For those on more modest incomes, supporting themselves, let alone a family, is nigh on impossible.

Ironically, the boom in the tech industry in this region, a boom Facebook has been at the forefront of, has been a major contributor to the crisis. As Peter Cohen from the Council of Community Housing Organizations explained it:

> The tech boom is a clear factor … When you're dealing with this total concentration of wealth and this absurd slosh of real estate money, you're not dealing with housing that's serving a growing population. You're dealing with housing as a real estate commodity for speculation.[4]

Zuckerberg's apparent generosity, it would seem, is a small contribution to a large problem that was created by the success of the industry he is involved in. What his giving illustrates is how even the meaning of generosity has been rewritten in the CEO society. In one sense, the housing grants (enough to buy just one and a half average Menlo valley homes) are trying to put a sticking plaster on a problem Facebook and other Bay Area technology corporations aided and abetted. It would appear that Zuckerberg was redirecting a fraction of the spoils of neoliberal tech capitalism, in the name of generosity, to try to address the problems of wealth inequality created by a social and economic system that allowed those spoils to be accrued in the first place.

It is easy to think of Mark Zuckerberg as some kind of CEO hero, a once regular kid whose genius made him one of the richest men in the world, and who decided to use that wealth for the benefit of others. The image he portrays is of an altruism untainted by self-interest. The corporate spin is that this is generosity at its most pure, meted out by the hands of the CEO with a heart of gold. A quick scratch of the surface reveals that the structure of Zuckerberg's charity enterprise is informed by much more that good-hearted altruism. Even while many have applauded Zuckerberg for his generosity, the nature of this apparent charity was openly questioned from the outset.

The wording of Zuckerberg's 2015 letter could easily have been interpreted as meaning that he was intending to donate $45 billion to charity. As investigative reporter Jesse Eisenger reported at the time, the Chan Zuckerberg Initiative through which this giving was to be funnelled is not a not-for-profit charitable foundation but a limited liability company.[5] This legal status has significant practical implications, especially when it comes to tax. As a company, the Initiative can do much more than charitable activity; its legal status gives it rights

to invest in other companies, and to make political donations. Effectively the company does not restrict Zuckerberg's
decision making as to what he wants to do with his money;
he is very much the boss. Moreover, as Eisenger described
it, Zuckerberg's bold move yielded a huge return on investment in terms of public relations for Facebook, even though
it appeared that he simply "moved money from one pocket to
the other" while being "likely never to pay any taxes on it".[6]

As described in *Forbes Magazine* by Robert Wood, Zuckerberg's generosity is "incredibly tax efficient" because
"donating appreciated stock is a much better tax move than
selling it and donating the sales proceeds ... [and] since Mr.
Zuckerberg will get credit on his tax return for the market
value of what he donates, he can use that to shelter billions
of other income".[7] The creation of the Chan Zuckerberg
Initiative, decidedly not a charity organisation, means that
Zuckerberg can control the company's investments as he
sees fit, while accruing significant commercial, tax and
political benefits. All of this is not to say that Zuckerberg's
motives do not include some expression of his own generosity or some genuine desire for humanity's wellbeing and
equality, as championed on the Chan Zuckerberg Initiative
website where he is positioned as having "a deep commitment to building strong communities".[8] What it does
suggest, however, is that when it comes to giving, the CEO
approach is one where there is no apparent incompatibility
between being generous, seeking to retain control over what
is given and the expectation of reaping benefits in return. It
is such a reformulation of generosity, one in which it is no

longer seen as incompatible with control and self-interest, that is a hallmark of the CEO society.

The rising social stock of the CEO

The modern CEO is very much at the forefront of the political and media stage. While often this sees CEOs become vaunted celebrities, it also leaves them open to becoming scapegoats for economic injustice both large and small. They are the public face of organisations, and, as such, are the first to be blamed for corporate scandals. Whoever might actually be at fault, if it happened under the chief executive's watch then they are in the public firing line. More broadly, CEOs have been castigated for their negative role in creating a modern free market that benefits the few at the expense of the many.[9] For CEOs, and the CEO society more generally, to thrive, such criticism needs to be headed off.

The enhanced public accountability of CEOs is related to a renewed corporate focus on their wider social responsibility. Firms must now balance, at least rhetorically, a dual commitment to profit and social outcomes. This has been reflected in the promotion of the 'triple bottom line' that combines social, financial and environmental priorities in corporate reporting.[10] This turn toward social responsibility represents a distinct problem for CEOs. While firms may be willing to sacrifice some short-term profit for the sake of preserving their public reputation, this same bargain is rarely on offer to CEOs, who are judged on their quarterly reports and how much they are serving the fiscal interests of their shareholders. Thus, whereas social responsibility strategies may win public kudos, in the private confines of the boardroom it is often a different story, especially when the budget is being scrutinised.

There is a further economic incentive for CEOs to avoid making fundamental changes to their operations in the name of social justice in that a large portion of CEO remuneration consists of company stock and options. Accepting fair trade policies and closing sweatshops may be good for the world but is potentially disastrous for a firm's immediate financial success. What is ethically valuable to the voting and buying public is not necessarily of concrete value to corporations or personally beneficial to their top executives. Many firms have sought to resolve this contradiction through high-profile philanthropy. Exploitative labour practices or corporate malpractices are swept under the rug as companies publicise tax efficient contributions to good causes. This is a relatively small price to pay compared to changing fundamental values and practices. Likewise, for CEOs, giving to charity is a prime opportunity for doing good without having to sacrifice (and possibly even enhancing) their overriding commitment to making profit at any social cost. They can appear privately good while not having to address their profoundly negative impact on the public good. Charitable activity permits current and former CEOs from Mark Zuckerberg to Bill Gates to be philanthropic rather than economically progressive or politically democratic.

There is an even more straightforward financial consideration at play in some cases. Charity can be an absolute boon to capital accumulation. The renowned economist William Lazonick shows that the stock-based payment structure for CEOs incentives short-term gain over long-term investment:

> Five years after the official end of the Great Recession, corporate profits are high, and the stock market is booming. Yet most Americans are not sharing in the recovery. While the top 0.1% of income recipients – which include most of the highest-ranking corporate executives – reap almost all the income gains, good jobs keep disappearing, and new employment opportunities tend to be insecure and underpaid. Corporate profitability is not translating into widespread economic prosperity. The allocation of corporate profits to stock buybacks deserves much of the blame. Consider the 449 companies in the S&P 500 index that were publicly listed from 2003 through 2012. During that period those companies used 54% of their earnings – a total of $2.4 trillion – to buy back their own stock, almost all through purchases on the open market. Dividends absorbed an additional 37% of their earnings. That left very little for investments in productive capabilities or higher incomes for employees.[11]

Consistent with this, corporate philanthropy has been shown to have a positive effect on perceptions by stock market analysts,[12] making it a particularly appealing strategy for CEOs, even in terms of their personal wealth. Charity can be used as a quick fix to a systematic neoliberal problem

– a sticking plaster for the social harm caused by marketisation, privatisation, financialisation and executisation. At the personal level, CEOs can take advantage of promoting their individual charity to distract from other less savoury activities. Moreover, as an executive a CEO can cash in on the capital gains to be made from introducing high-profile charity strategies.

Corporate social responsibility

In order fully to understand the reformulation of generosity in the CEO society we need to look back at how CEO philanthropy has changed over the years. Business leaders have a long history of charitable giving. One needs to think only of the Carnegie, Rockefeller and Ford Foundations in the United States. The question of contemporary CEO philanthropy is one very much caught up in debates and practices associated with corporate social responsibility (CSR) as it has developed since the mid-20th century. In Archie Carroll's influential model of CSR it is meeting economic responsibilities that forms the foundation on which other corporate responsibilities can be built.[13] That is to say, a corporation would not be in a position to meet any broader responsibilities if it did not first achieve solid commercial and financial stability and success. Once that is in place, Carroll maintains, a corporation must also ensure that it meets its legal responsibilities to play the game of business by the rules, as well as its ethical responsibilities to do what is 'right' and 'fair'. At the pinnacle of corporate responsibility, according to Carroll's model, is the philanthropic responsibility to give back directly to the community to improve the general quality of life of its members. Zuckerberg's involvement with causes such as housing crisis relief in San Francisco is clearly an example of such philanthropy-based CSR initiatives.

CSR, as crowned by philanthropic generosity, is widely regarded as the dominant approach to management of an organisation's ethics in terms of its relationship to the communities of which it is a part. Historically, the concern over the responsibilities of business started to be broadly discussed in the 1950s. Specifically, applying the term 'social responsibility' to business organisations is generally credited to economist Howard R. Bowen. In his book *The Social Responsibilities of the Businessman* published in 1953, Bowen asked the direct question: "what responsibilities to society may businessmen reasonably be expected to assume?"[14] Bowen's response was to suggest that these responsibilities should be much broader than just seeking financially related goals such as increased profit, capital growth and so forth. In contrast he evinced that what businesses should do is to "pursue those policies, to make those decisions, or to follow those lines of action which are desirable in terms of the objectives and values of society".[15] For Bowen, corporate responsibility was understood in relation to social costs and benefits as well as social values, rather than stemming entirely from economic matters.

Today CSR is largely accepted as a normal part of business, but much of the response to Bowen at the time was to argue that business responsibilities and social responsibilities, somewhat like oil and water, should not be mixed. The most famous advocate of this anti-CSR position was Nobel prize-winning economist Milton Friedman. Friedman is best known for his unapologetic statement that 'the social responsibility of business is to increase profits', the title of his famous essay published in *The New York Times* in 1970.[16] While the proponents of CSR were concerned with the responsibilities of the 'businessman', Friedman directed his discussion in terms of the implications for the economy when the ownership and control of corporations are separated. That is, where shareholders own the corporation but professional managers direct it. Friedman was clear in stating that a business itself cannot be said to have moral responsibilities; it is only to individuals that such responsibility can be attributed. With this individual focus, his attention was directed at the responsibilities of the executives of large publicly listed corporations. He argued that the responsibilities of these executives should be understood as follows:

> In a free-enterprise, private-property system, a corporate executive is an employee of the owners of the business. He has direct responsibility to his employers. That responsibility is to conduct the business in accordance with their desires, which generally will be to make as much money as possible while conforming to the basic rules of the society.[17]

For Friedman the manager is understood first and foremost as an employee who is paid to do a job. As such, the CEO, for example, is responsible not for deciding what goals the organisation should pursue, but for achieving the business goals set out by the business owners who employ them. If a manager were to do otherwise, for example by pursuing socially valuable goals, then according to Friedman their motives would be political rather than commercial, and hence inappropriate.

Although Friedman was defending the free market system of which corporations are prime movers, he was not suggesting that matters of social value are unimportant. He argued instead that laissez-faire capitalism was the way that those social values can be realised. Managers should be socially responsible, according to Friedman; it is just that: "there is one and only one social responsibility of business – to use its resources and engage in activities designed to increase its profits so long as it stays within the rules of the game, which is to say, engages in open and free competition without deception or fraud".[18] Friedman was not an immoral person who valorised greed; rather he saw social values and business values as two separate domains. Within such a view, corporate managers are responsible for maximising organisational returns, so long as they operate within the rules "embodied in law and ... embodied in ethical custom".[19]

The debate between Friedman and the early advocates of CSR does not contest capitalism as an economic system, but rather suggests two different views on how that system should operate. These debates are a matter of history but they are still salient today, albeit having been recast in the CEO society. Considering the administration of contemporary organisations, management scholar Timothy Devinney articulates the question of whether corporate responsibility should extend beyond:

> Enhancing the society by creating and delivering products and services consumers want, providing employment and career opportunities for employees, developing markets for suppliers, and paying taxes to governments and returns to shareholders and other claimants on the rents generated by the corporation.[20]

Devinney suggests that in today's business world there are two conceptions of CSR. The first is a narrow conception where, as with Friedman, social responsibility is met by pursing business objectives. The second, wider connection maintains that businesses should hold themselves directly responsible for meeting broader social needs.

The giving pledge

The CEO society has witnessed a change in corporate social responsibility that has moved beyond the dichotomy that Devinney reports. Zuckerberg's engagement in philanthropy is a case in point, in that it both builds on and defies Friedman's critique. As an employee, Friedman's businessperson is at arm's length from the firm such that they should not spend corporate funds on social initiatives. Zuckerberg cannot be criticised on this level, given that not only is he part-owner of Facebook, but also his investment in the Chan Zuckerberg Initiative comes from his personal wealth (in the form of

Facebook shares) rather that the company's funds. Nevertheless, the separation is far from clear. Zuckerberg's activities
can still be regarded as a form of CSR given the insoluble
connection between his identity and that of the company. In
one sense Zuckerberg's celebrity CEO status means that he
is Facebook. Legal distinctions between the corporation and
the CEO-owner are less relevant than the social integration
of the two that are central to Zuckerberg's celebrity CEO
approach to managing Facebook.

The new form of billionaire CEO philanthropy that
Zuckerberg personifies is a specific feature of the CEO
society. Zuckerberg was by no means the first contemporary CEO to promise and initiate large-scale donations of
wealth to self-nominated good causes. In the CEO society it
is positively a badge of honour for the world's most wealthy
businesspeople to create vehicles for them to give away their
wealth. This has been institutionalised in what is known as
'The Giving Pledge', a new-style philanthropy campaign
initiated by magnates Warren Buffett and Bill Gates in 2010.
This is self-described as follows:

> The Giving Pledge is an effort to help address society's
> most pressing problems by inviting the world's wealth-
> iest individuals and families to commit to giving more
> than half of their wealth to philanthropy or charitable
> causes either during their lifetime or in their will.[21]

The campaign targets billionaires around the world, encouraging them to give away the majority of their wealth. There

is nothing in the Pledge that specifies what exactly the donations will be used for, or even whether they are to be made now or willed after death; it is just a general commitment to using private wealth for ostensibly public good. It is not legally binding either, but rather is a moral commitment on the part of those signing up.

There is a long list of people and families who have made the pledge. Mark Zuckerberg and Priscilla Chan are there, and so are some 156 others, including household names such as Richard and Joan Branson, Michael Bloomberg, Barron Hilton and David Rockefeller. It would seem that many of the world's richest people simply want to give their money away to good causes. This all amounts to what human geographers Iain Hay and Samantha Muller believe is a 'golden age of philanthropy' where, since the late 1990s bequests to charity from the super-rich have escalated to the hundreds of billions of dollars.[22] These new philanthropists bring to charity an "entrepreneurial disposition",[23] yet one that has been criticised for "diverting attention and resources away from the failings of contemporary manifestations of capitalism"[24] as well as serving as a substitute for public spending withdrawn by the state.

Essentially, what we are witnessing is the transfer of responsibility for public good from democratic institutions and into the hands of the wealthy, so as to be administered by an executive class. In the CEO society, it is thus revealed, the exercise of social responsibilities is no longer debated in terms of whether corporations should or shouldn't be responsible for more than their own business interests.

Instead it is about how philanthropy can be used to reinforce the politico-economic system that enables such
obscene amounts of wealth to be accrued to such a small
number of people in the first place. Zuckerberg's investment
in solutions to the Bay Area housing crisis is a microcosmic
example of this broader trend.

The reliance on billionaire businesspeople for charity is
a part of what has been called 'philanthrocapitalism'. Philanthrocapitalism manifests in absolving the apparent antimony
between charity (traditionally focused on giving) and capitalism (based on the pursuit of economic self-interest). As
historian Mikkel Thorup explains, the claim of philanthrocapitalism is that:

> capitalist mechanisms are superior to all others (espe-
> cially the state) when it comes to not only creating
> economic but also human progress; that the market and
> market actors are or should be made the prime creators
> of the good society; that capitalism is not the cause but
> the solution to all the major problems in the world; that
> the best thing to do is to extend the market to hitherto
> personal or state processes; and, finally, that there is no
> conflict between the rich and the poor but rather that the
> rich are the poor's best and possibly only friend.[25]

It is apparent that the golden age of philanthropy is not just
about benefits that accrue to individual givers, but, more
broadly, this new philanthropy serves to legitimise capitalism, as well as to extend it further and further into all

domains of human endeavour. This also clarifies the relationship between the new philanthropy and the CEO society by demonstrating how corporate logics and practices have come to extend beyond the traditional commercial focus of the boardroom, leaving little untouched by the culture of corporate capitalism. Philanthrocapitalism is about much more than the simple act of generosity it portrays itself as, instead involving the social inculcation of neoliberal values as personified in the billionaire CEOs who have led its charge. Central to this is that philanthropy is recast in the same terms through which a CEO would consider a business venture. Charitable giving is translated into a business model that employs market-based solutions characterised by efficiency and quantified costs/benefits.[26]

As summarised by law professor Garry Jenkins, philanthrocapitalism has two primary features.[27] The first is the application of management discourses and practices from business corporations and adapting them to charitable endeavours. The focus is on entrepreneurship, market-based approaches and performance metrics. The second is that this application should be funded by super-rich businesspeople and managed under the leadership of those experienced in business. The result, at a practical level, is that philanthropy is undertaken by CEOs in a manner similar to how they would run businesses, with both bolstering capitalist forms of exchange and organisation as being both natural and desirable for all. As part of this, charitable foundations have changed in recent years, "increasingly directive, controlling, metric focused, and business oriented with respect to their interactions with grantee public charities in an attempt to demonstrate that the work of the foundation is 'strategic' and 'accountable'".[28] This is far from a benign shift to a different and better way of doing things in a CEO style, a style based on claiming to be able to "'save the world' through business thinking and market methods".[29] Instead, the risk of philanthrocapitalism is a takeover of charity by business interests, such that generosity to others is appropriated into the overarching dominance of the CEO model of society and its corporate institutions.

Responsible CEOs, irresponsible corporations

Corporate social responsibility, as discussed above, has been criticised for providing companies with a moral cover to act in quite exploitive and socially damaging ways. However, in the current era social responsibility, by being portrayed as an individual character trait of chief executives themselves, has allowed corporations to be run as irresponsibly as ever. This goes straight to the heart of what precisely the role of a CEO is and should be. While holding substantive responsibilities, they are also figureheads, the public face of complex and otherwise rather anonymous corporate ventures. To this effect, they are the stewards of a company's reputation, its most public champion and most strident defender. According to one study of CEOs:

> [they] believe it is they who own the management of reputation. All recognised that reputation is perhaps the

most important single asset the company has, and many went on to say that they are simply the stewards of that reputation for the period they are in office.[30]

CEOs' very public engagement in philanthrocapitalism can be understood as a key component of this reputation management. It is part of the marketing of the firm itself, as the good deeds of its leaders come to signify the overall goodness of the conglomerate.

Ironically, philanthrocapitalism also grants corporations the moral right, at least within the public consciousness, to be socially irresponsible. The trumpeting of the CEOs' personal generosity can grant an implicit right for their corporations to act ruthlessly and with little consideration for the broader social effects of their firms' activities. This reflects a productive tension at the heart of modern CSR: the more moral a CEO, the more immoral their company can in theory seek to be. As the figurehead, it is the chief executive's actions that matter, masking the damage being done by the corporations that they officially head up. The Gates Foundation is a prime example of this rather paradoxical contemporary relationship between the ethics of the CEO and the corporations they run. This is a foundation that is publicly lauded for its generosity. With an endowment of over US$40 billion, $28 billion of which were donated by Bill Gates himself, it is the epitome of 'venture philanthropy'.[31] The Foundation's website sets out its mission:

We seek to unlock the possibility inside every individual. We see equal value in all lives. And so we are dedicated to improving the quality of life for individuals around the world. From the education of students in Chicago, to the health of a young mother in Nigeria, we are catalysts of human promise everywhere.[32]

Yet this charity distracts from Microsoft's very questionable record as a responsible corporation. This is, of course, a corporation that in 2001 was sued by the US government for being a monopoly, a case which it lost, then settled after an appeal. The details of whether or not Microsoft was monopolistic miss the more important point that such threats can be downplayed by the perceived moral actions of its founder and chief Bill Gates. This represents the split personality of corporate responsibility in the present age: it is totally fine for corporations to maximise their success at the expense of society so long as their leading executive gives back.

This tension is even starker when seen in light of the human rights abuses that Microsoft has been linked to in its manufacturing practices. In 2016, the company was accused by Amnesty International of the worst forms of child labour abuse in the mining of cobalt essential for the making of its 'smart' products. Quoting Mark Durmett, a human rights researcher at Amnesty:

> The glamorous shop displays and marketing of state-of-the-art technologies are a stark contrast to the children carrying bags of rocks, and miners in narrow man-made tunnels risking permanent lung damage ... It is high time the big brands took some responsibility for the mining

of the raw materials that make their lucrative products. The dangers to health and safety make mining one of the worst forms of child labor. Companies whose global profits total $125 billion cannot credibly claim that they are unable to check where key minerals in their productions come from.[33]

It is more than a little ironic that the Gates Foundation is committed to ending the very global poverty that Microsoft is alleged to be in no small part responsible for perpetuating.

At the very heart of this irony is how such CEO responsibility patently ignores the deeper structural and political problems of global capitalism. Similar to the CSR that gave it birth, this CEO responsibility papers over the difficult tensions between the stated charitable mission and the forms of exploitation that are essential to their company's continued expansion and profitability. A prime example of these contradictory priorities is the stance taken by Microsoft in regard to censorship. The company has been accused of aiding authoritarian regimes in China and Thailand to use their technology to 'trap' dissidents and repress dissent.[34] Perhaps if Bill Gates truly wants to save the world he should start by taking a long, hard look at the company he founded.

The CEO autocrat

The hypocrisy revealed by CEOs claiming to be dedicated to social responsibility and charity also exposes a deeper authoritarian morality that prevails in the CEO society.

Philanthrocapitalism is commonly presented as the social justice component of an otherwise amoral global free market. As we have been discussing, critics, of course, take a much dimmer view of this generosity, highlighting its use to advance an overall corporate agenda. At best, corporate charity is a type of voluntary tax paid by the 1% for their role in creating such an economically deprived and unequal world. Yet this 'giving' culture also helps support and spread a distinctly authoritarian form of economic development that mirrors the autocratic leadership style of the executives who predominantly fund it.

Significantly, CEO charity has the aim of transforming the values and practices of development to better match those of a business venture. Returning to the Gates Foundation, beneath its laudatory goals is a fine print that reveals its overwhelming market bias. It proclaims, in this regard, that "Every year, millions of people find ways to transition out of poverty – by adopting new farming technologies, investing in new business opportunities, or finding new jobs".[35] This reflects the capitalist ethos shaping the development agenda more generally, one on full display in the policies of microfinancing discussed at the end of the previous chapter. Implicit in these charitable ventures is the idea once again that CEOs can empower the poor through their timeless business wisdom.

The marketisation of global charity and empowerment has dangerous implications that transcend economics. It also has a troubling emerging political legacy, one in which democracy is sacrificed on that altar of executive style empowerment. Politically, the free market is posited as a fundamental requirement for liberal democracy. However, recent analysis reveals instead the deeper connection between processes of marketisation and authoritarianism. In particular, a strong government is required to implement these often unpopular market changes.[36] The image of the powerful autocrat is, to this effect, transformed into a potentially positive figure as a forward-thinking political leader who can guide their country on the correct market path in the face of 'irrational' opposition.

Charity becomes a conduit for CEOs to fund these 'good' authoritarians. Needed are elite networks for brokering direct and indirect relationships between corporate leaders and their market-minded authoritarian political counter-parts. The Clinton Foundation is perhaps the most obvious and notorious example of this linking of economic and polit-ical autocrats in a common project of global 'empowerment' and 'development'. It has made a veritable not for (official) profit industry of providing corporations with access to these sympathetic market despots. Criticisms of the foundation have, understandably, largely focused on the more straight-forward revelations about repressive governments buying influence. WikiLeaks uncovered emails from the founda-tion showing that it had accepted donations from Qatar, for instance, at a time when its government was being severely criticised for its horrendous labour conditions and the suspect way it won the right to the 2020 World Cup. According to Craig Minassian, a foundation spokesman:

Since 2002, Qatar has been among our hundreds of thousands of donors who have supported the Clinton

Foundation's overall humanitarian work including making life-saving HIV/AIDS treatment available to millions of people in more than 70 countries, combating childhood obesity here in the United States and working to empower girls and women around the world.[37]

However, the foundation also provided the opportunity for a high-ranking government official from Qatar to appear "onstage with Bill Clinton to discuss efforts to help improve agriculture and feed the hungry with technology designed to cool soccer stadiums",[38] thus granting the Qatar administration much-needed international legitimacy and goodwill.

This is far from the only way that authoritarianism and charity can mutually reinforce each other. Just as significant is the encouragement of projects and donations to countries that are supportive of free market empowerment projects. This involves specifically the promotion of notorious human rights abusers as paragons of good governance. Central to these efforts is such people being recast as comparable in worth to political CEOs, doing whatever is necessary to drive forward their country's economic growth and development. The Clinton Foundation again exemplified this troubling trend. It has helped to fund and promote a range of development projects in Rwanda with the ostensible aim of strengthening public health initiatives for the country's poorest citizens. Yet these projects largely revolve around a market logic whereby charitable investment is meant to help cultivate a more empowered capitalist population. Undoubtedly, following its destructive genocide in the 1990s, the past decades have seen substantial economic gains in Rwanda, although according to World Bank figures 45% of its population still in live in poverty. For the majority of those this is extreme poverty and the Rwandan economy is still overly dependent on foreign aid. Just as telling, according to the World Economic Forum, "in the long term, the government aims to transform Rwanda from a low-income agriculture-based economy to a knowledge-based, service-oriented economy with a middle-income status by 2020".[39]

Politically Rwanda is led by the autocratic President Paul Kagame, a close personal associate of former President Bill Clinton whom the *New York Times* has described as the "Global elite's favourite strongman".[40] In the face of mounting criticism of this relationship, Clinton has privately praised Kagame as someone who can "GSD" (get stuff done).[41] One supporter, Gerald Mpyisi, the managing director of the Institute of Management and Leadership, defended Kagame's methods in explicitly corporate terms:

> The president is running the country like a CEO of a company who ensures that every director is accountable for their department. That is why, despite the lack of resources, you still find things happening. I believe for a country in the third world to develop there has to be a certain element of organising the population. The west tries to use its standards in the developing world and it isn't fair.[42]

Such an approach sees values associated with democracy and human rights easily jettisoned in the name of the types of governance associated with a strong executive-type ruler. The logic of the CEO society is that these market-friendly autocrats deserve generosity, for they are fundamentally dedicated to goals of helping the deprived populations that they rule with an iron fist. The benefits of such a charitable relationship flow two ways between the authoritarian executive and the CEO autocrat. The former is able to 'responsibly' support a corporate-friendly politician while the latter is able to present their reign as legitimate while ruthlessly maintaining power. It is, furthermore, not surprising that these economic and political leaders make such compatible bedfellows; they both rely on an authoritarian vision of market leadership that emphasises efficiency, productivity and instrumentality over deliberation or shared decision making.

Political CSR

The development of philanthrocapitalism in recent years also marks the increasing encroachment of business into the provision of public goods. This encroachment is not limited to the activities of individual billionaires, however, and is also becoming a part of the activities of large corporations under the rubric of corporate social responsibility. This is especially the case for large multinational corporations whose global activities combined with their wealth and power give them significant political power. This relationship between CSR and politics has been referred to as 'political CSR'. This notion of political CSR, as originally developed by business ethics professors Andreas Scherer and Guido Palazzo, recognises that for large corporations "CSR is increasingly displayed in corporate involvement in the political process of solving societal problems, often on a global scale".[43] Such CSR initiatives see organisations cooperating and collaborating with governments and civic bodies as well as international institutions, so that the historically different purposes of the state and the corporations are increasingly eroded.

CSR has thus served to 'politicise' large organisations in that:

> some of the observable CSR activities, such as developing corporate codes of behaviour in collaboration with critical NGOs, exposing corporate CSR performance to third party control, linking corporate decision making to civil society discourses, and shifting corporate attention and money to societal challenges beyond immediate stakeholder pressure, point to politicization of the corporation.[44]

Ethics researcher Glen Whelan identifies two reasons for the growing engagement of corporations in global and national political processes.[45] The first is that many of the global and national environments in which corporations are located do not have the socio-political structures common to the liberal democracies of so-called advanced economies. The second is that large global corporations are already involved in quasi-government activities through the setting of standards and codes and the provision of public goods. The implication of this is that with CSR many large organisations become involved in activities that were traditionally the domain of government, meaning that, as Scherer and Palazzo argue, the division between the activities of businesses and those of states is not as clear as it perhaps once was, especially under conditions of globalisation.[46] As they identify, under the banner of CSR organisations have engaged in activities such as public health provision, education, the protection of human rights, addressing social problems such as AIDS and malnutrition, protection of the natural environment, promotion of peace and social stability.

In understanding the development of political CSR as a business practice, it is important to remember its political and historical context. Concurrent with the growth of CSR has been a politico-economic shift towards a neoliberal global economic agenda characterised by an expansion in corporate power enacted by heroically valorised CEOs. This expansion has been achieved through, inter alia, the privatisation of former government-owned industries, trade liberalisation on a global scale and market deregulation. The more recent emphasis on political CSR alerts us to the fact that large organisations today can have significant economic and political power on a global scale. Moreover, this means that the actions of such organisations, and the way that they regulate those actions, have far-reaching social consequences. The balanced tipped in 2000 when the Institute for Policy Studies in the United States reported that in comparing corporate revenues with gross domestic product (GDP), fifty-one of the largest economies in the world were corporations, and forty-nine were national economies. The biggest corporations were General Motors, Walmart, ExxonMobil and Ford, each of which was larger economically than Poland, Norway and Saudi Arabia.[47] As the heads of these corporations, CEOs are now quasi-politicians. One only has to think of the increasing power of the World Economic Forum, whose annual meeting in Davos in Switzerland sees corporate CEOs and senior politicians getting together with the ostensible goal of 'improving the world', a now time-honoured ritual that symbolises the global power and agency of CEOs.[48]

While CEOs might deploy a discourse of social responsibility to portray themselves, their corporations and the politico-economic system they represent as being focused on the noble pursuits of world improvement, the facts of its uptake yield a different conclusion. The UN's Peter Utting suggests, the development of CSR has not been the result of self-directed corporate initiatives for doing good deeds, but has been ushered in as a response to widespread CSR activism from non-governmental organisations (NGOs), pressure groups and trade unions.[49] Often this has been in response to the failure of governments to regulate large corporations. High-profile industrial accidents and scandals have also put pressure of organisations for heightened self-regulation. Management Professor James Post explains:

> it was the 1984 explosion at a Union Carbide chemical plant in Bhopal, India, that killed an estimated 25,000 people and became a major landmark in the global CSR story ... in the aftermath of Bhopal, the global chemical industry recognised that it was nearly impossible to

secure a license to operate without public confidence in industry safety standards. The Chemical Manufacturer's Association (CMA) adopted a code of conduct, including new standards of product stewardship, disclosure, and community engagement. Over time, the CMA's efforts raised the bar of corporate industrial performance around the world.[50]

As can perhaps be expected, the impetus was corporate self-interest rather than generosity, especially as industries and corporations globally "began to recognise the increasing importance of reputation and image".[51] There have been many industrial accidents bolstering this, whether it be the *Exxon Valdez* oil tanker spilling hundreds of thousands of barrels of oil in Alaska in 1989, or BP's Deepwater Horizon oil rig exploding in the Gulf of Mexico in 2010.

Another important case was the involvement of clothing companies Gap and Nike in a child labour scandal in 2001. This scandal took flight after the broadcast of a documentary by the BBC's *Panorama* television programme in October 2000 in the UK. The programme was entitled 'Gap and Nike: No Sweat?'[52] What it revealed was that despite both of these companies having made claims that they did not use sweatshop labour to produce their goods, this was in fact far from the case. Factories in Cambodia making Gap and Nike clothing were shown to operate under terrible working conditions involving children as young as twelve years old working seven days a week, being forced to do overtime, and enduring physical and emotional abuse from management. The public outcry that ensued demanded that organisations such as Gap and Nike take more responsibility for the negative human social impacts of their business practices.

While clothing and oil companies have been especially controversial, these scandals have had significant implications for CSR as it relates to many different industries and types of organisations. CSR was founded as a vehicle for harnessing the ill effects of the pursuit of corporate self-interest, although in the present era this has reversed such that CSR has developed into a means for further enhancing that self-interest while ostensibly claiming to be addressing the interests of others. When facing the threat of corporate scandal, CSR is seen as the vehicle through which corporate reputation can be boosted and the threat of government regulation mitigated. Again, here we see how corporations engage in seemingly responsible practices in order to increase their own political power, and to diminish the power of nation states over their own operations. CEOs are thus prompted to adopt CSR in order to avoid having their poor business practices made public, while also maintaining an aura of righteousness for the globalised market economy in which they operate.

The idea that organisations adopt CSR for the purposes of developing or defending a corporate reputation has in particular brought the ethics of CSR under critique. At the heart of this is the contention that rather than using CSR as a means of 'being good', corporations adopt it merely as a means of 'looking good', while not in any way questioning their basic ethical or political stance. Even Enron, before its legendary fraud scandal and eventual demise in 2001, was well known for its advocacy of social responsibility. As corporate governance expert John Roberts notes, "responsibility and the desire to be seen as ethical are very different",[53] with the latter often being the justification for CSR. The point Roberts makes is that while increasing social and economic pressures on organisations can yield a response where they seek to position themselves superficially as being interested in the good of others, the result may well be what he calls the "occluding of ethical sensibility" and moral responsibility.[54] Moreover, the irresponsibility of this occlusion is located in self-interest, such that "if ethical conduct is to be judged by its consequences, then the prime beneficiary of [corporate social responsibility] is the corporation itself".[55] Here corporate endorsement of a discourse of responsibility is "no more than the empty expression of pious wishes, which in practice amount to a flight from responsibility".[56]

The CEO as the model of generosity

CEOs position themselves as acting in the interests of society, with their ostensible do-gooding intended as a model for billionaires to come. There is no suggestion here that vast wealth inequality will abate through philanthropy. Commenting on the value and important of the Pledge, founder Warren Buffett singled out how proud he was of the younger signatories, stating:

> I tell them, every one of them is worth 10 of me because you're going to have young people, particularly in this

day and age, get wealthy very early and they're going to look to the people who are their heroes, whether it's Mark Zuckerberg or Brian Chesky.[57]

CEO generosity is epic in proportions, or at least that is how it is portrayed. Indeed, on an individual level it is hard to find fault with those rich people who have simply given away vast swathes of their wealth for charitable causes, or those corporations that champion socially responsible programmes. Beyond this individual level, however, things look somewhat different. What CSR, and philanthrocapitalism in particular, achieve more broadly is the social justification of extreme wealth inequality rather than being an antidote to it. We need to note here that, despite the apparent proliferation of giving promised by philanthrocapitalism, the so-called golden age of philanthropy is also an age of expanding inequality.

This is clearly spelled out in Oxfam's 2017 report, *An Economy for the 99%*.[58] The report highlights the injustice and unsustainability of a world suffering from widening levels of inequality. The simple fact is that since the early 1990s the top 1% of the world's wealthy people earned more than the entire bottom 50%. Why so? Oxfam's report places the blame firmly with corporations and the global market economies in which they operate. The statistics are alarming, with the world's ten biggest corporations having revenues that exceed the total combined revenues of the 180 least wealthy nations. Corporate social responsibility is not making any real difference. The report states:

when corporations increasingly work for the rich, the benefits of economic growth are denied to those who need them most. In pursuit of delivering high returns to those at the top, corporations are driven to squeeze their workers and producers ever harder – and to avoid paying taxes which would benefit everyone, and the poorest people in particular.[59]

Neither the philanthropy of the super-rich nor socially directed corporate programmes have any real effect on combating this trend, in just the same way that Zuckerberg's hand-out of $3 million will have a negligible effect of the San Francisco housing crisis. Instead, vast fortunes in the hands of the few, whether earned through inheritance, commerce or crime, continue to grow at the expense of the poor. In the end it is capitalism that is at the heart of philanthrocapitalism and the corporation that is at the heart of CSR, with even well-meaning endeavours serving to justify a system that is rigged in favour of the rich. As sociologist Linsey McGoey explains, this is achieved through a conflation of the objectives of businesses with those of charity.[60] What is particular about this is not that rich people are supporting charitable endeavours, but rather how the new approach involves "an openness that deliberately collapses the distinction between public and private interests in order to justify increasingly concentrated levels of private gain".[61] It is thus without apparent contention or irony that one might ask the question, "does corporate philanthropy increase firm value?", as if to suggest that it would be controversial if the answer was no.[62] For acolytes of the business benefits of corporate philanthropy, like strategy professor Paul Godfrey, the logic behind this is laid out with brute honesty:

1. corporate philanthropy can generate positive moral capital among communities and stakeholders;
2. moral capital can provide shareholders with insurance-like protection for a firm's relationship-based intangible assets; and
3. this protection contributes to shareholder wealth.[63]

Moral capital! In the CEO society corporate logic such as this rules supreme and ensures that any activities thought of as generous and socially responsible ultimately have a payoff in terms of self-interest. If there was ever a debate between the ethics of genuine hospitality, reciprocity and self-interest it is not to be found here.[64] It is with the CEO logic that the mechanisms for redressing the inequality created through wealth generation are placed in the hands of the wealthy, and in a way that ultimately benefits them. The worst excesses of neoliberal capitalism are morally justified by the actions of those very people who represent and continue to benefit from those excesses. Wealth redistribution is placed in the hands of the wealthy, and social responsibility in the hands of those who have exploited society for personal gain.

Meanwhile, inequality extends, and both corporations and the wealthy find ways to avoid the taxes that the rest of us pay. In the name of generosity, we find a new form of corporate rule, refashioning another dimension of human endeavour in its own interests. Such is a society where CEOs are no longer content to do business; they must control public goods as well. In the end, while the Giving Pledge's website might feature more and more smiling faces of smug-looking CEOs, the real story is of a world characterised by gross inequality that is getting worse year by year.

7

The bad faith of CEO salvation

The CEO society has continued to develop, brazenly undeterred by the economic and political crises that have afflicted our times. Even as the promise of the free market continues to prove itself hollow for the majority of the world's citizens, the idolisation of chief executives continues. This idolisation relies on spreading hope fuelled by dazzling dreams of economic, political and personal fulfilment, buttressed by the idea that if you fail it is your fault for not being good enough. Only by being decisive, efficient, innovative and, when necessary, ruthless can success in all areas of 21st century existence be achieved. At least that's how the story goes.

These characteristics of the CEO society do not rely on any subtle or ideologically driven forms of interpretation; they are admitted openly by their pundits and beneficiaries. Take for example comments made by Eric Trump, defending his father's long-standing refusal to release his tax returns for public scrutiny. Before coming to those comments, we need to recall here that during Trump senior's campaign in 2016 this issue of the tax returns was a recurring topic of discussion.

It is also notable that there is a long history in US politics of presidents making their tax affairs public, with the last president not to do so being Richard Nixon. In the forty years since then, public disclosure has been accepted practice; a means for politicians to be financially transparent as well as to more generally demonstrate their honesty. While campaigning Trump continually indicated that he intended to release his returns, while delaying actually doing so by claiming that his taxes were under audit. As early as May 2016 he claimed the audit would mean that the tax returns would not be public until after the election. By September of that year he was backtracking further, saying he would only release them if his Democratic rival Hillary Clinton released hers. In January 2017, already in office, when asked if he thought people wanted to see his tax returns he said: "I won, I mean, I became president, no, I don't think they care at all".[1]

Fast-forward a few months to April 2017 and still no disclosure, despite unrelenting public pressure. In response, President Trump turned to Twitter, proclaiming: "I did what was almost an impossible thing to do for a Republican – easily won the Electoral College! Now Tax Returns are brought up again?" His logic was simple: because he saw himself as the ultimate 'winner', there was no reason for the public to hold him to account for anything other than his greatness. That same month Eric Trump fleshed this view out when he was interviewed on an Orlando, Florida radio station. Like Donald, Eric announced that his father's tax returns were "irrelevant". Why so? According to Eric:

It's funny how taxes work. They sort of punish the hardest working and most productive members of our society while taking nothing from those who would rather be lazy and beg on the streets. That's kind of not fair. What we have here is a system that flat out punishes those who want to contribute and make their lives better and at the same time, rewards those who want to be nothing more than dead weight. The worst part is, I'm not saying something that's revolutionary here; this system has been in place ever since the country was established. My father, regardless of the fact that he's president, is just one person out of millions of those who are capable enough to be successful but are simultaneously struck down by our tax system. That's a catastrophe.[2]

On one level what we had here was a Park Avenue silver-spooner lecturing radio listeners about the value of hard work, and how wealth is a just reward for personal effort. Notwithstanding the irony, young Trump also laid bare a specific logic of what justice means in the CEO society. That is, the rich are rich because they deserve to be, and the poor and destitute are in that position because they are lazy losers. By this account, taxing the rich is akin to a form of punishment that mistreats the best people in society: those who have managed to garner the world's riches for themselves. As if this was not enough, Eric followed up with the statement that his father had plans to issue an executive order that would cancel taxes for "extra productive people in the U.S. economy". Would this serve Trump senior's self-interest? Of course not, said Eric, it would be meant as a public gesture of goodwill to the deserving:

> a sort of 'thank you' from him to the entrepreneurs, businessmen and other hard-working Americans who have done their duties thus far. As for the rest, I guess they'll just have to find some other way to get free meals once the economy starts favoring those who are willing to actually get off their butts and go to work. No more freeloaders, that's where we're going with this. Bottom line, if you've got two working legs and a minimally func-tioning brain, you can sustain yourself. And you're going to have to pretty soon.[3]

Eric was parroting the idea, central to the CEO society, that the vast inequality that characterises our time is justified as being both natural and moral; a simple consequence of hard work and initiative. Moreover, 'winners' like Trump, who enjoy untold levels of fortune and power, have been elevated over the rest of us and so should not be subject to the same rules.[4] Of course, if the vast majority of people who do not enjoy such wealth buy this message, they are rendered both malleable and passive. In the CEO society the poor are poor not because they have been robbed of opportunities, or because they have been exploited or discriminated against, it is because they are not good enough to be rich!

We need to bear in mind here that the Trump campaign ran in the same year that saw the leak of what were known as the 'Panama papers'. This leak involved millions of financial documents from the Panamanian law firm Mossack Fonseca being made public; documents that showed without doubt how corporations and high net worth individuals, including businesspeople and politicians, were employing complex and secretive financial arrangement to ensure that they paid as little tax as possible. Contra Eric Trump's rich kid moralising, this was hardly about getting rich through hard work, and more about staying rich through cunning and legally dubious financial dealings. Remember too that 2016 was also a year where corporate tax avoidance was a central feature of public debate internationally. It was in this year, for example, that the European Union fined Apple €13.5 billion for tax evasion in Ireland, a ruling which also showed how the Irish government gave Apple illegal tax benefits in exchange for jobs and investment.[5]

The debates, and justifications, for tax avoidance are a litmus test of the veracity of the CEO society and its dubious morality. Reflected here is one of the ultimate paradoxes of the modern political economy. Neoliberalism has been popularly assailed for the damage it has perpetuated, whether it be broadening inequality, heightened economic deprivation or persistent underdevelopment. This is a condition that presents a progressively dystopian future where everything and everyone is just a commodity to be financially exploited. This dystopia, however, comes with its own inbuilt remedy, embodied in the salvationary figure of the CEO. The worse the ideological peril that present-day hyper-capitalism finds itself in, the stronger the appeal of its most dominant figure. The CEO thrives as the market struggles. This is effectively what Eric Trump's statement repeats: that his father's opaque tax dealings are not a sign of him having something to hide, but rather they symbolise that he is in fact the biggest winner of them all and that because of this he should not be punished by talk about his taxes. The moral of their story is that 'winner-takes-all' is the way things should be. The consequences of this social idolisation of capitalism's highest officer are wide-ranging and profound. This is a call to a form of perverse hero worship that entrenches the market (and the exploita-tion that it relies upon) as a founding ideology and basis for identity, even as it is being revealed as a fundamentally flawed and inequitable socio-economic system. Moreover, it limits the political and economic imagination to the narrow and out-dated solutions of the free market, unencumbered by pesky social sanction or legal regulation. In perhaps one of modern history's ultimate contradictions, the 'fact' we are presented with is that capitalism can only (and should only) be saved by capitalists. The cost of this misguided and stubborn faith in this executive religion is short-term suffering and our long-term destruction.

The threat of executive freedom

At the heart of the free market is the promise to individuals of the right to pursue their desires and happiness. Its appeal is in proclaiming that the 'sky is the limit', regardless of our background; that through hard work and talent we can all achieve our dreams. That its reality fails to live up to this vaunted ideal does little to detract from its capacity to grip the popular imagination. This is a cultural fantasy of market freedom that represents so much more than the ability to freely sell your labour, start a business, or market a product. It is the belief that all things are personally possible. The figure of the CEO, star athlete, or celebrity actor all play into this tantalising myth.[6]

This promise of freedom is underpinned by a deep irony, in that it is precisely the economically unequal conditions of the marketplace that people are seeking to free themselves from. This desire to be free both from and through the market is exacerbated by neoliberalism. As economic anxiety and disparity grow, so too does the fantasy that it is within one's power to achieve the financial security so desperately desired. It is thus not surprising that self-help discourses are so popular in this era.[7]

The idolisation of CEOs reflects this paradoxical fantasy. CEOs personify the longing to control the market rather than being a wage slave to its whim. Executives epitomise the possibility of personal agency in an age when it seems to be in increasingly short supply. According to social policy scholar Erzsébet Bukodi, "there is a clear change in the direction of mobility. Over the past four decades, the experience of upward mobility has become less common, and going down the social ladder has become more common".[8] In this context, aspiring to CEO freedom might not only be delusional but also dangerous. Sociologists Frank Dobbin and Jiwook Jung, in analysing the economically destructive role played by this hyper-capitalist form of agency in the latter half of the 20th century, found that executives focused almost exclusively on profit making brought the world to the brink of total financial collapse.[9] Perhaps even more dangerous is that this executive agency continues to persist long after the devastating effects of this crisis. It limits freedom to the narrow confines of being a market 'winner'. Everything is reduced to perception management, creating the appearance that one is in control while trampling over broader concerns of economic justice and environmental sustainability.

A complete CEO takeover?

On the path to economic growth and financial gain there can be no inefficient stragglers; that is the morality of the CEO society. 'Losers' must be left to lose as the minority class of winners claim the spoils for themselves. It is the imaginary CEO who can ruthlessly make those 'hard decisions' about what and who must be preserved and what and who must be liquated. As Bruce Springsteen critically presaged in his 1983 song *Atlantic City*, "down here it's just winners and losers, and don't get caught on the wrong side of that line". But in the casino capitalism of the CEO society, more and more people get pushed over that very line in a world characterised by dramatically increasing inequality.

Despite this inequality, the CEO mentality has vaulted out of the boardroom in an attempt to take over the wider world. Of course the expansion of globalisation has, above all, been an expansion of corporate wealth and power internationally.[10] As part of this, finance has become the not so secret power behind the modern throne of politics, setting the terms and conditions for what governments can 'responsibly' do.[11] At the heart of this global rule is an executive ethos whose market rationality and obsession with wealth is prioritised at the expense of all other social and environmental consider-ations. The CEO takeover attempt runs so much deeper than just global economic pre-eminence. It is a hostile takeover, frighteningly successful, of society by the corporation and the values it embodies; a takeover that threatens to shake and reshape the very foundations of our modern psyche. It works to colonise more than just organisations and institutions; it has formed the very basis for defining who we are and who we want to be. Regardless of what we desire, it is reinforced that our dreams are only achievable through a business-like cost–benefit analysis that allows one person to pitilessly maximise gains and minimise losses at the expense of others.[12] We must be the leaders of our own existence.inc!

As much as it enables new ways of being, the CEO society sets the limits to our contemporary imagination. No matter how many executives show themselves to be morally reprehensible or socially irresponsible, and no matter how questionable their function is to our economic system gener-ally, the values they symbolise continue to be pushed. There is nothing beyond the ideological horizon of their capitalist vision and lifestyle. It is their peculiar form of 'wisdom' that wants to guide the present and determine future possibilities. It is the CEO spirit that animates so much of human devel-opment. Progress, hence, is reduced to a series of financial opportunities. The figure of the CEO represents a particu-larly profound problem for modern-day capitalism. On the one hand, it symbolises all that is wrong with the current system, with CEOs the personification of a status quo rife with immorality and greed. On the other hand, CEOs are raised up as the ultimate problem solvers, economic visionaries who can successfully cure all of society's ills. Along these lines, organisational theorist Edward Wray-Bliss evinces that "evilness and goodness have become personified in the figure of the chief executive officer in contemporary, particularly US, business culture".[13] In Wray-Bliss's sense, it is still the capitalist who has been given the task of solving the problems created by capitalism.

At the heart of this historical condition is the reversal of the free market itself from being an economic solution to being a pressing social problem. The initial appeal of neoliberalism, especially in the 1970s and 1980s, was that it could break through and transform the economic stagnation and cultural malaise of the later post-war era. It offered the vision of a dynamic post-bureaucratic world which promised to "emancipate individuals from the formalistic constraints of bureaucracy, arranging them instead in organic and fluid networks".[14] As the Berlin Wall fell and the spectre of socialism appeared to fall with it, the 1980s offered the possibility of a brave new world of market-driven optimism. As Margaret Thatcher was so fond of saying, there was no alternative. In the US context, speaking of Ronald Reagan's supposed "legacy of optimism and common sense" a decade after his death, former Republican congressman and current media commentator Joe Scarborough wrote in *Time* magazine that:

Those men who gathered in Philadelphia set a course for America that has always pointed toward the future. Along the way, our ship of state was violently tossed by slavery, a historically bloody civil war, a staggering depression and two world wars. But America was sustained by its people's inner strength and determined optimism. Men like Reagan continued to believe that the United States was headed toward a brighter future – until they hit the turbulence of the '60s and '70s, when the national identity felt tremors of doubt.[15]

But the doubt had to be abated, and the appeal of renewed hopefulness that Reagan was able to create went much deeper than mere rationality; it was a dream of collective progress and individual prosperity that played into the hopes and fears of an entire society. Suddenly it was in the free market that we trusted.

The popularity and celebrity of executives has simply been a symptom of this wider mass embrace of the free market faith. CEOs were touted as the fearless leaders who could single-handedly turn industries around and deliver profit and jobs. In this respect, today's CEOs play a similar function to government in the decades following the Second World War. The expansive liberal democratic state in both the US and Western Europe was going to produce a more equitable and tolerant society. Likewise in the latter half of the century, corporations and the financial titans in charge of them promised to produce a dynamic and meritocratic modern economy where wealth would be available to all.

The 2008 financial crisis, as a puncturing of the neoliberal promissory balloon, was as much a threat to the future as it was to the immediate present. It was not just houses that were being lost, but the prospect of a brighter tomorrow. In the United States, then President Obama exemplified these fears and hopes when he declared to the nation and world in 2009:

> The answers to our problems don't lie beyond our reach. They exist in our laboratories and our universities; in our fields and our factories; in the imaginations of our entrepreneurs. What is required now is for this country to pull together, confront boldly the challenges we face, and take responsibility for our future once more.[16]

However, instead of infinite economic growth there was now seemingly inescapable material and environmental ruin on the horizon. As anthropologist James Ferguson observed at the time, neoliberalism had ceased to be a harbinger of socio-economic prosperity, and had "become the name for a set of highly interested public policies that have vastly enriched the holders of capital". Prosperity? No. What we had was "increasing inequality, insecurity, loss of public services, and a general deterioration of quality of life for the poor and working classes".[17] What was once triumphantly proclaimed as the 'end of history'[18] was now a nightmare reality of political oligarchy and economic despair to which there really did not appear to be any alternative.

Emerging out of this deep-seated insecurity was a new crisis narrative of recovery revolving around the CEO. As discussed previously, crisis evokes a paradoxical nostalgia for a romanticised past period of stability. Trump's campaign slogan, 'make America great again', was grist to a well-worn mill. This appeals to desires for a collective return to an idealised, if not entirely imagined, time when it appeared that security and endless progress seemed assured.[19] The potential opportunities for a more revolutionary response in this case were limited due to neoliberalism's continued domination of the political and economic imagination. While the free market certainly enriched a select few economic and political elites, it left the rest of the world poor in ideological options. With few places else to go, there was a mass reinvestment in the power and promise of the CEO. These corporate leaders did much more than escape prosecution for the financial crisis. They were rehabilitated as the only people able to heal a sick market system. In the wake of an almost total global economic meltdown, the figure of the CEO was resurrected to save a dying capitalist order.

Brand CEO

If there is anything we have learned from neoliberal capitalism, it is that successful branding is crucial to the success of companies and their top leaders.[20] Reputation often trumps reality in the cutthroat financial world of buying and selling. It's not what you are but what people think you are worth that matters. Following the 2008 financial crisis, CEOs were in need of some serious popular rebranding themselves. The image they had garnered as ruthless profiteers and cold-hearted boardroom operators was no longer polit-ically credible or culturally acceptable. Required was a fresh vision of these business titans as more socially conscious and morally responsible.

The rebranding has worked! As a headline in the UK newspaper *The Guardian* recently lamented: "Seven years ago, Wall Street was the villain. Now it gets to call the shots".[21] This executive reboot was far from straightforward, however. Most notably, it was hard to ignore the misdeeds of past and present CEOs. Even in the popular imagination movies such as 2015's *The Big Short* demonstrated (once again!) how corporate greed had gone on manipulative overdrive in the lead-up to the financial crisis.[22] Every week seemed to bring to light a damning new case of corporate tax evasion or exec-utive malfeasance. There were also widespread demands for CEOs to be held accountable for the near-global economic meltdown that they were largely responsible for causing. The United States was a conspicuous case. It is worth quoting Pulitzer Prize-winning financial reporter Jesse Eisinger in the *New York Times* at length, in this respect:

> American financial history has generally unfolded as a series of booms followed by busts followed by crack-downs. After the crash of 1929, the Pecora Hearings seized upon public outrage, and the head of the New York Stock Exchange landed in prison. After the savings-and-loan scandals of the 1980s, 1,100 people were prosecuted, including top executives at many of the largest failed banks. In the '90s and early noughts, when the bursting

of the Nasdaq bubble revealed widespread corporate accounting scandals, top executives from WorldCom, Enron, Qwest and Tyco, among others, went to prison. The credit crisis of 2008 dwarfed those busts, and it was only to be expected that a similar round of crackdowns would ensue.[23]

This was hardly easy material upon which to suddenly affix a halo of corporate righteousness, and the same principle applied globally to developed and developing economies alike. Questions about whether corporations could really serve both their shareholders and the public interest were asked at a level of seriousness never before encountered in recent times.

There was also a more fundamental, but less immediately visible, contradiction at the core of this rebranding attempt. Notably, how could market solutions effectively address market-created problems? If capitalism was the 'sick patient', were capitalists really its best chance for a cure? One would think that 'no' was a sensible answer, but returning once again to the words of Barack Obama in 2009, in the immediate aftermath of the crisis: "I think we applied the right medicine; I think the patient is stabilised; there's still wounds that have to heal and there's still emergencies that could arise, but I think that you've got some pretty good care being applied".[24] Not everyone agreed, and the free market policies under the name of 'austerity' that were widely implemented across the United States and Europe seemed if anything to be holding back recovery rather speeding it up.[25] CEOs and their fellow elites, for their part, appeared more than happy to reap the rewards of these policies while the rest of society continued to suffer. As well-known author and activist Naomi Klein carefully observes:

> Here is what we need to understand: a hell of a lot of people are in pain. Under neoliberal policies of deregulation, privatisation, austerity and corporate trade, their living standards have declined precipitously. They have lost jobs. They have lost pensions. They have lost much of the safety net that used to make these losses less frightening. They see a future for their kids even worse than their precarious present. At the same time, they have witnessed the rise of the Davos class, a hyper-connected network of banking and tech billionaires, elected leaders who are awfully cosy with those interests, and Hollywood celebrities who make the whole thing seem unbearably glamorous. Success is a party to which they were not invited, and they know in their hearts that this rising wealth and power is somehow directly connected to their growing debts and powerlessness.[26]

This reflected one of the 21st century's most profound and serious tensions. How could policy makers and citizens rebuild society away from a free market ideology when all they had were capitalist tools? The fundamental problem was not just that CEOs continued to hold sway over the world's economy but that their executive power was the only one known and available. The executive conundrum that afflicts modern society is that it is forced to rely on its ruler's wisdom for its own preservation and liberation. CEOs have won the historical battle of ideas by default. The free market's present triumph over its ideological rivals looms heavily as our doomed future defeat.

The appeal of the CEO is that for all their own practical failings they reflect what can appear as a timeless universal wisdom for achieving personal success and collective advancement. Fantasy wrestles with reality as CEOs symbolise a knowledge written deep within Western culture and handed down to us from on high on how to best realise our goals. Their idealised presence holds out the possibility of taking control of one's life and shaping it to one's own will. At the level of society, this proffers a belief in our power to direct our shared fate rather than letting it be determined by the supposedly inevitable forces of 'progress'. The CEO is thus god-like in their perceived function. At their purest, they are the personification of agency at a time when it seems in particularly short supply.

As Joshua Rothman wrote in the *New Yorker*, "[m]any of today's challenges are too complex to yield to the exercise of leadership alone. Even so, we are inclined to see the problems of the present in terms of crises and leaders".[27] Never was the CEO way such an easy solution, at least insofar as it might solve the anxiety of our time. To this effect, Rothman quotes WestPoint English professor Elizabeth Samet, who notes that:

> Crises of leadership are the order of the day at the beginning of the twenty-first century. If we live in a world of crisis we also live in a world that romanticizes crisis

– that finds in it fodder for an addiction to the twenty-four-hour news cycle, multiple information streams, and constant stimulation.[28]

Samet further proclaims that it is precisely this pathological commitment to crisis that leads us to embrace "the false prophets, the smooth operators, the gangsters, and the demagogues" as saviours. The CEO is chief amongst these shady characters.

In this spirit CEOs are the mythical heroes in a world where simply getting a job can prove an almost insurmountable obstacle. Despite their human frailties and failures in 'real life', we are pressured to accept their seemingly divine right to have power over us. This is all part of the corporate apparatus that preserves itself through the glorification of itself and its leaders.[29] The attraction of the CEO is the ability to experience for ourselves, even if only partially, this transcendent power. With little to no ideological or institutional alternative apparently available, this is as close to feeling empowered as can sometimes seem currently possible. Romanticising the CEO is a way to channel this idealised image of the all-conquering executive into the struggles of our own lives. Clearly there are CEOs who are corrupt and others who are without scruples. Some have even done significant jail time, such as Enron's Jeff Skilling, WorldCom's Bernard Ebbers and Tyco's Dennis Kozlowski. Such cases, however, do not undermine the truth of the awesome faith that CEOs still represent. Executives, like some priests, may prove to be sinners but this is seen as a reflection of their human frailty rather than a cause for religious doubt. Indeed, what remains sacred is the unrelenting belief that the market driven skills, thinking and practices of the idealised CEO is the only path to our moral and material improvement.

The CEO society is built on the belief in a supernatural salvation, with believers gaining strength from being able discipline themselves to the impossible ideals of these faiths. The market is gospel, the good word, in an uncertain world full of ungodly temptations. Just as Christians traditionally held fast and avoided the seven deadly sins, so too must we ward off the grave market sins of being inefficient, unproductive and unprofitable. Any deviation from this CEO orthodoxy is akin to a blasphemy that would rebuke the executive's self-evident truth and power. It is indeed telling that top executives are often described in messianic terms – as 'saviours' of their companies and 'visionaries' of a new world. This plays into a deeper 'market fundamentalism' that glorifies both corporations and CEOs.[30] In the words of Nobel prize-winning economist Joseph Stiglitz:

> From a historical point of view, for a quarter of a century the prevailing religion of the West has been market fundamentalism. I say it is a religion because it was not based on economic science or historical evidence. It was sold by Thatcher in the UK and by Reagan in the USA. It made reference to some old ideas in economics, specifically to Adam Smith's notion of the invisible hand, which is the argument that firms who pursue their self-interest

and the maximization of profits would lead, as if by an invisible hand, to general societal well-being.[31]

Similarly, there is an abiding fundamentalist ideology that believes in the saving powers of CEOs, themselves positioned as the saviour that has been bequeathed to the earthly world. CEOs have come to perform not only a corporate miracle but also a social one. The good ones are supposed to be able to bring a company back from the dead, just as they can make a lame economy walk again. Similarly, salvation is available for any one of us that follows their tried and true path.

Faith in both capitalism and its CEO offspring stands as an easily accessible form of modern common sense, even for free market unbelievers. One does not have to be a faithful Christian to accept the goodness of Christian values. Indeed, not believing in the implausible biblical stories of Christ as being a literally divine child of a virgin mother does not necessitate abandoning the golden rule as a sound piece of moral wisdom. Similarly, the value of being efficient, productive and innovative like a CEO is simply obvious, regardless of any wider ethical or political criticisms one may have of contemporary capitalism generally. Pivotal, in this respect, is to spread the word of this executive salvation to all who are in need of it. This is perhaps above all else the age of self-help.[32] But just as, according to certain Christian factions, God helps those who help themselves, in the CEO society we all have to help ourselves to as much as we can. For the CEO, as a cultural figure, the obligation is to help others by introducing them to, and ensuring they dutifully follow, a righteous executive lifestyle. The failure to do so brings with it not only the wrath of the CEO gods but also the condemnation of their pious earthly followers.

Bad faith

For all its other supposed faults, an executive mentality is widely praised for the freedom it offers people, and the knowledge it portends for how to manage a complex, precarious and disempowering existence. While actual CEOs are a main contributor to the present-day plague of mass alienation, their feted wisdom is embraced as the magic bullet for individually escaping such a dispiriting fate. It is the holy wisdom of how to be a modern winner rather than a loser. It offers the heavenly keys to earthly success, showing people the path to freedom and prosperity.

The liberty promised by embracing the CEO society reflects the possibility of the contemporary person's embrace of their own lack of agency. The danger that this courts is the false acceptance of the CEO society and lifestyle as humanity's only choice. Moreover, such an acceptance highlights an ideological bondage to a socially unjust and personally debilitating system. Resistance is imperative because at stake is not just the triumph of a free market but rather the short-sighted relief of buying into the only, and drastically limited, form of freedom currently on offer. And this freedom might well be slavery, as George Orwell predicted,[33] but today it is delivered as much by the corporations as it is by governments.

The conditions of the CEO society echo the notion of 'bad faith' first introduced by the French existential philosopher

Jean-Paul Sartre. This idea of bad faith refers to the potential unwillingness of individuals to realise and pursue their
radical freedom due to being overly attached to an existing
and dominant identity. To this end:

> it is precisely this person who I have to be ... and who I
> am not. It is not that I do not wish to be this person or
> that I want this person to be different. But rather there is
> no common measure between his being and mine. It is a
> 'representation' for others and for myself, which means
> that I can be he only in representation.[34]

Identity, insofar as it is understood as being predicated on
identifying with someone else, represents paradoxically the
freedom to be unfree, through the willing imprisonment in a
predetermined and narrow sense of self. As such, the slavish
devotion to the permanency of an eternally transformable
status quo ends up as a prison.

The neoliberal celebration of free market liberal democracy on which the CEO society is erected is a prime example
of modern bad faith. It has the tragic ability to enchant us with
its visions of a prosperous free market full of heroic CEOs, and
in doing so limits social possibilities to the narrow ideological
horizons of capitalism and corporate rule. The demise of state
communism in the Soviet Union and the Eastern bloc became
the catalyst, if not an excuse, for surrendering our historical
freedom completely to the forces of the market. It also proffered the belief that neoliberalism was the only economic,
political and social choice we had left. A similar case of bad

faith followed the 2008 financial crisis in respect of the resurrection of the CEO as a cultural hero. Here, as we discussed earlier, the executive was clearly demonised on an individual basis. Indeed, as a group they were widely condemned for their greed and culpability. However, since then the figure of the CEO, their perceived abilities and mindsets, have been raised again to the level of heroic expectations.

The contemporary obsession with being like a CEO makes tragic sense. A tell-tale sign of such bad faith, a refusal to explore one's free choice and the external obstacles preventing one from doing so, is an attempt to completely embody the idealised image of this prevailing identity and ideology. Sartre uses the everyday example of observing the waiter who is committed to completely embodying the ideal of the waiter. Sartre writes:

> Let us consider this waiter in the cafe. His movement is quick and forward, a little too precise, a little too rapid. He comes toward the patrons with a step a little too quick. He bends forward a little too eagerly; his voice, his eyes express an interest a little too solicitous for the order of the customer. Finally there he returns, trying to imitate in his walk the inflexible stiffness of some kind of automaton while carrying his tray with a recklessness of a tight-rope walker by putting it in a perpetually unstable, perpetually broken equilibrium which he perpetually re-establishes by a light movement of the arm and hand.[35]

Likewise, the self-disciplining function of the CEO society is founded in no small part on the attempt to be the perfect executive, at least of one's own life, given the impossibly of doing otherwise and being successful. The only choice that this ultra-competitive reality presents, at least on its own terms, is to take on the ruthless and calculative mentality of an idealised business titan. A failure to do so, in the mentality of the CEO society, means giving up on the possibility of achieving one's goals and dreams.

In the end, what the CEO society tries to rob us of is choice and liberty. If successful, it takes from us of the promise of democracy itself. The CEO society does more than just spread and shape ever more spheres of existence, whether they concern work, politics, community, family, charity or education. As Sartre prophetically declared, "They are in bad faith – they are afraid – and fear, bad faith have an aroma that the gods find delicious. Yes, the gods like that, the pitiful souls".[36] Indeed, the CEO god tries to steal from us our ability to search for alternative ways of life and organising, confining the entirety of human desire and ethics to its narrow managerial and capitalist worldview. Whether one wants to make money or save the environment, we are cajoled to do so according to CEO values and standards.

Existential freedom, as far as the CEO society would have it, is found in the ability to embody or strive for 'what is not'. More precisely, it is the capacity to imagine being something different to what one currently is and working toward realising that self-becoming project. For the person of the new millennium, it might easily be imagined that all there is to aspire to is to be like a CEO. There is no 'what is not' other than the disappointment felt in not meeting the executive ideal. It is an at times comfortable but ultimately debilitating forsaking of our freedom. It is misguided faith that proposes the saving power of strong business leadership both for society and ourselves. Yet despite its romantic appeal, the idolisation of the CEO means travelling down a road to nowhere. It forces upon us the bad faith of CEO salvation. It is absolutely fundamental for our mass survival and flourishing that we are saved from these saviours and from their acolytes.

Afterword

The high cost
of the CEO society

The development of the CEO society has been as decisive as it has been wide-ranging, yet so has resistance to it. The disasters of the early months of the Trump presidency are a case in point, leaving many wondering whether the idea that a country could be run like a business was a good idea.[1] Global protests, highlighted especially by the Women's Marches around the world, represented a backlash against not just the threat of right-wing populist movements led by senior corporate executives, but also against the very executive values inspiring those movements.

Despite resistance, both the threat and the reality of the CEO society remain strong. There continues to be an abiding belief that entrepreneurs and business titans can show us the way to economic, political and social progress. This is so even when actual CEOs repeatedly reveal themselves as morally tainted and corrupt. Regardless of how far from grace individual CEOs fall, the desire to be the master of the universe in all areas of our existence survives. This obsession with corporate leadership has dramatically transformed our world, and our selves. It has threatened to turn us all into self-interest calculating, value-obsessed, efficient executive stereotypes. By now, for many it is assumed to be entirely natural to draw on the quasi-mystical knowledge of CEOs to create a profitable economy, politics and life.

As we have highlighted in this book, CEOs are the magical gurus in whom all of us are coaxed to put our modern faith. Their knowledge and practices will supposedly lead to our individual and collective salvation. Tellingly, this reverence for the heroic CEO persists even when belief in the dogma of the free market is showing signs of significant wear and tear. New progressive movements are arising all over the world challenging the global rule of corporations and their neoliberal political minions. That the executive continues, therefore, to be a false idol of progress is both telling and troubling. The CEO society embodies one of the most confounding and fundamental contradictions of late capitalism.

There is a profoundly paradoxical socio-economic dynamic at work. Even at times when the cultural stock of the market falls, people invest even more intensely in the salvationary power of the strong executive to rescue them, in the way that Steve Jobs rescued Apple, and Donald Trump was expected by many to rescue America. Ultimately, the persistent belief in the CEO is shorting our present world and our future. It is buying into the false hopes of business rhetoric for confronting complex contemporary global problems. It is ignoring the potential for more creative and emancipatory solutions, concentrating instead on the ultimately empty short-term corporate thinking of top executives. In doing so, our economic and ecological survival is placed at grave risk. The vitalisation of the myth of the CEO is as central to the free market's legitimacy as it is to global democratic society's collective downfall. It is a historical race to the bottom that has come to shape all areas of modern existence such that even the so-called winners might be destined to lose. Theirs is a gilded victory that is unbearably narrow in what it makes socially possible, and undeniably limited in the value it can provide. There is quite a price to pay to maintain such an executive existence: from the perpetuation of an (un)free market with its rising tide of inequality and authoritarianism to the constriction of all thought and action by the instrumental tyranny of a repressive capitalist logic. This is the unconscionably high cost of a CEO society that we are all forced to bear.

This book is intended as a bold provocation against executive fundamentalism, and a call to resist it. It goes beyond a mere plea to keep such corporate fanaticism within the private confines of the boardroom and the marketplace, and aims to strike at the heart of this prevailing global worship of the CEO and all that it symbolises. It is a critical warning of its far-reaching destruction of the possibility for creating a democratic, sustainable and just present and future. It is also a clarion call to a better critical understanding of how the CEO is threatening to colonise not just the world but also our very selves. In the end, it is our hope that we might find a way to fire the CEO from our collective imaginations so that we can start building a more progressive, free and democratic economy and society.

Notes

Introduction

1 Alex Malley, *The Naked CEO: The Truth You Need to Build a Big Life* (Milton: Wiley, 2015), back cover.

2 Liz Hobday, "Allegations of Bullying Levelled against CPA Boss", in *7.30* (Australian Broadcasting Corporation, 2017).

3 Linsey McGoey, "Philanthrocapitalism and Its Critics", *Poetics* 40, no. 2 (2012).

4 Nina Atwood, *Date Like a CEO: Leadership in Life and Love for Men* (Dallas: Atwood, 2015).

5 Miranda P. Charles, *The Unmasked CEO* (Captured by Love #7) (Sydney: MPC Romance Publishing, 2017).

6 Anna DePalo, *Second Chance with the CEO* (Fort Erie: Harlequin, 2016).

Chapter 1: Welcome to the CEO society

1 Stanley Weiser and Oliver Stone, *Wall Street: Original Screenplay* (Glendale: Oaxatal Productions, 1987).

2 Timothy Shenk, "Booked #3: What Exactly Is Neoliberalism?", *Dissent*, 2 April 2015. https://www.dissentmagazine.org/blog/booked-3-what-exactly-is-neoliberalism-wendy-brown-undoing-the-demos.

3 Thomas Klikauer, "What Is Managerialism?", *Critical Sociology* 41, no. 7 8 (2015): 1107.

4 Larry Julian, *God Is My CEO: Following God's Principles in a Bottom-Line World*, 2nd ed. (Avon: Adams, 2014).

5 Ibid., 300.

6 Ma Chi, "CEO Courses for 3-Year-Old Kids: Grooming Future Elites or Glorified Babysitting?", *China Daily*, 19 August 2016,

n.p. http://www.chinadaily.com.cn/china/2016-08/19/content_ 26533865.htm.

7   Michael A. Peters, *Poststructuralism, Marxism, and Neoliberalism: Between Theory and Politics* (Lanham, MD: Rowman & Littlefield, 2001).

8   Adam Smith, *The Wealth of Nations* (Middletown: Shine, 2014; repr., 1776), 10.

9   Michel Foucault, *The Birth of Biopolitics: Lectures at the Collège De France, 1978 1979* (Houndmills: Springer, 2008), 130.

10 Donald Trump, "Transcript: Donald Trump's Victory Speech", *New York Times*, 9 November 2016, n.p. http://www.nytimes. com/2016/11/10/us/politics/trump-speech-transcript.html.

11 Carl Rhodes and Peter Bloom, "Both Trump and Clinton Would See the US Run Like a Corporation", *The Conversation*, 3 November 2016. https://theconversation.com/both-trump-and-clinton-would-see-the-us-run-like-a-corporation-68059.

12 Klikauer, "What Is Managerialism?", 1107.

13 David A. Fahrenthold, "Trump Recorded Having Extremely Lewd Conversation About Women in 2005", *The Washington Post*, 8 October 2016, n.p. https://www.washingtonpost.com/ politics/trump-recorded-having-extremely-lewd-conversation-about-women-in-2005/2016/10/07/3b9ce776-8cb4-11e6-bf8a-3d26847eeed4_story.html.

14 Peter Bloom and Carl Rhodes, "Corporate Authoritarianism and the New American Anti-Democracy", *Common Dreams*, 23 October 2016. https://www.commondreams.org/views/2016/10/ 23/corporate-authoritarianism-and-new-american-anti-democracy.

15 Peter Bloom and Carl Rhodes, "Trump and the Dangerous Rise of Executive Salvation", *The Sociological Review Blog*, 22 November 2016. https://www.thesociologicalreview.com/blog/ trump-and-the-dangerous-rise-of-executive-salvation.html.

16 Abby Phillip, "Clinton Slams Trump's Hypocrisy in Using Undocumented Labor to Build D.C. Hotel", *The Washington Post*, 26 October 2016, n.p. https://www.washingtonpost.com/news/ post-politics/wp/2016/10/26/clinton-slams-trump-for-using-undocumented-labor-to-build-d-c-hotel/.

17 Merriam-Webster, "CEO", in *Merriam-Webster's Collegiate Dictionary 11th Edition* (Springfield, MA: Merriam-Webster, 2004), 201.

18 James D. Richardson, comp., *A Compilation of the Messages and Papers of the Presidents, 1789 1897*, vol. 7 (New York: Bureau of National Literature and Art, 1901), 399.

19 Herman Melville, *White-Jacket; or, the World in a Man-of-War* (London: Bentley, 1850), 35.

20 Alexander L. Peterman, *Elements of Civil Goverment* (New York etc.: American Book Company, 1891), 40.

21 Martin Kornberger, Carl Rhodes and Renéten Bos, "The Others of Hierarchy: Rhizomatics of Organising", in *Deleuze and the Social* (Edinburgh: Edinburgh University Press, 2006).

22 Klaus P. Hansen, "The Mentality of Management: Self-Images of American Top Executives", in *The Politics of Management Knowledge*, ed. Stewart R. Clegg and Gill Palmer (London: Sage, 1996), 36.

23 Jo Littler, "Celebrity CEOs and the Cultural Economy of Tabloid Intimacy", in *Stardom and Celebrity: A Reader*, ed. Su Holmes and Sean Redmond (London: SAGE Publications Ltd, 2006).

24 Robert van Krieken, *Celebrity Society* (London: Routledge, 2012), 124.

25 Jack Welch and John A. Byrne, *Jack: Straight from the Gut* (New York: Warner, 2003).

26 Louis V. Gerstner, *Who Says Elephants Can't Dance? How I Turned around IBM* (New York: Harper Business, 2003).

27 Phil Knight, *Shoe Dog: A Memoir by the Creator of Nike* (London: Simon and Schuster, 2016).

28 Donald J. Trump's Hair, *The Autobiography of Donald Trump's Hair* (Seattle: Createspace, 2016).

29 Sloan Wilson, *The Man in the Grey Flannel Suit* (New York: Cardinal, 1955).

30 William H. Whyte, *The Organization Man* (New York: Simon and Schuster, 1956).

31 Ibid., 17.

32 Gideon Haigh, "Bad Company: The Cult of the CEO", *Quarterly*

Essay 10 (2003). https://www.quarterlyessay.com.au/essay/2003/ 06/bad-company#.

33 Marcus Buckingham and Curt Coffman, *First, Break All the Rules, What the World's Greatest Managers Do Differently* (New York: Simon and Schuster, 1999).

34 AFL-CIO, "Executive Pay Watch", accessed 9 November, 2015. http://www.aflcio.org/Corporate-Watch/Paywatch-2016.

35 Gretchen Gavett, "CEOs Get Paid Too Much, According to Pretty Much Everyone in the World", *Harvard Business Review* (2014). https://hbr.org/2014/09/ceos-get-paid-too-much-according-to-pretty-much-everyone-in-the-world.

36 Mathew L. A. Hayward, Violina P. Rindova and Timothy G. Pollock, "Believing One's Own Press: The Causes and Consequences of CEO Celebrity", *Strategic Management Journal* 25, no. 7 (2004).

37 Paresha N. Sinha, Kerr Inkson and James R. Barker, "Committed to a Failing Strategy: Celebrity CEO, Intermediaries, Media and Stakeholders in a Co-Created Drama", *Organization Studies* 33, no. 2 (2012): 224.

38 Littler, "Celebrity CEOs"

39 Jenni Dean, *Be the CEO of Your Own Body* (Port Melbourne: Dean, 2011).

40 Atwood, back cover.

41 Ellen Ernst Kossek and Brenda A. Lautsch, *CEO of Me: Creating a Life That Works in the Flexible Job Age* (Upper Saddle River: Prentice Hall, 2007).

42 Wendy Brown, *Undoing the Demos: Neoliberalism's Stealth Revolution* (Brooklyn: Zone, 2015).

43 Gérard Duménil and Dominique Lévy, *The Crisis of Neoliberalism* (Cambridge, MA: Harvard University Press, 2011).

44 Thomas Picketty, *Capital in the Twenty-First Century* (Cambridge, MA: Harvard University Press, 2014).

45 Brown, *Undoing the Demos*, 22.

46 Kerry A. Dolan, "Forbes 2017 Billionaires List: Meet the Richest People on the Planet", *Forbes*, 20 March 2017. https://www.forbes.com/sites/kerryadolan/2017/03/20/forbes-2017-billionaires-list-meet-the-richest-people-on-the-planet/.

47 Maurizio Lazzarato, "Neoliberalism in Action: Inequality, Insecurity and the Reconstitution of the Social", *Theory, Culture & Society* 26, no. 6 (2009).

48 Angela M. Eikenberry and Jodie Drapal Kluver, "The Marketization of the Nonprofit Sector: Civil Society at Risk?", *Public Administration Review* 64, no. 2 (2004): 132. Also see Norman Fairclough, "Critical Discourse Analysis and the Marketization of Public Discourse: The Universities", *Discourse & Society* 4, no. 2 (1993); Daniel J. Lair, Katie Sullivan and George Cheney, "Marketization and the Recasting of the Professional Self", *Management Communication Quarterly* 18, no. 3 (2005); Lester M. Salamon, "The Marketization of Welfare: Changing Nonprofit and for-Profit Roles in the American Welfare State", *Social Service Review* 67, no. 1 (1993).

49 See Emanuel S. Savas, *Privatization: The Key to Better Government*, Public Administration and Public Policy (London: Chatham House, 1987); John Vickers and George K. Yarrow, *Privatization: An Economic Analysis* (Cambridge, MA: MIT Press, 1988).

50 William L. Megginson and Jeffry M. Netter, "From State to Market: A Survey of Empirical Studies on Privatization", *Journal of Economic Literature* 39, no. 2 (2001): 321.

51 Thomas I. Palley, "Macroeconomics and Monetary Policy: Competing Theoretical Frameworks", *Journal of Post Keynesian Economics* 30, no. 1 (2007): 1.

52 Colin Crouch, *The Strange Non-Death of Neo-Liberalism* (Oxford: Wiley, 2013); Aihwa Ong, *Neoliberalism as Exception: Mutations in Citizenship and Sovereignty* (Durham, NC: Duke University Press, 2006); Henk Overbeek and Bastiaan van Apeldoorn, *Neoliberalism in Crisis* (London: Palgrave Macmillan, 2012).

53 John Dewey, "Democracy and Educational Administration", *School and Society* 45 (1937).

54 Ibid., 457.

Chapter 2: The idolisation of the CEO

1 Mark Whitehouse, "Crisis Compels Economists to Reach for New Paradigm", *The Wall Street Journal*, 4 November 2009, n.p. https://www.wsj.com/articles/SB125720159912223873.

2   Tom Wolfe, *Bonfire of the Vanities* (New York: Farrar Straus Giroux, 1987).

3   Paul A. Dillon, "Why Doing the Right Thing Can Bring You Success in the Global Marketplace", *The CEO Magazine*, 25 July 2017. http://media.the-ceo-magazine.com/guest/why-doing-right-thing-can-bring-you-success-global-marketplace.

4   Reuters, "U.S. Drugmaker Turing to Roll Back 5,000 Percent Price Hike", *Reuters*, 23 September 2015, n.p. http://www.reuters.com/article/us-usa-healthcare-turing/u-s-drugmaker-turing-to-roll-back-5000-percent-price-hike-idUSKCN0RM2RU20150922.

5   HBR, "Measuring the Return on Character", *Harvard Business Review*, April 2015, n.p. https://hbr.org/2015/04/measuring-the-return-on-character.

6   See Picketty, *Capital in the Twenty-First Century.*

7   Peter Vanham, *Before I Was CEO: Life Stories and Lessons from Leaders before They Reached the Top* (Hoboken: Wiley, 2016).

8   G. William Domhoff, *Who Rules America? The Triumph of the Corporate Rich* (New York: McGraw-Hill, 2014).

9   Rakesh Khurana, "The Curse of the Superstar CEO", *Harvard Business Review* 80, no. 9 (2002); Rakesh Khurana, *Searching for a Corporate Savior: The Irrational Quest for Charismatic CEOs* (Princeton, NJ: Princeton University Press, 2002).

10 Khurana, "The Curse of the Superstar CEO", 60.

11 Khurana, *Searching for a Corporate Savior.*

12 Edwin S. Hunt and James Murray, *A History of Business in Medieval Europe, 1200 1550* (Cambridge: Cambridge University Press, 1999), 132.

13 Smith, *The Wealth of Nations.*

14 P. McNulty, "A Note on the History of Perfect Competition", *Journal of Political Economy* 75, no. 4, Part 1 (1967): 396.

15 John Stuart Mill, *Principles of Political Economy*, vol. 1 (Boston: Little and Brown, 1848), 286.

16 William H. Young, *Ordering America: Fulfilling the Ideals of Western Civilization* (Bloomington: Xlibris, 2010), 376.

17 See for instance John Micklethwait and Adrian Wooldridge, *The Company: A Short History of a Revolutionary Idea* (London: Phoenix, 2005).

18 Sean D. Cashman, *America in the Gilded Age*, 2nd ed. (New York: NYU Press, 1993); Rebecca Edwards, *New Spirits: Americans in the Gilded Age, 1865 1905* (New York: Oxford University Press, 2006); Alan Trachtenberg, *The Incorporation of America: Culture and Society in the Gilded Age* (New York: Hill and Wang, 2007).

19 See David M. Boje and Robert D. Winsor, "The Resurrection of Taylorism: Total Quality Management's Hidden Agenda", *Journal of Organizational Change Management* 6, no. 4 (1993); Craig R. Littler, "Understanding Taylorism", *The British Journal of Sociology* 29, no. 2 (1978); Charles S. Maier, "Between Taylorism and Technocracy: European Ideologies and the Vision of Industrial Productivity in the 1920s", *Journal of Contemporary History* 5, no. 2 (1970); Stephen P. Waring, *Taylorism Transformed: Scientific Management Theory since 1945* (Chapel Hill: University of North Carolina Press, 1994).

20 Hindy Lauer Schachter, "The Role Played by Frederick Taylor in the Rise of the Academic Management Fields", *Journal of Management History* 16, no. 4 (2010): 442 43.

21 Karl Marx, *Capital: A Critique of Political Economy* (London: Penguin Harmondsworth, 1976; first published 1885), 342.

22 Ibid., 339.

23 Jill Lepore, "Not So Fast", *New Yorker*, 12 October 2009. https://www.newyorker.com/magazine/2009/10/12/not-so-fast.

24 Jerry Useem, "Tyrants, Statesmen, and Destroyers (a Brief History of the CEO) Today's Disgraced Chieftains Are the Product of 100 Years of Evolution", *Fortune*, 18 November 2002. http://archive.fortune.com/magazines/fortune/fortune_archive/2002/11/18/332249/index.htm.

25 Joseph A. Schumpeter, *Capitalism, Socialism, and Democracy* (London: Routledge, 1994; first published 1943).

26 Ibid., 83.

27 David Harvey, *A Brief History of Neoliberalism* (Oxford: Oxford University Press, 2005), 3.

28 See Werner Bonefeld, "Social Constitution and the Form of the Capitalist State", in *Open Marxism Volume 1: Dialectics and History*, ed. Werner Bonefeld, Richard Gunn and Kosmas Psychopedis

(London: Pluto Press, 1992); Peter Burnham, "Open Marxism and Vulgar International Political Economy", *Review of International Political Economy* 1, no. 2 (1994).

29 John A. Byrne, *Chainsaw: The Notorious Career of Al Dunlap in the Era of Profit-at-Any-Price* (Darby: Diane, 2005).

30 See Ian Maitland, "Virtuous Markets: The Market as School of the Virtues", *Business Ethics Quarterly* 7, no. 1 (2015); Antonella Picchio, *Social Reproduction: The Political Economy of the Labour Market* (Cambridge: Cambridge University Press, 1994).

31 Marion Fourcade and Kieran Healy, "Moral Views of Market Society", *Annual Review of Sociology* 33, no. 1 (2007).

32 Ibid., 287.

33 Max Weber, *The Protestant Ethic and the Spirit of Capitalism* (New York: Allen and Unwin, 1930).

34 See David Brion Davis, *The Problem of Slavery in the Age of Revolution, 1770 1823* (Ithaca, NY: Cornell University Press, 1975); Eric Eustace Williams, *Capitalism and Slavery* (Chapel Hill: University of North Carolina Press, 1944).

35 Kenan Malik, *The Meaning of Race: Race, History and Culture in Western Society* (New York: New York University Press, 1996), 225.

36 In Tom Ward, "Jeff Bezos: 'It's Time for America to Go Back to the Moon, This Time to Stay'", *Futurism*, 24 July 2017. https://futurism.com/jeff-bezos-its-time-for-america-to-go-back-to-the-moon-this-time-to-stay/.

37 Walter Isaacson, "The Genius of Jobs", *New York Times*, 29 October 2011. http://www.nytimes.com/2011/10/30/opinion/sunday/steve-jobss-genius.html.

38 Joseph E. Stiglitz, *Globalization and Its Discontents* (New York: Norton, 2002).

39 Khurana, *Searching for a Corporate Savior*.

40 William Davies, "Elite Power under Advanced Neoliberalism", *Theory, Culture & Society* 34, no. 5 6 (2017): 227.

41 Valentina Zarya, "Employers Are Quietly Using Big Data to Track Employee Pregnancies", *Fortune*, 17 February 2016. http://fortune.com/2016/02/17/castlight-pregnancy-data/.

42 Gil Press, "6 Predictions for the $203 Billion Big Data Analytics Market", *Forbes*, 20 January 2017. https://www.forbes.com/sites/gilpress/2017/01/20/6-predictions-for-the-203-billion-big-data-analytics-market/.

43 Peter Bloom, "Cutting Off the King's Head: The Self-Disciplining Fantasy of Neoliberal Sovereignty", *New Formations* 88 (2016).

44 Wolfe, *Bonfire of the Vanities*.

45 Ibid., 78.

46 See Warwick Tie, "The Psychic Life of Governmentality", *Culture, Theory and Critique* 45, no. 2 (2004).

47 Nell Merlino, "On Being Your Own CEO", *Huffpost*, 8 July 2012. http://www.huffingtonpost.com/nell-merlino/woman-ceo_b_1497682.html.

48 Matthew Jussim, "Fit at 50: CEO and Entrepreneur Eric Schiffer's Tips for Staying in Shape and Building Confidence", *Men's Health*, 13 July 2017. http://www.mensfitness.com/weight-loss/success-stories/fit-50-ceo-and-entrepreneur-eric-schiffers-tips-staying-shape-success.

49 Sheryl O'Loughlin, "I'm a CEO Who's Been Married to an Entrepreneur for 19 Years Here's How We Make It Work", *CNBC*, 20 December 2016. https://www.cnbc.com/2016/12/20/im-a-ceo-whos-been-married-to-an-entrepreneur-for-20-years-heres-how-we-make-it-work.html.

50 Jeremy Gilbert, "What Kind of Thing Is 'Neoliberalism'?", *New Formations: A Journal of Culture/Theory/Politics* 80, no. 80 (2013): 9.

51 Allan Cox, *The CEO in You*, rev. 3rd ed. (Chicago: Harrier Press, 2015), xii.

52 Dennis Green, "Under Armour CEO: Trump Is 'a Real Asset for the Country'", *Business Insider*, 8 February 2017, n.p. https://www.businessinsider.com/under-armour-ceo-praises-trump-2017-2.

53 Joanna Latimer and Rolland Munro, "Driving the Social", *The Sociological Review* 54 (2006): 40.

54 See also Peter P. Bloom and Paul J. White, "The Moral Work of Subversion", *Human Relations* 69, no. 1 (2016).

Chapter 3: Competing in the executive economy

1 Richard Feloni, "33 War Strategies That Will Help You Win in Business", *Business Insider*, 15 August 2014, n.p. https://www.businessinsider.com.au/war-strategies-to-win-in-business-2014-8.

2 Trent Dalton, "Queen's Birthday Honours 2017: Alan Joyce's Immigrant Song, Fair-Go Ethos", *The Australian*, 12 June 2017, n.p. http://www.theaustralian.com.au/in-depth/queens-birthday-honours/queens-birthday-honours-2017-alan-joyces-immigrant-song-fairgo-ethos/news-story/980c06a7022c31c1b270279076025d29.

3 Ed Michaels, Helen Handfield-Jones and Beth Axelrod, *The War for Talent* (Boston: Harvard Business School Press, 1997).

4 James R. Faulconbridge et al., "The 'War for Talent': The Gatekeeper Role of Executive Search Firms in Elite Labour Markets", *Geoforum* 40, no. 5 (2009).

5 Martin Gilens and Benjamin I. Page, "Testing Theories of American Politics: Elites, Interest Groups, and Average Citizens", *Perspectives on Politics* 12, no. 3 (2014): 577.

6 E.g. Haigh, *Bad Company*, 10; Khurana, "The Curse of the Superstar CEO"; Khurana, *Searching for a Corporate Savior*.

7 Gerald F. Davis, Mina Yoo and Wayne E. Baker, "The Small World of the American Corporate Elite, 1982 2001", *Strategic Organization* 1, no. 3 (2003).

8 Tom Farley, "Nyse President: I Owe Every Job I've Ever Had to Networking", *Fortune*, 7 July 2015, n.p. http://fortune.com/2015/07/07/tom-farley-networking-tips/.

9 Benjamin Barber, *Jihad Vs. Mcworld* (New York: Times Books, 1995), 23.

10 Joshua Barkan, *Corporate Sovereignty: Law and Government under Capitalism* (Minneapolis: University of Minnesota Press, 2013).

11 In Henry A. Giroux, *Politics after Hope: Barack Obama and the Crisis of Youth, Race, and Democracy* (New York: Routledge, 2015), 7.

12 Maurizio Lazzarato, *Signs and Machines: Capitalism and the Production of Subjectivity*, trans. Joshua David Jordan (Los Angeles: Semiotext(e), 2014), 25.

13 Hilary Osborne, "Amazon Accused of 'Intolerable Conditions' at Scottish Warehouse", *The Guardian*, 12 December 2016, n.p. https://www.theguardian.com/technology/2016/dec/11/amazon-accused-of-intolerable-conditions-at-scottish-warehouse.

14 Davies, "Elite Power under Advanced Neoliberalism", 19.

15 Morten Bøås and Desmond McNeill, *Multilateral Institutions* (London: Pluto Press, 2003), 1.

16 Barkan, *Corporate Sovereignty*; Carl Rhodes, "Democratic Business Ethics: Volkswagen's Emissions Scandal and the Disruption of Corporate Sovereignty", *Organization Studies* 37, no. 10 (2016).

17 Jolle Demmers, Alex E. Fernández Jilberto and Barbara Hogenboom, *Good Governance in the Era of Global Neoliberalism* (London: Routledge, 2004), 2.

18 See Gareth Porter, "Trade Competition and Pollution Standards: 'Race to the Bottom' or 'Stuck at the Bottom'", *The Journal of Environment & Development* 8, no. 2 (1999); Nita Rudra, *Globalization and the Race to the Bottom in Developing Countries: Who Really Gets Hurt?* (Cambridge: Cambridge University Press, 2008); William K. Tabb, "Race to the Bottom?", in *Implicating Empire: Globalization & Resistance in the 21st Century World Order*, ed. Stanley Aronowitz and Heather Gautney (New York: Basic Books, 2003).

19 United Nations Global Compact, "Global Financial Crisis: Why Corporate Sustainability Is More Important Than Ever", *Corporate Social Responsibility Newswire*, 17 October 2008. http://www.csrwire.com/press_releases/21649-Global-Financial-Crisis-Why-Corporate-Sustainability-Is-More-Important-Than-Ever-.

20 Christopher Harress, "The Sad End of Blockbuster Video: The Onetime $5 Billion Company is Being Liquidated as Competition from Online Giants Netflix and Hulu Prove All Too Much for the Iconic Brand", *International Business Times*, 5 December 2013. http://www.ibtimes.com/sad-end-blockbuster-video-onetime-5-billion-company-being-liquidated-competition-1496962.

21 Leslie Kwoh, "When the CEO Burns Out: Job Fatigue Catches up to Some Executives Amid Mounting Expectations; No More Forced Smiles", *Wall Street Journal*, 7 May 2013, n.p. https://www.

wsj.com/articles/SB100014241278873236876045784691240085 24696.

22 Harry Levinson, "When Executives Burn Out", *Harvard Business Review*, July August 1996, n.p. https://hbr.org/1996/07/when-executives-burn-out.

23 Matthew J. Hoffarth, "Executive Burnout", *Business History Review* 90, no. 4 (2017).

24 Caroline O'Donovan and Priya Anand, "How Uber's Hard-Charging Corporate Culture Left Employees Drained", *Buzzfeed*, 18 July 2017, n.p. https://www.buzzfeed.com/carolineodonovan/how-ubers-hard-charging-corporate-culture-left-employees.

25 Marx, *Capital*, 367. Also see Mark Neocleous, "The Political Economy of the Dead Marx's Vampires", *History of Political Thought* 24, no. 4 (2003); Chris Rasmussen, "Ugly and Monstrous: Marxist Aesthetics", *James A. Rawley Graduate Conference in the Humanities* 7 (2006).

26 André Spicer and Peter Fleming, "Intervening in the Inevitable: Contesting Globalization in a Public Sector Organization", *Organization* 14, no. 4 (2007): 533.

27 James Arnt Aune, *Selling the Free Market: The Rhetoric of Economic Correctness* (New York: Guilford, 2002).

28 Khurana, *Searching for a Corporate Savior*.

29 In Yoni Appelbaum, "'I Alone Can Fix It'", *The Atlantic*, 21 July 2016, n.p. https://www.theatlantic.com/politics/archive/2016/07/trump-rnc-speech-alone-fix-it/492557/.

30 Megan McArdle, "The Cult of the CEO", *The Atlantic*, 28 February 2008. https://www.theatlantic.com/business/archive/2008/02/the-cult-of-the-ceo/2849/.

31 Ruth Sunderland, "Superheroes and Supervillains – Why the Cult of the CEO Blinds Us to Reality", *The Guardian*, 13 June 2010, n.p. https://www.theguardian.com/business/2010/jun/13/tony-hayward-terry-leahy-corporate-governance.

32 Peter Bloom and Carl Cederström, "'The Sky's the Limit': Fantasy in the Age of Market Rationality", *Journal of Organizational Change Management* 22, no. 2 (2009).

33 Ibid., 172.

34 In Dawn Kent Azok, "First 'Apprentice' Winner Spotlights Entrepreneurs, Talks Trump During Alabama Visit", 21 September 2015, n.p. http://www.al.com/business/index.ssf/2015/09/first_apprentice_winner_spotli.html.

35 David Prosser, "The Cult of the CEO", *Independent*, 14 June 2010, n.p. http://www.independent.co.uk/news/business/analysis-and-features/the-cult-of-the-ceo-2000460.html.

36 Carl Rhodes and Peter Bloom, "The Cultural Fantasy of Hierarchy: Sovereignty and the Desire for Spiritual Purity", in *Reinventing Hierarchy and Bureaucracy – from the Bureau to Network Organizations*, ed. Thomas Diefenbach and Rune Todnem (Bingley: Emerald, 2012).

37 Rowena Mason and Jill Treanor, "David Cameron: Inquiry into Co-Op Bank May Be Needed", *The Guardian*, 21 November 2013, n.p. https://www.theguardian.com/business/2013/nov/20/david-cameron-inquiry-co-op-bank-paul-flowers.

38 Alessia Contu, Christopher Grey and Anders örtenblad, "Against Learning", *Human Relations* 56, no. 8 (2003): 935.

39 Carl Rhodes and Oriana Milani Price, "The Post-Bureaucratic Parasite: Contrasting Narratives of Organizational Change in Local Government", *Management Learning* 42, no. 3 (2011).

40 Christian Maravelias, "Post Bureaucracy – Control through Professional Freedom", *Journal of Organizational Change Management* 16, no. 5 (2003): 547.

41 Quoted in Janet Lowe, *Jack Welch Speaks: Wit and Wisdom from the World's Greatest Business Leader* (Hoboken, NJ: Wiley, 2008), 219.

42 Sherry B. Ortner, "Resistance and the Problem of Ethnographic Refusal", *Comparative Studies in Society and History* 37, no. 1 (1995): 196.

43 Carl Rhodes and Alison Pullen, "Editorial: Neophilia and Organization", *Culture and Organization* 16, no. 1 (2010).

44 Donald J. Trump and Tony Schwartz, *Trump: The Art of Deal* (New York: Random House, 1987).

45 Picketty, *Capital in the Twenty-First Century*.

46 Bernard Gazier, "Employability the Complexity of a Policy Notion", in *Employability: From Theory to Practice*, ed. Patricia Weinert (Somerset: Transaction Publishers, 2001), 23.

47 Glenn Kessler, "Trump's False Claim He Built His Empire with a 'Small Loan' from His Father", *Washington Post*, 3 March 2016. https://www.washingtonpost.com/news/fact-checker/wp/2016/03/03/trumps-false-claim-he-built-his-empire-with-a-small-loan-from-his-father/.

48 Jessica Chasmar, "Donald Trump: I Consult Myself on Foreign Policy, 'Because I Have a Very Good Brain'", *The Washington Times*, 17 March 2016, n.p. http://www.washingtontimes.com/news/2016/mar/17/donald-trump-i-consult-myself-on-foreign-policy-be/.

49 Nigel Thrift, "Performing Cultures in the New Economy", in *Cultural Economy: Cultural Analysis and Commercial Life*, ed. Paul du Gay and Michael Pryke (London: Sage, 2002).

50 Noel M. Tichy and Stratford Sherman, *Control Your Destiny or Someone Else Will* (New York: Collins, 2005).

51 Ronald W. McQuaid and Colin Lindsay, "The Concept of Employability", *Urban Studies* 42, no. 2 (2005); Colin Cremin, "Living and Really Living: The Gap Year and the Commodification of the Contingent", *Ephemera* 7, no. 4 (2007).

52 Zig Ziglar and Tom Ziglar, *Born to Win: Find Your Success* (Issaquah, WA: Made for Success Publishing, 2017).

53 See Carl Rhodes and Alison Pullen, "Critical Business Ethics: From Corporate Self-Interest to the Glorification of the Sovereign Pater", *International Journal of Management Reviews* (2017).

54 See Kornberger, Rhodes and Bos, "The Others of Heirarchy"; Rhodes and Bloom, "The Cultural Fantasy of Hierarchy".

55 In Jessica Shambora, "Amex CEO Ken Chenault: Define Reality and Give Hope", *Fortune*, 12 May 2009. http://fortune.com/2009/05/12/amex-ceo-ken-chenault-define-reality-and-give-hope/.

Chapter 4: The CEO politician

1 M. J. Lee, "Carly Fiorina Announces Presidential Bid", *CNN*, 5 May 2015, n.p. http://edition.cnn.com/2015/05/04/politics/carly-fiorina-presidential-announcement/index.html.

2   Rory Carroll and Rupert Neate, "Carly Fiorina Will Run for President as a Successful Tech CEO. Silicon Valley Says That's a Fantasy", *The Guardian*, 4 May 2015, n.p. https://www.theguardian.com/us-news/2015/may/03/carly-fiorina-run-for-president-hewlett-packard.

3   David Corn, "Can a CEO Who Laid Off Thousands, Botched a Merger, and Left with $21 Million Become President?", *Mother Jones*, 4 May 2015, n.p. http://www.motherjones.com/politics/2015/05/carly-fiorina-hewlett-packard-2016-gop/.

4   Brown, *Undoing the Demos*.

5   Andreas Georg Scherer and Guido Palazzo, "The New Political Role of Business in a Globalized World: A Review of a New Perspective on CSR and Its Implications for the Firm, Governance, and Democracy", *Journal of Management Studies* 48, no. 4 (2011).

6   Carl Rhodes, "Volkswagen Outrage Shows Limits of Corporate Power", *The Conversation*, 30 September 2015, n.p. https://theconversation.com/volkswagen-outrage-shows-limits-of-corporate-power-48302.

7   Mark Lyons and Bronwen Dalton, "Australia: A Continuing Love Affair with the New Public Management", in *Governance and Regulation in the Third Sector: International Perspectives*, ed. Susan Phillips and Steven Rathgeb Smith (London: Taylor & Francis, 2011); Adam Dahl and Joe Soss, "Neoliberalism for the Common Good? Public Value Governance and the Downsizing of Democracy", *Public Administration Review* 74, no. 4 (2014).

8   Max Weber, *The Theory of Social and Economic Organization* (New York: Oxford University Press, 1947), 358.

9   Ann Ruth Willner, *The Spellbinders: Charismatic Political Leadership* (London: Yale University Press, 1985).

10   Torben Iversen, "Political Leadership and Representation in West European Democracies: A Test of Three Models of Voting", *American Journal of Political Science* (1994).

11   See for instance Barbara Kellerman, ed., *Political Leadership: A Source Book* (Pittsburgh, PA: University of Pittsburgh Press, 1986).

12 Mike McArdle, "The Era of Bill Clinton is Over", *Democratic Underground*, 11 November 2002. https://www.democratic underground.com/articles/02/11/11_clinton.html.

13 Anthony Giddens, *The Third Way: The Renewal of Social Democracy* (Cambridge: Polity Press, 1998).

14 Fred I. Greenstein, *The Presidential Difference: Leadership Style from FDR to Clinton* (New York: Free Press, 2000), 7.

15 Vidyadhar Date, "Is the CEO Model of Political Leadership the Answer?", *Economic and Political Weekly* 44, no. 8 (2009).

16 In Ben Schiller, "The Rise of MBA Politicians", *Financial Times*, 17 January 2011, n.p. https://www.ft.com/content/96d634f0-1ffd-11e0-a6fb-00144feab49a.

17 Haigh, *Bad Company*, 10.

18 Brown, *Undoing the Demos*, 17.

19 Haigh, *Bad Company*, 10.

20 Lou Cannon and Carl M. Cannon, *Reagan's Disciple: George W. Bush's Troubled Quest for a Presidential Legacy* (New York: PublicAffairs, 2007), 219.

21 Quoted in Mike Allen, "Management Style Shows Weaknesses: Delegation of Responsibility, Trust in Subordinates May Have Hurt Bush", *The Washington Post*, 2 June 2004, n.p. http://www.washingtonpost.com/wp-dyn/articles/A7869-2004Jun1.html.

22 Haigh, *Bad Company*, 10.

23 Donald F. Kettl, *Team Bush: Leadership Lessons from the Bush White House* (New York: McGraw-Hill, 2003), 31.

24 Ronald Kessler, *A Matter of Character: Inside the White House of George W. Bush* (New York: Sentinel, 2004).

25 Quoted in Schiller, "The Rise of MBA Politicians", n.p.

26 Steve Strauss, "Ask an Expert: A Look at Leadership Traits", *USA Today*, 18 February 2013, n.p. https://www.usatoday.com/story/money/columnist/2013/02/18/steve-strauss-leader-entrepreneur/1927581/.

27 Pasuk Phongpaichit and Chris Baker, *Thaksin: The Business of Politics in Thailand* (Copenhagen: Nordic Institute of Asian Studies, 2004), 101.

28 Ibid.

29 Duncan McCargo, "Network Monarchy and Legitimacy Crises in Thailand", *The Pacific Review* 18, no. 4 (2005): 512.

30 Bill Briggs, "10 Business Leaders with Politics in Their Blood", *NBC News* (2013), http://www.nbcnews.com/id/39800329/ns/business-us_business/t/business-leaders-politics-their-blood/.

31 Quoted in ibid.

32 Carl Rhodes, "Breaking Democracy's Promise in Tony Abbott's Team Australia", *New Matilda*, 19 January 2015. https://newmatilda.com/2015/01/19/breaking-democracys-promise-tony-abbotts-team-australia/.

33 Wenlei Ma, "If Tony Abbott Was CEO, Would He Be Sacked for His Performance?", *Daily Telegraph*, 3 February 2015, n.p. http://www.news.com.au/finance/economy/if-tony-abbott-was-ceo-would-he-be-sacked-for-his-performance/news-story/5bee751697ed87b7e718c08887d8f04a.

34 Jonathan Chew, "5 Things You Should Know About Australia's New PM Malcolm Turnbull", *Fortune Magazine*, 14 September 2015. http://fortune.com/2015/09/14/malcolm-turnbull-australia-prime-minister/.

35 Matthew Knott, "Don't Expect a 'Fistful of Dollars' Election Campaign: Malcolm Turnbull", *Sydney Morning Herald*, 29 January 2016, n.p. http://www.smh.com.au/federal-politics/political-news/dont-expect-a-fistful-of-dollars-election-campaign-malcolm-turnbull-20160128-gmgkeq.html.

36 Ibid.

37 Kim Stephens, "Shorten in Election Mode as Queensland Labor Kicks Off 2016 Campaign", *Sydney Morning Herald*, 30 January. http://www.smh.com.au/federal-politics/political-news/shorten-a-man-in-election-mode-as-queensland-labor-kicks-off-2016-campaign-20160130-gmho9l.html.

38 Mark Kenny, "The Tricky Politics of Sunday Penalty Rates for Malcolm Turnbull", *Sydney Morning Herald*, 21 December 2015. http://www.smh.com.au/federal-politics/political-opinion/the-tricky-politics-of-sunday-penalty-rates-for-malcolm-turnbull-20151221-glshu4.html.

39 Brown, *Undoing the Demos*.

40 Ibid., 25.

41 Ibid.

42 Ibid.

43 Ibid., 26 27.

44 Gilbert, 9.

45 Brown, *Undoing the Demos*, 80.

46 Mark Blyth, *Austerity: The History of a Dangerous Idea* (Oxford: Oxford University Press, 2013).

47 Mark Blyth, "The Austerity Delusion: Why a Bad Idea Won over the West", *Foreign Affairs* 92, no. 3 (2013).

48 Alasdair Roberts, *The Logic of Discipline: Global Capitalism and the Architecture of Government* (Oxford: Oxford University Press, 2010).

49 Paul Posner and Jón Blöndal, "Democracies and Deficits: Prospects for Fiscal Responsibility in Democratic Nations", *Governance* 25, no. 1 (2012): 28.

50 See Joseph J. Thorndike, "A Lost Age of Fiscal Heroes? Not So Much", *Huffpost*, 10 July 2013. https://www.huffingtonpost.com/joseph-j-thorndike/a-lost-age-of-fiscal-hero_b_3249676.html.

51 Anne M. Tucker, "The Citizen Shareholder: Modernizing the Agency Paradigm to Reflect How and Why a Majority of Americans Invest in the Market", *Seattle University Law Review* 35 (2012): 1299.

52 Lynne Phillips and Suzan Ilcan, "Capacity-Building: The Neoliberal Governance of Development", *Canadian Journal of Development Studies / Revue canadienne d'*études du développement 25, no. 3 (2004): 397.

53 In Tom Lutey, "Trump: 'We're Going to Win So Much, You're Going to Be So Sick and Tired of Winning'", *Billings Gazette*, 26 May 2016, n.p. http://billingsgazette.com/news/government-and-politics/trump-we-re-going-to-win-so-much-you-re/article_2f346f38-37e7-5711-ae07-d1fd000f4c38.html.

54 Leonard D. White, *The City Manager* (Chicago: University of Chicago Press, 1926).

55 Eugene Lewis, "The Political Leader as Entrepreneur", in *Political Leadership: A Source Book*, ed. Barbara Kellerman (Pittsburgh, PA: University of Pittsburgh Press, 1986), 250.

56 Ibid., 252.

57 Inger Boyett, "New Leader, New Culture, 'Old' University", *Leadership & Organization Development Journal* 17, no. 5 (1996).

58 Brown, *Undoing the Demos*, 27.

59 Neil Brenner, "Global, Fragmented, Hierarchical: Henri Lefebvre's Geographies of Globalization", *Public Culture* 10, no. 1 (1997).

60 Matt Broomfield, "Women's March against Donald Trump is the Largest Day of Protests in US History, Say Political Scientists", *The Independent*, 23 January 2017. http://www.independent.co.uk/news/world/americas/womens-march-anti-donald-trump-womens-rights-largest-protest-demonstration-us-history-political-a7541081.html.

61 Tim Wallace and Alicia Parlapiano, "Crowd Scientists Say Women's March in Washington Had 3 Times as Many People as Trump's Inauguration", *New York Times*, 22 January 2017. https://www.nytimes.com/interactive/2017/01/22/us/politics/womens-march-trump-crowd-estimates.html.

62 Momentum, "About Momentum", accessed 21 August 2017. http://www.peoplesmomentum.com/about.

63 Our Revolution, "About Our Revolution", accessed 21 August 2017. https://ourrevolution.com/about/.

Chapter 5: The CEO as a model for living

1 Edward J. O'Boyle, "Requiem for Homo Economicus", *Journal of Markets & Morality* 10, no. 2 (2017).

2 Jason Read, "A Genealogy of Homo-Economicus: Neoliberalism and the Production of Subjectivity", *Foucault Studies* 6 (2009); Peter Fleming, *The Death of Homo Economicus: Work, Debt and the Myth of Endless Accumulation* (London: Pluto Press, 2017).

3 Carl Cederström and André Spicer, *The Wellness Syndrome* (Cambridge: Polity Press, 2015).

4 Ankita Rathore, "11 Famous Entrepreneurs and CEOs with Unusual Hobbies You Won't Believe", *The Hacker Street*, 24 July 2016. https://thehackerstreet.com/11-famous-entrepreneurs-unusual-hobbies/.

5   Jacob Morgan, "Is Happiness the New ROI?", *Forbes*, 12 September 2015. https://www.forbes.com/sites/jacobmorgan/2015/09/12/is-happiness-the-new-roi/.

6   David Clarke, "Are Today's CEOs Tomorrow's Early Adopters?", LinkedIn, 2 May 2017, https://www.linkedin.com/pulse/todays-ceos-tomorrows-early-adopters-david-clarke/.

7   In William Heinecke, *The Entrepreneur: 25 Golden Rules for the Global Business Manager* (Singapore: Wiley, 2012).

8   Craig Glenday, *Guinness World Records 2015* (Vancouver: Jim Pattison Group, 2015), 9.

9   Jayanthi Sunder, Shyam V. Sunder and Jingjing Zhang, "Pilot CEOs and Corporate Innovation", *Journal of Financial Economics* 123, no. 1 (2017).

10 Josh Lipton, "Meet Gopro's Thrill-Seeking Founder Nick Woodman", *CNBC*, 26 June 2014, n.p. https://www.cnbc.com/2014/06/26/meet-gopros-thrill-seeking-founder-nick-woodman.html.

11 Donald C. Hambrick and Phyllis A. Mason, "Upper Echelons: The Organization as a Reflection of Its Top Managers", *Academy of Management Review* 9, no. 2 (1984).

12 Shrinivas Pandit, *Exemplary CEOs: Insights on Organisational Transformation* (New Delhi: Tata McGraw-Hill, 2005).

13 Rose Cathy Handy, *Going from Homeless to CEO* (Toronto: Burnham Books, 2012).

14 Ibid., back cover.

15 Robin S. Sharma, *The Saint, the Surfer, and the CEO: A Remarkable Story About Living Your Heart's Desires* (Carlsbad, CA: Hay House, 2006).

16 Paul Krugman, "Why We're in a New Gilded Age", *New York Review of Books*, 8 May 2014. http://www.nybooks.com/articles/2014/05/08/thomas-piketty-new-gilded-age/.

17 Aaron Sorkin, *Steve Jobs: Screenplay* (Hollywood: Universal Pictures, 2015).

18 John Schwatrz, "Contrite over Misstep, Auto Chiefs Take to Road", *New York Times*, 2 December 2008, n.p. http://www.nytimes.com/2008/12/03/business/03jets.html.

19 Quoted in William D. Cohan, "Wall Street Executives from the Financial Crisis of 2008: Where Are They Now?", *Vanity Fair*, April 2015, n.p. https://www.vanityfair.com/news/2015/03/wall-street-executives-2008-jamie-dimon-cancer.

20 Quoted in ibid.

21 Melanie Haiken, "More Than 10,000 Suicides Tied to Economic Crisis, Study Says", *Forbes*, 12 June 2014. https://www.forbes.com/sites/melaniehaiken/2014/06/12/more-than-10000-suicides-tied-to-economic-crisis-study-says/.

22 Andrew Farlow, *Crash and Beyond: Causes and Consequences of the Global Financial Crisis* (Oxford: Oxford University Press, 2013), 344.

23 Carl Rhodes, Alison Pullen and Stewart R. Clegg, "'If I Should Fall from Grace...': Stories of Change and Organizational Ethics", *Journal of Business Ethics* 91, no. 4 (2009); Peter Bloom, "Back to the Capitalist Future: Fantasy and the Paradox of Crisis", *Culture and Organization* 22, no. 2 (2016).

24 Barack Obama, "Address before a Joint Session of the Congress", *The American Presidency Project*, 24 February 2009, n.p. http://www.presidency.ucsb.edu/ws/?pid=85753.

25 Sachs in Georg Simmel, *The Philosophy of Money*, trans. Tom Bottomore and David Frisby (London: Routledge, 2011; first published 1900), 256.

26 David Beer, LSE Blogs, 24 May, 2016, http://blogs.lse.ac.uk/politicsandpolicy/55395-2/.

27 AFL-CIO, "Executive Pay Watch".

28 Lucinda Shen, "Ousted Ford CEO Mark Fields Is Being Paid a Lot of Money to Leave the Company", *Fortune*, 25 May 2017. http://fortune.com/2017/05/25/ford-ceo-mark-fields-severance-package/.

29 Colin Cremin, "Never Employable Enough: The (Im)Possibility of Satisfying the Boss's Desire", *Organization* 17, no. 2 (2010): 137.

30 Weber, *The Protestant Ethic and the Spirit of Capitalism*.

31 Neely Steinberg, *Skin in the Game: Unleashing Your Inner Entrepreneur to Find Love* (Boston: Love Trep, 2014).

32 Ibid., 20.

33 Catherine Clifford, "13 Inspiring Quotes on Leadership and Success from Starbucks CEO Howard Schultz", *CNBC*, 2 December 2016, n.p. https://www.cnbc.com/2016/12/02/13-inspiring-quotes-on-leadership-and-success-from-starbucks-ceo-howard-schultz.html.

34 Cederström and Spicer, *The Wellness Syndrome*; Peter Bloom, "Work as the Contemporary Limit of Life: Capitalism, the Death Drive, and the Lethal Fantasy of 'Work–Life Balance'", *Organization* 23, no. 4 (2016).

35 Elizabeth Dukes, iOFFICE (blog), 28 October 2015, https://www.iofficecorp.com/blog/4-ways-executives-are-killing-their-work-life-balance.

36 Rachel Feintzeig, "Male CEOs Tell Us Their Work Life Rules", *Wall Street Journal*, 14 June 2016. https://www.wsj.com/articles/male-ceos-tell-us-their-work-life-rules-1465896602.

37 Kossek and Lautsch, *CEO of Me*.

38 Ibid., 5.

39 Allan Cox, *Your Inner CEO: Unleash the Executive Within* (Franklin Lakes, NJ: Career Press, 2007), 40.

40 Keiko Krahnke, Robert A. Giacalone and Carole L. Jurkiewicz, "Point Counterpoint: Measuring Workplace Spirituality", *Journal of Organizational Change Management* 16, no. 4 (2003): 397.

41 Bloom, "Back to the Capitalist Future", 3.

42 Sheryl Sandberg and Nell Scovell, *Lean In: Women, Work, and the Will to Lead* (New York: Random House, 2013).

43 Laura Stampler, "CEO Dads Open up About Balancing Fatherhood and Work", *Time*, 15 September 2014. http://time.com/3342431/work-life-balance-fatherhood-ceos/.

44 Gary A. Cohen, "How You Can Become the CEO of Your Life", *Washington Post*, 7 October 2016, n.p. https://www.washingtonpost.com/news/capital-business/wp/2016/10/07/how-you-can-become-the-ceo-of-your-life/.

45 Suzanne Bates, *Discover Your CEO Brand: Secrets to Embracing and Maximizing Your Unique Value as a Leader* (New York: McGraw Hill, 2011).

46 Sean Kelly, "5 Surefire Ways to Maximize Your Life, Starting This Morning", *Entrepreneur*, 31 July 2014, n.p. https://www.entrepreneur.com/article/236024.

47 Sandberg and Scovell, *Lean In*.

48 Ronen Shamir, "The Age of Responsibilization: On Market-Embedded Morality", *Economy and Society* 37, no. 1 (2008): 7.

49 Maurizio Lazzarato, *The Making of the Indebted Man: An Essay on the Neoliberal Condition*, trans. Joshua David Jordan (Cambridge: Semiotext(e), 2012).

50 Ibid., 8 9.

51 See Jana Costas and Christopher Grey, "The Temporality of Power and the Power of Temporality: Imaginary Future Selves in Professional Service Firms", *Organization Studies* 35, no. 6 (2014).

52 See Albert Hyunbae Cho, "Politics, Values and Social Entrepreneurship: A Critical Appraisal", in *Social Entrepreneurship*, ed. Johanna Mair, Jeffrey Robinson and Kai Hockerts (London: Palgrave Macmillan UK, 2006); Ana María Peredo and Murdith McLean, "Social Entrepreneurship: A Critical Review of the Concept", *Journal of World Business* 41, no. 1 (2006); Christian Seelos and Johanna Mair, "Social Entrepreneurship: Creating New Business Models to Serve the Poor", *Business Horizons* 48, no. 3 (2005).

53 Richard Smith, "Green Capitalism: The God That Failed", *Real World Economics Review*, no. 56 (2011); Kyla Tienhaara, "Varieties of Green Capitalism: Economy and Environment in the Wake of the Global Financial Crisis", *Environmental Politics* 23, no. 2 (2014); Michael Watts, "Preface: Green Capitalism, Green Governmentality", *American Behavioral Scientist* 45, no. 9 (2002).

54 Andrew Barry, "Ethical Capitalism", in *Global Governmentality: Governing International Spaces*, ed. Wendy Larner and William Walters (London: Routledge, 2004).

55 Shamir, "The Age of Responsibilization".

56 John Mackey and Raj Sisodia, *Conscious Capitalism, with a New Preface by the Authors: Liberating the Heroic Spirit of Business* (Cambridge, MA: Harvard Business Review Press, 2013).

57 See Gregor Campbell, "Microfinancing the Developing World: How Small Loans Empower Local Economies and Catalyse Neoliberalism's Endgame", *Third World Quarterly* 31, no. 7 (2010).

58 Shahid Khandker, The World Bank (blog), 21 March 2011. http://blogs.worldbank.org/developmenttalk/microcredit-deserves-support-to-benefit-the-poor.

59 See Wendy Parkins and Geoffrey Craig, *Slow Living* (Oxford: Berg, 2006).

Chapter 6: The generous CEO?

1 Richard Scheinin, "Chan Zuckerberg Initiative Gives $3.6 Million to Fight Housing Crisis", *Mercury News*, 6 February 2017, n.p. http://www.mercurynews.com/2017/02/06/chan-zuckerberg-initiative-gives 3 6-million-to-fight-housing-crisis/.

2 Mark Zuckerberg, "A Letter to Our Daughter", *Facebook*, 2 December 2015, n.p. https://www.facebook.com/notes/mark-zuckerberg/a-letter-to-our-daughter/10153375081581634.

3 Zillow, "Menlo Park Home Prices & Values", accessed 28 February 2017. https://www.zillow.com/menlo park-ca/home-values/.

4 Maria L. La Ganga, "Ordinary People Can't Afford a Home in San Francisco. How Did It Come to This?", *The Guardian*, 5 August 2016, n.p. https://www.theguardian.com/business/2016/aug/05/high-house-prices-san-francisco-tech-boom-inequality.

5 Jesse Eisinger, "How Mark Zuckerberg's Altruism Helps Himself", *ProPublica*, 3 December 2015. https://www.propublica.org/article/how-mark-zuckerbergs-altruism-helps-himself.

6 Ibid.

7 Robert W. Wood, "The Surprising Math in Mark Zuckerberg's $45 Billion Facebook Donation", *Forbes*, 2 December 2015, n.p. https://www.forbes.com/sites/robertwood/2015/12/02/the-surprising-math-in-mark-zuckerbergs-45-billion-facebook-donation/.

8 "About | Chan Zuckerberg Initiative", accessed 28 February 2017. http://www.chanzuckerberg.com/about.

9 Natalie Sabadish and Lawrence Mishel, *CEO Pay and the Top 1%: How Executive Compensation and Financial-Sector Pay Have*

Fueled Income Inequality, vol. 331, Issue Brief (Washington, DC: Economic Policy Institute, 2012).

10 Tanya J. Hall, "The Triple Bottom Line: What Is It and How Does It Work?", *Indiana Business Review* 86, no. 1 (2011).

11 William Lazonick, "Profits without Prosperity", *Harvard Business Review* 92, no. 9 (2014): 46.

12 George Emmanuel Iatridis, "Corporate Philanthropy in the US Stock Market: Evidence on Corporate Governance, Value Relevance and Earnings Manipulation", *International Review of Financial Analysis* 39, no. Supplement C (2015).

13 Archie Carroll, "The Pyramid of Corporate Social Responsibility: Toward the Moral Management of Organizational Stakeholders", *Business Horizons* 34, no. 4 (1991).

14 Howard R. Bowen, *Social Responsibilities of the Businessman* (New York: Harper & Brothers, 1953), xi.

15 Ibid., 6.

16 Milton Friedman, "The Social Responsibility of Business Is to Increase Its Profits", *New York Times*, 13 September 1970, 32. http://www.nytimes.com/1970/09/13/archives/article-15-no-title.html.

17 Ibid.

18 Milton Friedman, *Capitalism and Freedom* (Chicago: University of Chicago Press, 1982), 133.

19 Friedman, "The Social Responsibility of Business", 32.

20 Timothy M. Devinney, "Is the Socially Responsible Corporation a Myth? The Good, the Bad, and the Ugly of Corporate Social Responsibility", *Academy of Management Perspectives* 23, no. 2 (2009): 44.

21 The Giving Pledge, "The Giving Pledge: Frequently Asked Questions", accessed 1 March 2017. https://givingpledge.org/faq.aspx.

22 Iain Hay and Samantha Muller, "Questioning Generosity in the Golden Age of Philanthropy", *Progress in Human Geography* 38, no. 5 (2014).

23 Ibid., 647.

24 Ibid., 649.

25 Mikkel Thorup, "Pro Bono? On Philanthrocapitalism as Ideological Answer to Inequality", *Ephemera* 13, no. 3 (2013): 556.

26 Delacey Tedesco, "American Foundations in the Great Bear Rainforest: Philanthrocapitalism, Governmentality, and Democracy", *Geoforum* 65, no. Supplement C (2015).

27 Garry W. Jenkins, "Who's Afraid of Philanthrocapitalism?", *Case Western Reserve Law Review* 61, no. 3 (2011).

28 Ibid., 1.

29 Ibid., 5.

30 Quoted in Kristien Vermoesen and Raf Weverbergh, "Should Your CEO Be the Face of Your Company? And If So: How, When and Why?", FINN, 2013, accessed 1 March 2016. http://www.finn.be/blogs/should-your-ceo-be-face-your-company-and-if-so-how-when-and-why.

31 Tara Weiss and Hannah Clark, "'Venture Philanthropy' Is New Buzz in Business", *Forbes*, 26 June 2006. http://www.nbcnews.com/id/13556127/ns/business-forbes_com/t/venture-philanthropy-new-buzz-business/.

32 Gates Foundation, "Who We Are", accessed 2 May 2017. https://www.gatesfoundation.org/Who-We-Are.

33 In Anthony Cuthbertson, "Apple, Samsung and Microsoft Accused of 'Worst Forms' of Child Labor Abuse", *Newsweek*, 19 January 2016, n.p. http://www.newsweek.com/apple-samsung-and-microsoft-linked-child-labor-abuse-claims-417313.

34 See for instance Nick Mathiason, "Microsoft in Human Rights Row", *The Guardian*, 1 February 2004. https://www.theguardian.com/technology/2004/feb/01/business.microsoft.

35 Gates Foundation, "Financial Services for the Poor", accessed 2 May 2017. http://www.gatesfoundation.org/What-We-Do/Global-Development/Financial-Services-for-the-Poor.

36 See Bloom, "Cutting Off the King's Head".

37 Quoted in Rosalind S. Helderman, "Hacked Emails Show Extent of Foreign Government Donations to Clinton Foundation", *The Washington Post*, 16 October 2016, n.p. https://www.washingtonpost.com/politics/hacked-emails-show-extent-of-foreign-government-donations-to-clinton-foundation/2016/10/16/ce871a82-9319-11e6-a6a3-d50061aa9fae_story.html.

38 Ibid.

39 Rosamond Hutt, "5 Things to Know About Rwanda's Economy", *World Economic Forum*, 7 April 2016, n.p. https://www.weforum. org/agenda/2016/04/5-things-to-know-about-rwanda-s-economy/.

40 Jeffrey Gettleman, "The Global Elite's Favorite Strongman", *The New York Times*, 4 September 2013, n.p. http://www.nytimes. com/2013/09/08/magazine/paul-kagame-rwanda.html.

41 Kevin Sack and Sheri Fink, "Rwanda Aid Shows Reach and Limits of Clinton Foundation", *New York Times*, 18 October 2015, n.p. https://www.nytimes.com/2015/10/19/us/politics/rwan-da-bill-hillary-clinton-foundation.html.

42 Quote in David Smith, "Paul Kagame's Rwanda: African Success Story or Authoritarian State?", *The Guardian*, 11 October 2012, n.p. https://www.theguardian.com/world/2012/oct/10/paul-kag-ame-rwanda-success-authoritarian.

43 Andreas Georg Scherer and Guido Palazzo, "Toward a Political Conception of Corporate Responsibility: Business and Society Seen from a Habermasian Perspective", *The Academy of Management Review* 32, no. 4 (2007): 1111.

44 Ibid., 1115.

45 Glen Whelan, "The Political Perspective of Corporate Social Responsibility: A Critical Research Agenda", *Business Ethics Quarterly* 22, no. 4 (2015).

46 Scherer and Palazzo, "The New Political Role of Business in a Globalized World".

47 John Cavanagh and Sarah Anderson, "Top 200: The Rise of Corporate Global Power" (Washington, DC: Institute for Policy Studies, 2000).

48 Christina Garsten and Adrienne Sörbom, "Magical Formulae for Market Futures: Tales from the World Economic Forum Meeting in Davos", *Anthropology Today* 32, no. 6 (2016).

49 Peter Utting, "Corporate Responsibility and the Movement of Business", *Development in Practice* 15, no. 3 4 (2005).

50 James E. Post, "The United Nations Global Compact", *Business & Society* 52, no. 1 (2013): 59.

51 Ibid.

52 Paul Kenyon, "Gap and Nike: No Sweat?", *Panorama* (London: BBC, 2000).

53 John Roberts, "The Manufacture of Corporate Social Responsibility: Constructing Corporate Sensibility", *Organization* 10, no. 2 (2003): 251.

54 Ibid., 255.

55 Ibid., 257.

56 Ibid., 263.

57 Richard Feloni, "Warren Buffett Says These Billionaires' Letters Might Be More Valuable Than Their Money", *Business Insider*, 22 September 2016, n.p. https://www.businessinsider.com.au/warren-buffett-says-giving-pledge-letters-are-more-valuable-than-money-2016-9.

58 Deborah Hardoon, *An Economy for the 99%: It's Time to Build a Human Economy That Benefits Everyone, Not Just the Privileged Few* (Oxford: Oxfam, 2017).

59 Ibid., 3.

60 McGoey, "Philanthrocapitalism and Its Critics".

61 Ibid., 187.

62 Weichieh Su and Steve Sauerwald, "Does Corporate Philanthropy Increase Firm Value? The Moderating Role of Corporate Governance", *Business & Society* (2015).

63 Paul C. Godfrey, "The Relationship between Corporate Philanthropy and Shareholder Wealth: A Risk Management Perspective", *Academy of Management Review* 30, no. 4 (2005): 777.

64 Carl Rhodes and Robert Westwood, "The Limits of Generosity: Lessons on Ethics, Economy, and Reciprocity in Kafka's *The Metamorphosis*", *Journal of Business Ethics* 133, no. 2 (2016).

Chapter 7: The bad faith of CEO salvation

1 Donald Trump, "Transcript of President-Elect Trump's News Conference", *CNBC*, 11 January 2017, n.p. https://www.cnbc.com/2017/01/11/transcript-of-president-elect-donald-j-trumps-news-conference.html.

2 Alex Stevan, "Eric Trump: 'My Father's Tax Return Is Irrelevant Because We're Going to Cancel Taxes for "Extra Productive

People" Anyway'", *Newslo*, 16 April 2017, n.p. http://politicalo. com/eric-trump-fathers-tax-return-irrelevant-going-cancel-tax-es-extra-productive-people-anyway/.

3 Ibid.

4 Rhodes, "Democratic Business Ethics".

5 Carl Rhodes and Peter Bloom, "Apple and Ireland Are Betting on 'Nation Inc' and a World of Shareholder Citizens", *The Conversation*, 6 September 2016. https://theconversation.com/ apple-and-ireland-are-betting-on-nation-inc-and-a-world-of-shareholder-citizens-64956.

6 Bloom and Cederström, "'The Sky's the Limit'".

7 See Tie, "The Psychic Life of Governmentality".

8 Erzsébet Bukodi cited in Martin Thomas, "Social Mobility Increases. Downwards", Worker's Liberty: Reason in Revolt, accessed 3 December 2014. http://www.workersliberty.org/ story/2017-07-26/social-mobility-increases-downwards.

9 Frank Dobbin and Jiwook Jung, "The Misapplication of Mr. Michael Jensen: How Agency Theory Brought Down the Economy and Why It Might Again", *Markets on Trial: The Economic Sociology of the U.S. Financial Crisis: Part B* (2010).

10 See Bélen Balanya, Ann Doherty and Olivier Hoedeman, *Europe Inc.: Regional and Global Restructuring and the Rise of Corporate Power* (London: Pluto Press, 2015); William K. Carroll, *The Making of a Transnational Capitalist Class: Corporate Power in the 21st Century* (London: Zed, 2010); Jeffrey S. Juris, *Networking Futures: The Movements against Corporate Globalization* (North Carolina: Duke University Press, 2008).

11 Peter Bloom, *Authoritarian Capitalism in the Age of Globalization* (Cheltenham: Edward Elgar, 2016); David Craig and Doug Porter, *Development Beyond Neoliberalism? Governance, Poverty Reduction and Political Economy* (London: Routledge, 2006); Harvey, *A Brief History of Neoliberalism*.

12 Peredo and McLean, "Social Entrepreneurship.

13 Edward Wray-Bliss, "Leadership and the Deified/Demonic: A Cultural Examination of CEO Sanctification", *Business Ethics: A European Review* 21, no. 4 (2012): 434.

14 Maravelias, "Post Bureaucracy", 547.

15 Joe Scarborough, "Reagan: A Legacy of Optimism and Common Sense", *Time*, 4 June 2014, n.p. http://time.com/2815630/reagan-a-legacy-of-optimism-and-common-sense/.

16 Obama, "Address before a Joint Session of the Congress".

17 James Ferguson, "The Uses of Neoliberalism", *Antipode* 41 (2010): 170.

18 Francis Fukuyama, *The End of History and the Last Man* (New York: Free Press, 1992).

19 See Bloom, "Back to the Capitalist Future".

20 See Mary Jo Hatch and Majken Schultz, "Bringing the Corporation into Corporate Branding", *European Journal of Marketing* 37, no. 7/8 (2003).

21 Joel Kotkin, "Seven Years Ago, Wall Street Was the Villain. Now It Gets to Call the Shots", *The Guardian*, 4 January 2015, n.p. https://www.theguardian.com/commentisfree/2015/jan/04/obama-wall-street-democrats-big-finance.

22 Adam McKay, *The Big Short* (Hollywood: Paramount, 2015).

23 Jesse Eisinger, "Why Only One Top Banker Went to Jail for the Financial Crisis". *The New York Times*, 30 April 2014. https://www.nytimes.com/2014/05/04/magazine/only-one-top-banker-jail-financial-crisis.html.

24 Office of the Federal Register, "Public Papers of the Presidents of the United States: Barack Obama, 2009" (Washington, DC: National Archives and Record Administration, 2011), 404.

25 Blyth, "The Austerity Delusion"; Blyth, *Austerity*.

26 Naomi Klein, "It Was the Democrats' Embrace of Neoliberalism That Won It for Trump", *The Guardian*, 10 November 2016, n.p. https://www.theguardian.com/commentisfree/2016/nov/09/rise-of-the-davos-class-sealed-americas-fate.

27 Joshua Rothman, "Shut up and Sit Down: Why the Leadership Industry Rules", *New Yorker*, 29 February 2016, n.p. https://www.newyorker.com/magazine/2016/02/29/our-dangerous-leadership-obsession.

28 Elizabeth D. Samet, ed., *Leadership: Essential Writings by Our Greatest Thinkers* (New York: Norton, 2015), xxvi.

29 Rhodes and Pullen, "Critical Business Ethics".

30 Ibid.

31 D. Joseph Stiglitz, "Moving Beyond Market Fundamentalism to a More Balanced Economy", *Annals of Public and Cooperative Economics* 80, no. 3 (2009): 346.

32 See Tie, "The Psychic Life of Governmentality".

33 George Orwell, *1984: A Novel* (London: Secker and Warburg, 1949).

34 Jean-Paul Sartre, *Being and Nothingness* (New York: Philosophical Library, 1956), 102.

35 Ibid., 101.

36 Jean-Paul Sartre, *No Exit and the Flies* (Adelaide: Adelaide University Press, 1943), 44.

Afterword: The high cost of the CEO society

1 See Clare Foran, "Can Trump Fix Government by Running It Like a Business?", *The Atlantic*, 29 March 2017. https://www.theatlantic.com/politics/archive/2017/03/trump-kushner-government-business-innovation/521064/; Henry Mintzberg, "The U.S. Cannot Be Run Like a Business", *Harvard Business Review*, 31 March 2017. https://hbr.org/2017/03/the-u-s-cannot-be-run-like-a-business.

Index

Abbott, Tony, 128–30
agency, 88, 104, 155, 219–20, 229,
    233; capitalist, 50; of CEOs, 80;
    executive, 106
Amazon, 65, 68, 86
American Express, 113
Amnesty International, 195
analytics: health care, 68; peoxple,
    68, 86
Annan, Kofi, 124
anxiety, 50, 71, 157, 161, 229;
    economic, 2, 41, 219;
    performance, 91
Apple, 3, 31, 66, 149, 173, 217, 240
austerity, 2, 133, 135, 153, 169,
    227, 228
Australia, 6, 34, 41, 72, 93, 128, 130
Australia Institute, The, 129
authoritarianism, 1, 39, 44, 53, 129,
    198, 199, 241
authority, 28, 30; administrative, 30;
    capitalist, 62; charismatic, 119,
    123; corporate, 96 elite, 113;
    executive, 45, 139; legitimate,
    64; paradox of, 59–64; political,
    45, 118, 122; state, 24
Axelrod, Beth, 82

Barber, Benjamin, 84
Bauman, Zygmunt, 85
Beer, David, 157
Belfort, Jordan, 70
Berlusconi, Silvio, 13, 124
Bezos, Jeff, 65
bigdata, 68, 86–7

Black Lives Matter, 45
Blair, Tony, 121
Blockbuster, 91
Blo ndal, Jón, 134
Bloomberg, Michael, 190
Bøås, Morten, 88
Bonfire of the Vanities, 69–70
Bowen, Howard R., 185
BP oil spill in the Gulf of Mexico,
    5, 205
branding, 20, 225
Branson, Joan, 190
Branson, Richard, 11, 31, 67, 108,
    143, 144, 190
Britain, 102, 121, 139
Brown, Wendy, 18, 36, 131, 132,
    133, 138
Buffett, Warren, 11, 14, 189, 207
Bukodi, Erzsébet, 219
bureaucracy, 41, 102, 222; ideal
    type, 62
Bush, Billy, 26
Bush, George W., 124, 125

Cambodia, 205
Cameron, David, 100
capitalism, 1, 2, 43, 57, 64, 84,
    164–5, 240; benefits of, 156;
    conscious, 174; critique of,
    76; ethical, 173; financial,
    38; global, 5; green, 173;
    laissez-faire, 187; and poverty,
    175; theological foundations of,
    111; as vampiric, 56, 93
Card, Andrew, Jr., 125

Carnegie Foundation, 184
Carroll, Archie, 184–5
CEO: adventurous, 144–55;
    autocrat, 196–201; brand,
    225–33; celebrity, 14, 30,
    35, 59, 143, 189; cult of, 33,
    124; curse of, 49–53; fantasy,
    96–101; generous, 177–211; as
    hero, 3–6, 11, 19, 24, 28–35,
    49, 59, 73, 88, 95, 96, 106, 121,
    150, 155, 179, 230, 234–5,
    240; idolisation of, 47–78, 213;
    male, 162, 166; and masculinity,
    43, 145; as the model of
    generosity, 207–11; myth
    of, 94, 155, 241; as political
    leader, 123–7; politician, 28,
    115–40; president, 118, 125,
    126; responsible, 193–6; as role
    model, 6, 11, 39, 48, 53, 73,
    83, 145, 148, 161; salaries, 34,
    157; salvation, 1–15, 213–37;
    thrill-seeking, 144–5; values,
    11, 15, 48, 173, 236; worship of,
    15, 59, 66, 241; as villain, 5, 59
CEO Magazine, 49
Chan Zuckerberg Initiative, 177–80,
    188
Chan, Priscilla, 177, 190
Chao, Elaine, 125
charisma, 11, 35, 51–2, 88, 120
charismatic authority, 119, 123
charismatic leadership, 43, 106, 121,
    123
Chenault, Ken, 113
Cheney, Dick, 125
Chile, 34
China, 21, 196
Christian, 232–3
Christianity, 21
Chrysler, 43
Chung, Yu Jung, 124
CISCO systems, 143

citizens, 85
class, 51; capitalist, 58;
    contradiction, 110; interests,
    36; political, 122; privilege, 73
Clif Bar, 74
climate change, 6
Clinton Foundation, 198, 199
Clinton, Bill, 121, 199, 200
Clinton, Hillary, 27, 214
Co-Op Bank, 100
Cohen, Gary, 167
Cohn, Gary, 151
collective decision making, 45
competition, 7, 17, 40, 53–4, 64, 81,
    84–5, 91, 103, 112, 187
Conaway, Chuck, 98
Cook, Tim, 173
Corbyn, Jeremy, 139, 156
corporate: authority, 96; culture,
    20, 32, 118; democracy, 139;
    feminist, 166; globalisation, 2,
    93; greed, 19; leadership, 10,
    52, 117, 127, 240; management
    practices, 7; misconduct,
    67; political lobbying, 12;
    politics, 13; power, 35, 89, 203;
    righteousness, 227; scandals,
    5, 11, 43, 99, 112, 181, 206;
    self-interest, 67, 205; social
    domination, 41; sovereignty, 85;
    strategy, 20; tax avoidance, 217;
    tax evasion, 226; values, 38, 39,
    35–40, 134
Corporate Social Responsibility
    (CSR), 14, 184–8, 206–7, 208;
    activism, 204; ethics of, 206;
    political, 201–7; and politics,
    201
corporation: monstrous, 93; as a
    legal body, 55; as villain, 89
corruption, 154; political, 3
Council for Citizens Against
    Government, 135

Cox, Allan, 164
CPA Australia, 8
creative destruction, 58
creativity, 48, 130, 148
Cremin, Colin, 158
culture: anti-democratic, 28;
    authoritarian, 26; corporate,
    20, 32, 118, 165; crisis, 91;
    industries, 34; neoliberal, 94;
    of corporate capitalism, 192;
    popular, 30; self-help, 74;
    Western, 229; workaholic,
    92

Davies, Will, 87
Davis, Gerald, 83
Davos, 143, 204
dehumanisation, 68, 86, 88, 96
democracy, 14, 38, 53, 73, 106,
    116, 132, 137–40, 197, 236;
    American, 26; and the CEO way
    of life, 44–5; corporate, 139;
    industrial, 79; liberal, 1, 5, 41,
    45, 140, 156, 198, 223, 234;
    pseudo-, 39; retreat from, 129;
    as a social ideal, 45; as a way of
    life, 44–5
deregulation, 203, 228
Devinney, Timothy, 187–8
Dewey, John, 44
diversity, 51, 106, 118
Dobbin, Frank, 219
downsizing, 60
Dragon's Den, 149
Duménil, Gérard, 36
Dunlap, Al 'Chainsaw', 60
Durmett, Mark, 195
dystopia, 19, 25, 217

Eastman Kodak, 91
Ebbers, Bernard, 98, 230
economic anxiety, 2, 41, 219
economic competeveness, 118

economic elites, 89, 107, 108, 146,
    225
economic growth, 52, 89, 127, 132,
    158, 199, 220, 224
economic inequality, 169
economic insecurity, 161, 1269
economic justice, 172, 220
economic life, 7, 23, 36, 40, 81, 112
economic power, 28, 96, 148, 203
economic self-interest, 141, 191
'economic suicides', 153
economics, 53; liberal, 54; trickle-
    down, 56, 65
economy: executive, 111–13;
    Frankenstein, 155; market, 24,
    156, 206
education, 23, 39, 40, 72, 131, 203;
    free, 20; management, 78;
    spending on, 130
efficiency, 8, 19, 40, 123, 136, 201
Ek, Daniel, 107
elites, 41, 227; corporate, 83;
    economic, 89, 107, 108, 146,
    225; global, 73; financial, 42,
    47; political, 225; social, 108
elitism, 82–3
Ellison, Larry, 143
employability, 12, 108; fetishising
    of, 158
empowerment, 82, 97, 158, 165, 169,
    198; free market, 199; market,
    80; marketisation of, 197;
    promise of, 158; trickle-down,
    73–8
Enron, 206, 230
entrepreneurship, 22, 34, 48, 53, 57,
    113, 149, 150, 192; indigenous,
    174; social, 173
environmental apocalypse, 18
environmental degradation, 71, 97
environmental justice, 172
environmental sustainability, 118,
    220

equality, 9, 22, 106, 130; gap, 107; social, 131
ethics, 27, 185, 236; of the CEO, 194; of Corporate Social Responsibility, 206; entrepreneurial, 159; of genuine hospitality, 210; sober, 65
Europe, 2, 227
European Union, 2, 217
Evans, Don, 125
executisation, 132–6, 184
executive burnout, 92
exploitation, 9, 36, 39, 45, 48, 60, 98, 158, 196; interpersonal, 14; reflexive, 158
Exxon Valdez, 205
ExxonMobil, 5, 85, 204

Facebook, 3, 31, 66, 68, 88, 145, 166, 177–80, 188, 189
Farlow, Andrew, 153
Ferguson, James, 224
Fields, Mark, 158
financial crisis (2008), 5, 10, 13, 18, 112, 127, 135, 142, 151, 152, 154, 172, 225, 226, 235
financialisation, 42, 75, 133, 184
Fiorina, Carly, 116
Fleming, Peter, 93
Flowers, Paul, 100
Ford Foundation, 184
Ford Motor Company, 158, 204
Ford, Henry, 56
Fortune Magazine, 130
Foucault, Michel, 23–4
Fourcade, Marion, 61
France, 34
fraud, 206; accounting, 60; securities, 49, 71
free will, 96, 104
freedom, 22, 40, 101–6, 130, 233; capitalist, 43; CEO, 219; executive, 218; exercise of, 50;

existential, 236; individual, 42, 88; market, 219; neoliberal promise of, 146; radical, 234
Friedman, Milton, 186–8

Gap, 205–6
Gates Foundation, 194, 196, 197
Gates, Bill, 14, 15, 31, 66, 108, 182, 189, 194, 195, 196
Gecko, Gordon, 17, 22, 23
General Electric, 31, 43, 104, 173
General Motors, 204
generosity, 14, 23, 179, 192, 197, 205; CEO as the model of, 207–11; CEOs' personal, 194; in the CEO society, 184; philanthropic, 185
gig economy, 21
Gilbert, Jeremy, 75
gilded age, 55, 148
Gilens, Martin, 82
Giving Pledge, The, 14, 211
globalisation, 71, 117, 138, 169, 203, 220
God, 155, 232; CEO as, 67, 233; Christian, 21; is my CEO, 21
Godfrey, Paul, 210
Goldman Sachs, 130, 151
Google, 66, 68
GoPro, 145
government, 24, 36, 55, 75, 118, 128, 133, 203; art of, 24; corporate encroachment on, 140; democracy as a system of, 44; intervention, 76; regulation, 206; role of, 88; small, 89; spending, 131; strong, 198
Grant, Ulysses S., 29
greed, 17, 89, 109, 154, 187, 222, 226, 235
'greed is good', 19, 22

Haigh, Gideon, 33

Handfield-Jones, Helen, 82
Harvard Business Review, 50
Harvard Business School, 56, 125
Harvey, David, 58
Hay, Iain, 190
Hayek, Friedrich, 102
health care, 23, 40, 131
health care analytics, 68
Healy, Kieran, 61
Hello Magazine, 107
Henry Ford Museum of American
    Innovation, 6
Hewlett-Packard, 116
Hilton, Barron, 190
homo economicus, 141–2
human rights, 195, 199, 200, 203
humanism, 86
Hungary, 34

Iacocca, Lee, 43
IBM, 68
Ilean, Suzan, 136
Immelt, Jeff, 173
immorality, 222
individualism, 12, 22, 33, 40, 49;
    competitive, 13, 45, 161
inequality, 2, 4, 11, 18, 36, 39, 40,
    45, 67, 72, 81, 83, 90, 98, 110,
    156, 197, 207, 208, 210, 211,
    216, 217, 241; authoritarian,
    45; created through wealth
    generation, 210; economic, 106,
    169; fuelled by neoliberalism,
    140; global, 175; structural, 109
injustice, 107, 181, 208
innovation, 6, 22, 37, 40, 52, 53,
    58, 66, 94, 112, 130, 145, 157;
    political, 88
Institute for Policy Studies, 203
Intel, 68
International Student Movement
    (ISM), 20
'invisible hand', 54, 231

Ireland, 217

Jack: Straight From the Gut, 31
Jenkins, Garry, 192
job creation, 53, 132
Jobs, Steve, 3, 31, 66, 145, 149, 240
Joyce, Alan, 81
JP Morgan Chase, 85, 152
Jung, Jiwook, 219
justice, 9, 99, 101, 106, 131, 215;
    economic, 58, 172, 220;
    environmental, 172; social, 8,
    14, 118, 131, 132, 172, 182, 197

Kagame, Paul, 200
Kennedy, John F., 65
Khandker, Shahid, 174
Khurana, Rakesh, 51
Klein, Naomi, 228
Kmart, 98
Knight, Phil, 31
Kossek, Ellen, 163
Kozlowski, Dennis, 230

labour, 175; child, 195, 205; dead,
    56; division of, 23; living, 56;
    precarious, 12; relations, 165;
    sweatshop, 205; wage, 63
LaTrobe University, 72–3
Lautch, Barbara, 163
Lazonick, William, 183
Lazzarato, Maurizio, 86, 171
leadership, 29, 30, 52, 79, 113, 237;
    autocratic, 197; charismatic,
    43, 106, 121; corporate, 10, 52,
    117, 127, 240; crisis, 229; crisis
    of, 43; democratic, 132–6;
    market, 201; political, 116,
    117, 140; public, 119; romantic
    vision of, 59; transformational,
    31
'leaning in', 166, 169
Lerner, Sandy, 143

Levander, Sofia, 107
Levison, Harry, 91
Lévy, Dominique, 36
liberal democracies, 27, 120, 202
liberalism, 23, 36, 55, 102, 141

Macke, John, 174
MacManus, Susan, 128
Malik, Kenan, 63
managerial class, 63–4
managerialism, 7, 19, 78
market, 24, 65, 117, 134; despots,
    198; economy, 36, 58, 60,
    102, 156, 206; economy, 4;
    efficiency, 22; empowerment,
    80; for votes, 45; free, 35, 54,
    59, 65, 67, 69–71, 74, 83, 94,
    102, 111, 152, 154, 181, 187,
    197, 213, 218, 222, 225, 228;
    fundamentalism, 67, 231; job,
    118; knowledge, 75; legitimacy,
    90; logic, 83; morality of, 61;
    rationality, 7, 12, 98, 103, 221;
    stock, 33, 60, 183
marketisation, 41, 43, 71, 75, 94,
    102, 140, 184, 198; of global
    charity, 197
Mars, Bruno, 107
Marx, Karl, 56, 93
masculinity, 43, 145
MBA (Masters of Business
    Administration), 12, 125
McArdle, Megan, 95
McGoey, Linsey, 209
McKinsey and Company, 82
McLoughlin, Sheryl, 74
McNeill, Desmond, 88
Melville, Herman, 29
meritocracy, 63, 72, 81, 84
Michaels, Ed, 82
microfinance, 174–5, 197
Microsoft, 31, 66, 68, 108,
    195–6

Mill, John Stewart, 54
Momentum, 2, 139
moral capital, 210
morality, 22, 49, 99, 103, 106, 169,
    217; authoritarian, 196; of the
    CEO society, 220; of the 'good
    CEO', 50; of markets, 61; of
    neoliberalism, 112, 173; public,
    54
Morrison, Denise, 73
Mossack Fonseca, 217
Muller, Samantha, 190
Musk, Elon, 3, 31, 173
myth of progress, 105

Napoleon, 113
neoliberal anxiety, 90
neoliberalism, 2, 5, 17, 19, 24, 32,
    36–44, 49, 68, 75, 85, 87, 103,
    112, 117, 124, 133, 136, 153,
    161, 171, 217, 224, 234; appeal
    of, 222; defining characteristic,
    24; ethos of, 22; internal
    dynamics of, 58; and leadership,
    117, 133, 135; morality of, 173;
    triumph of, 119
Netflix, 91
'new boys' network', 82
Nike, 31, 205–6
Nixon, Richard, 214
Nokia, 91
non-governmental organisations,
    20, 204
non-profit organisations, 20, 119
Norway, 204

Obama, Barack, 131–2, 151, 154–5,
    224, 227
Occupy Movement, 36, 45, 156
oligarchy, 82, 83, 90, 224
Oracle, 143
Ortner, Sherry, 104
Orwell, George, 233

Our Revolution, 139–40
Oxfam, 208

Page, Benjamin, 82
Page, Larry, 66
Palazzo, Guido, 201
Panama papers, 216–17
Paris climate accord, 173
paternalism, 61
patriarchy, 169
peopleanalytics, 68, 86
personal development, 172–6
Peterman, Alexander, 29
Peters, Michael, 22
Pfiffner, James, 125
pharmaceutical industry, 49
philanthrocapitalism, 14, 191–3,
    194, 197, 201, 208–9
philanthropy, 14, 182–5, 188–93,
    207–10; golden age of, 191, 208
Philips, Lynne, 136
Plank, Kevin, 77
Podemos, 2
Poland, 204
Political Corporate Social
    Responsibility, 201–7
political economy, 54, 217
politics, 131; American, 28; in the
    CEO society, 127; anti-CEO,
    139; anti-democratic, 28;
    bottom-up, 140; corporate,
    13, 28; democratic, 121, 139;
    executisation of, 139; global,
    117; influence of corporations
    on, 38; post-CEO, 139;
    progressive, 45, 139
Posner, Paul, 134
post-bureaucracy, 102–4
post-bureaucratic, 222
poverty, 43, 156; global, 196
power, 69, 139; centralisation of,
    129; corporate, 30, 35, 84,
    89, 203, 220; cultural, 148;

economic, 28, 96, 148, 203;
    elite, 28; executive, 43, 80,
    84–90, 175, 228; exercise of,
    62; neoliberal desire for, 105; of
    nation states, 206; political, 28,
    64, 201, 203, 206; shared, 45;
    socio-political, 137
powerlessness, 9, 71, 94, 96, 97
price-gouging, 49
privatisation, 41, 42, 75, 128, 139,
    184, 203, 228
privilege, 51, 63, 64, 81, 101, 152,
    176; economic, 111; structural,
    107; unearned, 80
productivity, 123, 136, 201
profit maximisation, 55, 60
profitability, 8, 40, 42, 92, 118, 123,
    136
profiteering, 19, 39, 60, 71
progressive: movements, 240;
    politics, 139, social alternative,
    45
Prosser, David, 99
public accountability of CEOs, 181
public goods, 14, 117, 201, 211

Qantas, 81
Qatar, 198–9

race to the bottom, 90, 175, 241
racism, 1, 63, 66
Reagan, Ronald, 31, 43, 57, 65, 102,
    222–3
Rebox, 91
religion, 218, 231–2
Republican, 116
resistance, 112, 233; to corporate
    democracy, 139; to the CEO
    society, 9, 239
responsibilisation, 169, 173
responsibility: CEO, 196; discourse
    of, 207; fiscal, 133; moral,
    207; for one's own success,

170; personal, 110, 173; philanthropic, 185; political, 117, 133; social, 117, 118, 181
revolution: conservative, 11; free market, 10, 48; industrial, 55, 59
revolutionary, 10, 225
right-wing populist movements, 239
robber baron, 48, 57, 59
Roberts, John, 207
Rock, Chris, 107
Rockefeller Foundation, 184
Rockefeller, David, 190
Roddick, Anita, 3
Romney, Mitt, 125
Rothman, Joshua, 229
Rumsfeld, Donald, 125
Rwanda, 199–200

Samet, Elizabeth, 229
Sandberg, Sheryl, 166
Sanders, Bernie, 1, 10, 139
Sartre, Jean-Paul, 234, 236
Saudi Arabia, 204
Scarborough, Joe, 222
Scherer, Andreas, 201
Schkreli, Michael, 49
Schultz, Howard, 109, 160
Schumpeter, Joseph, 58
scientific management, 55
self-help books, 148
self-interest, 10, 23, 45, 54, 89, 179, 207, 210; blinkered, 22; corporate, 205; economic, 141, 191; financial, 117; instrumental pursuit of, 38
sexism, 1, 169
Shamir, Ronen, 169
shareholder citizen, 135
shareholder value, 57, 67
Shark Tank, 149
Shiffer, Eric, 74
Shinawatra, Thaksin, 126–7, 129

Shkreli, Martin, 78
Shoe Dog, 31
Sisodia, Raj, 174
Skilling, Jeff, 230
slavery, 62–3
'small government', 75
Smith, Adam, 22, 54, 231
Snow, John, 125
'social entrepreneur', 173
social ethic, 32
social justice, 130, 172
social responsibility, 118
social welfare, 39, 117
socialism, 222
South Korea, 34, 124
sovereignty, 27; corporate, 85; political, 89
Soviet Union, 234
Spicer, André, 93
Spotify, 107
Springsteen, Bruce, 220
Starbucks, 109, 160
Stiglitz, Joseph, 67, 231
Stone, Oliver, 17, 19
Sunbeam, 60
Sunderland, Ruth, 97
sustainability: corporate, 90; environmental, 118, 220
Syriza, 2

Taiwan, 34
tax, 179, 209, 215; avoidance, 27, 217; carbon, 128; evasion, 217, 226; reform, 130, 131
Taylor, Frederick Winslow, 56
television, 30, 37, 98; 'reality', 99
Tesla Motors, 3, 31, 173
Thailand, 126, 129, 196
Thatcher, Margaret, 57, 102, 222
The Apprentice, 31, 37, 98–9
The Autobiography of Donald Trump's Hair, 32
The Big Short, 77, 226

INDEX

The Body Shop, 3
The Man in the Grey Flannel Suit, 32
The Organization Man, 32
Thorup, Mikkel, 191
Thrift, Nigel, 109
Toyota, 85
trickle-down economics, 56, 65
'triple bottom line', 181
Trump, Donald, 1, 6, 13, 15, 25, 30,
    37, 39, 52, 67, 74, 77, 95, 99,
    101, 109, 115, 136, 173, 240;
    'make America great again',
    225; tax returns, 213–14
Trump, Eric, 213, 214–16, 217, 218
Turing Pharmaceuticals, 49
Turnbull, Malcolm, 13, 130–1
Twitter, 214
Tyco, 230

Uber, 92
Under Armour, 77
Union Carbide, 204
United States, 1, 10, 25, 33, 39, 43,
    49, 55, 99, 102, 115, 121, 124,
    127, 131, 135, 139, 154, 173,
    178, 184, 223, 226, 227
'upper echelon theory', 146
Useem, Jerry, 57
Utting, Peter, 204

values, 7, 9, 43, 182, 221; business,
    117, 136; capitalist, 137;
    CEO, 11, 15, 37, 48, 124, 173,
    236; of the CEO society, 45;
    Christian, 232; commercial, 13;
    corporate, 38, 39, 35–40, 89,
    134; democratic, 25, 113, 137;
    economic, 10, 14; executive,
    104, 143, 170, 173; free market,
    47, 75, 105, 173; of individual
    competition, 85; market, 19,
    40, 41, 68, 75, 138; neoliberal,
    75; political, 120, 121;

self-oriented, 23; social, 35–40,
    44, 117, 185, 187
'venture philanthropy', 194
Virgin, 31, 143
Volkswagen, 5, 118

Wall Street, 17, 18, 47, 70, 226
Walmart, 85, 204
'war for talent', 82
Weber, Max, 61, 119, 120, 159
Welch, Jack, 31, 43, 74, 104
welfare state, 75, 102
wellness, 161
Whelan, Glen, 202
'whiteness', 63
Who Says Elephants Can't Dance?
    How I Turned Around IBM, 31
Whole Foods Markets, 174
Whyte, William H., 32
Wilson, Sloan, 32
Wolf of Wall Street, 70
Wolfe, Tom, 47, 69–70
Women's Marches, 139, 239
Woodman, Nick, 145
workaholic, 92, 142
workers, 80, 92, 131; exploitation of,
    93; healthy, 166; salaries, 34
workers' rights, 12
work–life balance, 161
World Bank, 175
World Economic Forum, 204
WorldCom, 98, 230
Wozniak, Steve, 149
Wray-Bliss, Edward, 222

Ziglar, Zig, 110
Zuckerberg, Mark, 3, 15, 31, 66, 88,
    107, 108, 145, 177, 179, 180,
    182, 185, 188–91, 208, 209

ZED

Zed is a platform for marginalised voices across the globe.

It is the world's largest publishing collective and a world leading example of alternative, non-hierarchical business practice.

It has no CEO, no MD and no bosses and is owned and managed by its workers who are all on equal pay.

It makes its content available in as many languages as possible.

It publishes content critical of oppressive power structures and regimes.

It publishes content that changes its readers' thinking.

It publishes content that other publishers won't and that the establishment finds threatening.

It has been subject to repeated acts of censorship by states and corporations.

It fights all forms of censorship.

It is financially and ideologically independent of any party, corporation, state or individual.

Its books are shared all over the world.

www.zedbooks.net
@ZedBooks